## Urban City Books

# Dysfunctional Family Not

**An Autobiography**

**By Shakenya Wardlaw**

**This book is based on actual events, however many of the names have been changed out of respect for the privacy and respect of family and friends.**



**ISBN# 978-0-9636678-1-6**

**Edited by Julius Justice**

**Published by Urban City Publishing**

**www.urbancitypublishing.com**

# Dysfunctional Family Not

**Table Of Contents**

# Chapter 1

## DYSFUNCTIONAL FAMILY NOT

### THE EARLY YEARS

*July 10, 2006- (Diary entry) It's funny how some things never change. As I drive around my old neighborhood, I still see many of the people I grew up with walking to and from. As I drive down Cope, its nothing like it was when I was a kid. Back then the streets would be packed with kids. I guess now that we're living in this technological age, the kids are just not interested in running around outside like we did.*

*As I get to the corner and turn up Forrest, I see this dude name Jerry that I grew up with. Back in the day he and his brothers were well known for getting that paper. He was the youngest of a fine line of hustlers. He and his brothers were no joke. After they got busted though, things have never been the same for them.*

*Things were not going too bad though because he was still driving a late 90's Lexus.*

*For somebody that had been in and out of prison I consider that pretty good. I'd seen people come out and do a lot worse. Since they been out they've been somewhat on the straight and narrow. When he spots me, he waves back and asks about my childhood friend Di. She was my dog. I tell him she's in the joint. That she caught a case and is doing two to eight years in prison. He then goes on to say that he doing good. That he's now married and has children. I tell him that I'm married also and have three children. That my oldest; Chavez, who I had as a teenager is now15. I still have family in the hood. My Aunt Mona still lives in the house that I grew up in. It was my grandmother's house. When I was a kid everybody and they momma lived there. At times there would be almost ten people at a time living there. It's nowhere near that now. My aunt doesn't play that people just popping up and moving in like my grandma did.*

*As I continue driving I see my brother Arcyle and he asks for a ride back to the west side and I tell him no. He's living with me but he really needs to get his shit together. I tell him that whatever way he got to the east side that's the way he needs to get back. I then continue on. After a minute or so, I reach Newport then turn down Marlborough, the street where my old middle school is located. I couldn't help but stop in front of the school as memories of my past began to cross my mind like an old movie from the past. Back in the day the school was called Jackson Middle. The sign now reads McNair. The school has also been upgraded some. It looks nothing like it did when I went there some 15 years ago. Some of the best years of my life were spent at Jackson. Those were the days. Back then I was known as "She Rock," the female beat boxer and I was good. I could out rap and out beat box anybody in the school. It didn't matter who they were. I didn't really have a crew but you would have thought I did, because everyday in between class in the hallway or during lunch me and a few fellas would huddle up and cause a scene. It would mainly be me and this boy name Kirk and sometimes this boy name Anthony would join in. The battles would be the greatest. Either someone would want to challenge me or wanted to challenge Kirk, but you best believe whoever was rapping chose me to keep the beat going.*

*My childhood was decent, pretty much like any other kid that grew up in the ghetto. I had my highs, my lows, good times, and bad times, things I fondly remember and things I had packed up, put up and locked up in the back of my mind. At least until I decided to write a book. One thing I can say, is I made it through. I was the oldest of four. We lived with my Grandma Erma along with Aunt Juanita, her son Travon, and my Aunt Mona who was my mother's youngest sister. We didn't have much money, probably because my mama worked for the government and from what I can gather they didn't pay much. They sent her a check every two weeks and between receiving the checks she also received food stamps.*

*The government also provided benefits. Our medical card was through this company called Medicaid. We didn't have to use it much though because if we did hurt ourselves and needed to go to the doctor, grandma would pull out one of her remedies and nine times out of ten, when she finished wrapping you up you were as good as new. I don't quite know what my mother did for the government all I know is she never left the house. To my understanding my mother would cash the checks, then give the money to my grandmother who would then place it in her bra and pass it out as she saw fit. I can still hear my grandmother now, yelling at my mother that she wasn't giving her any more money because she had given her enough for the week. But like clock work, two days later my mother would be back begging for more. Sometimes grandma was strong and stuck to her guns and other times she would give in and give her more money.*

*My Grandma Erma kept the family together. She was really family orientated and on top of that was a beautiful looking person. She was half Indian and half black. She was thick, a little chocolate, and had that long black wavy hair. On the flip side though, she was feisty, stern, and didn't take no stuff off of nobody. I can remember acting up, which for me was rare, and being sent out side to find a*

***switch suitable for the perfect ass whipping, and if it wasn't suitable I had to go back and find one that was. My grandmother was the community grandma. She didn't just love us, she loved everybody. She was everybody's grandma, mama, care giver, doctor, therapist; you name it, she was it. If you came over to our house and was hungry she fed you. If you needed something to wear she clothed, you. If you needed a place to stay she would fix up the couch, provide you a blanket and pillow, or let you sleep in one of the many beds we had around the house. For those with a government job or SSI, you got VIP treatment. If your intent was to stay awhile Grandma would make sure that she helped organize your money. She had no intent on anybody sticking around with money coming in who didn't contribute. There would be none of that getting your check, spending it all in a couple days and then looking for her for hand outs. She didn't play that.***

***Grandma also cooked all the time. Every morning before school, we had a hot meal. You didn't have to worry about going hungry around our house. During the week she washed our clothes, ironed them, and if necessary mended them and on Sunday she did it up big. There was nothing like those Sunday dinners. Yep... life with Grandma Erma was really good.***

As far back as I can remember, my dad has always been a wonderful man. He grew up on the east side in the Parkside projects. The projects were rough, but because my father was a musician he was able to avoid a lot of trouble by focusing on his music. Even back then the projects were known for its drugs, gangs, and women, so for him to avoid all three was an achievement.

My mom and dad never married. According to my dad he wanted to marry my mom, but because he knew he couldn't take care of her like he wished, he decided against marriage. Dad was a realist, at the time, he as well as mom were very young. They were teen parents. Plus, mom was high maintenance. So knowing that he would not be able to satisfy her in that way, he decided against getting married.

I can't help but feel a little bitter because like most children without both parents I think I would have been somewhat happier had they gotten married. Don't get me wrong though, grandma took good care of us, but there is nothing like having both parents at home. All growing up, I use to struggle with the what if's.

I remember my father coming to get me as far back as three years of age. After picking me up, we would take the long bus ride back to his mother's where I would stay for the weekend. On the way, I would fall asleep, wake up, fall asleep again and still be on the bus.

Even though my mom and dad did not work out he did eventually find him a nice young lady named Pamela. I remember meeting her for the first time when I was also three. She stayed on the west side with her mom and brother. She couldn't have been no more than 19 at the time. She was pretty, a nice size; about 4ft 11in, and maybe 100lbs. She was shaped nicely to be so little. She stayed in a big beautiful house. It was the biggest house I had ever seen. When you first entered the house, a foyer led you into the living room, which was nice. Upon entering, the first thing you noticed was the big glass crystal chandelier. It was beautiful. And so was the furniture, which I noticed right away, because unlike our house, it was covered in plastic. The living room also had a big picture window which looked out onto their street, which was lined with nice two story homes, freshly cut grass, trimmed bushes and tall healthy trees. There was also the dining room, the family room, and the kitchen. The family room was located down a few steps just right of the dining room. That's where I slept whenever I would visit. For its time, the kitchen was very modern; the stove was actually built into the wall. Now how cool was that. I may have been young but I knew enough to know that was not the norm.

The home also had a second level. My favorite part about the second floor was the master bedroom. It was unlike anything I had ever seen. You could also reach it through the bathroom leading out from the hall. As you walked through, the first thing you noticed was the tub, then an enclosed shower, with the sliding glass door, a walk in closet for towels and miscellaneous items, then the door leading to the bedroom. The master bedroom was Pam's room. The thing I remember most about her room was the two walk in closets as well as the dresser where she kept a large assortment of nice smelling perfumes.

Pam's mom had a nice sized bedroom too. The thing I liked most about her room was her bed; a king sized circular with the velvet headboard. As a child, the house seemed like a mansion. I remember walking through each room and feeling like Pam and her family were rich. I mean, what else was I to think.

When I would visit, my father would always try and make up for lost time and spoil me to no ends. I remember one time while taking the bus back home, I had eaten so much food and candy that I threw up all over everything. The whole ride home I couldn't hold anything down. I threw up on my dad, on the seats, on myself, and my dad took it all in stride. He used his shirt to wipe the vomit off of me, then sat me back on his lap like nothing happened. When we reached our stop, he picked me up, carried me to the house and handed me over to my mother. I remember him telling her about me getting sick, then kissing me good night, then turning and walking off into the night. My dad was my knight in shining armor.

My home was cool, we stayed on the east side in what most black people call the hood. When you first walked in the front door, immediately to the left, was my grandmother's room. We also had another bedroom on the first floor. That's where my Aunt Juanita and her son Travon slept. Upstairs was the attic. That was my Aunt Mona's room. I slept in the basement along with my mother, whom we called, Nana. But I spent a lot of time up in the attack in Aunt Mona's room. Her room was a far cry from Pam's. I remember my grandmother lining focus hope milk cans along the walls to help insulate the room. It didn't help very much though, because in the winter it got pretty cold up there. Nevertheless, Aunt Mona had the room set up really nice. It looked like a small living room. The most important piece of furniture up there was her stereo. I'm telling you, you could go up there and hang out, but you bet not touch her stereo and you bet not mess with her records. Them L.P.'s were her prize possessions. If she caught you messing with them she would break every finger on both hands. She didn't play when it came to her records.

I use to love going up there because the attic had these two big picture windows and you could see everything going on up and down the block.

Back downstairs what I considered cozy, a lot of people might consider cluttered. We had a couch in the living room, a couch in the dining room and this was in addition to the dining room table and other furniture which we had in those rooms. Between me, my brother Victor and my cousin Travon, we took turns sleeping on those couches. There was no rhythm or rhyme either, whoever got there first laid claim for the night. When we weren't sleeping on the couch or I wasn't in the basement we would jump in the bed with grandma. That was no easy thing either, because on any given night there could be up to five other people sleeping with her. Many nights I'd wake up with smelly feet in my face. Victor's feet were the worse. His feet would wake you from your sleep.

The basement was typical of many in Detroit. Cement floor, unfinished ceiling, and a big grey iron furnace located in the center of the floor. In addition to our beds which were located behind a hanging quilt curtain in the back of the basement there was also a washer and dryer located in the front. Also scattered about were three brown wooden dressers each filled to the brim with clothes. In fact, clothes were everywhere. They were piled from the floor to the ceiling. When kids would come to our house to play, they'd head straight to the basement.

There was never a dull moment in our house. There was always something going on. Somebody always moving in, moving out, leaving, coming, going. That house was always busy.

We didn't have much money, but as my crazy ass Aunt Mona use to say, we had a lot of love. Aunt Mona was the funny one out the family. She knew all the old folk's sayings and she didn't hesitate to quote them. She used them like people use bible scriptures, "The Book of Life said in Chap 2 Verse 3, a hard head makes a soft ass, can I get an amen." She would say things like that while we getting our asses whipped. I didn't get many whippings though; I was one of those kids that listened; well at least 70 ah 69.99% of the time. Back then some of the kids I grew up with never listened. Well maybe 40% of the time, but the rest was trial and error. I just didn't have a heavy problem doing what I was told. At best, and I know it got on people's nerves, but the worse thing I would do, would always ask, how come. Whenever Aunt Mona would ask me to do something, I would always ask, how come, and her silly ass would always have a funny ass come back like *"how come… how come,* cause if you don't I'm gone whip yo' little ass how come. How come that."

I learned at an early age that every one of those old sayings had some sort of meaning that could make my life a little easier… and lot less painful. At first some of them were a little confusing. Like, "a hard head makes a soft ass" I would constantly ask myself what the hell it meant. It took a couple ass whippings for me to figure it out and when I did I was all good. And, "you play with fire you get burned." I didn't figure that one out until much later. Then there were others, like, hard headed, (meaning) to keep doing something you were told to stop doing more than once. After awhile, hard headed became an adjective that was added to that person's name. As soon as you saw them, they would be referred to as such. "There go that hard headed ass such and such with his or her hard headed ass."

Growing up, Victor and I didn't have many name brand clothes and the ones we did get were hand me downs. For whatever reason, I think people felt sorry for us. But as a child, I couldn't understand why. But whatever, it was all good and we happily accepted them. My grandma called it being grateful. "Be glad somebody thought enough about you to fold them up, put them aside and bring them to you," she'd say.

Every day, from sun up to sun down, me, Travon, and Victor were together. We made up games and learned how to play together. Although we had friends, we didn't need them. We wrestled, flipped, raced, and just purely enjoyed life. Many times though, when Travon would leave with his mother, and Victor would leave with grandma, I would find myself alone. During such times I would ride my bike. I never went far, just a few houses one way, and a few houses the other, and never without first getting Nana's permission.

I remember this one time; I was out alone. I was riding my bike as usual, but this time I did something I was often warned not to do. I remember it like it was yesterday. It was a nice summer morning, wasn't noon yet so there wasn't a lot of people out. My mother had given me the speech that she gave me every time I'd go out and none of the neighbors were out. "Don't go past the Bells house, and in the opposite direction, don't go past Ms. June's house. Giving me a seven house range, which was cool, because I was only six. I couldn't go in the street, couldn't go in nobody's house and I couldn't go in anybody's back yard, and for the most part, I never did. But this one particular day for some reason all the nosy neighbors that were usually out were not out. My friends Cory, Tanisha, and Leonard were still in the house, and I was out having a ball. I liked being the only one out, because I didn't have to share the sidewalk. So I'm riding up and down the street and all a sudden, one of my neighbors, this man named Tione Bells, comes out, sits on his porch and commences to watch me ride by bike. So I start showing off. I'm riding with no hands, I'm burning rubber, I'm having a good time. All of a sudden I get to his house and turn around and he starts telling me how pretty I am. He tells me how good a job I'm doing, and being that I'd only recently stopped using training wheels, I'm geeked.

Tione had grown up with my mom and her sisters. He was about the same age as Nana, so that would have made him 24 or 25 at the time. He lived in the house with his mom and dad and his two younger brothers.

Anyway, after about the fourth time riding past he asked me to come in the house. He said that he wanted to show me something. So I laid down my bike and walked onto the porch. That's when he asked me if I liked kittens? And I said yea. He then asked if I wanted to see them, and again I said yea. I then asked him where they were and he said they were in the basement. I told him that Nana told me I couldn't go in nobody's house. He then said that my mother knew him and that he would tell her that I was just looking at the kittens if she asked. I figured, it's just baby kittens, so why not. So I said okay.

Tione then took a swift look around, then quickly walked in and closed the door behind us. I had been in the house a few times before, so I felt comfortable. His mother would give us kids candy and we would come in the house to get it. Plus, every day Tione, along with my mom and her friends would sit on the porch and drink beer.

As I followed him through the house I was excited about the kittens. I loved kittens and deep down was hoping that I might even get one. I didn't know if Nana would approve, but I hoped she would. When we reached the door leading to the basement, Tione slowly opened it, again looked around, then headed down the dimly lit stairs. When we reached the bottom of the steps, he led me into a dark closet where he said the cats were. At that point, I got scared because I was afraid of the dark. Plus, I didn't see any cats.

When I turned to leave, this fool had pulled out his dick, this weeda wada... and had this humongous thing pointed right up to my face. Okay. Aunt Mona had warned me about good touch, bad touch, but now I was at a lost. I was frozen in fright. I had seen my brother's little pee wee when he was a baby, but I had never seen anything like this. His thing was huge. He asked me to touch it, but I couldn't. I just stood there shaking. He then told me there was nothing to be afraid of and if I touched it, he would give me a kitten, so figuring my options, I touched it. After I touched it, he then asked me to kiss it. Again I nervously asked about the kittens. This time he said they were sleep and he would get one for me after I kissed his thing. So I kissed it. Then I kissed it again and before I knew it the tip of his weeda waada was in my mouth. I could barely breathe. He then put his hand on the top of my head, making it hard to push away. Finally, after a few minutes, he was done. I spit his cum out of my mouth, and looked up waiting for him to give me my kitten. Instead, looking stupid, he put his weeda wada back in his pants, and said he would bring it later because he thought he heard my mother calling my name.

As we hurried up the stairs, he asked if I liked whipped cream, and I said yes. He then said good, because next time he would put whip cream on it. That way it would taste better. He also told me unless I wanted to get in trouble I shouldn't tell anybody about what happened. That it was our little secret. He then wiped my mouth, walked me to the door, and let me out. Who knew our little secret was I'd just given this grown ass man a blow job.

As sickening as it sounds, I actually went back a second time; same scenario. Again, he told me about the kittens and like a fool I went to the basement looking for them again. This time, as soon as I got downstairs he pulled down my shorts and asked me to bend over so I could get a better look at the kittens. He kept saying they were in the corner. This time he rubbed his thing across my pocket book until the white stuff came out again, and for some reason, when it came out, I peed on myself. Out of fear, I asked him what I should tell Nana about my wet clothes, and he told me he didn't know; to make something up.

When we got upstairs, this time, his mother was standing in the living room. When she saw me, she looked surprised, but not shocked. She scolded him about having kids in the basement then told me to get my bike and hurry home.

After the second time, I started riding my bike in the opposite direction. The one time I did ride pass his house, he came outside, and asked me to come in, but I ignored him. After that, I never rode down there again.

## Chapter 2

### Starting school

All in all, my elementary years were fun. We caught the bus to and from school, so many of my friends didn't live on my block. The kids that did live on my block, I was closest to, like cousins, Rochelle and Kawana; brothers and sister, Tanisha, Cory, and Leonard, my girl Nico, and Ivan, who stayed next door. I spent most of my free time with Nico.

Some of the parents on our block were strict. My grandmother and mother didn't allow me to run wild, however they were not what I called strict. Now Nico's mother, Ms. Tina, she was strict. Whenever I played with her daughter, she would actually make us clean up her house before going home. She also didn't let many people in her house. I guess I was special.

Tina kept Nico nice and neat at all times. Unlike many of the kids on our block, her clothes always matched, and her hair was always french braided with beautiful colored beads adorning each row. Nico also had all the games. Among them included, Candyland, Sorry, Uno, and Trouble. Playing with her was like playing in a toy store. Nico was also very pretty. Her skin was what I called, California red. She also had a nice small pointed nose, small lips, a few freckles and she was skinny.

Ms. Tina was what I would label a good mom. She went to work, came home, cooked, cleaned and took good care of her daughter. Their house was small; she didn't have any furniture in the living room, but she had pretty wood floors that always looked like she had just put a fresh coat of wax on them. Ms. Tina could also cook her but off. She couldn't beat my grandma's cooking, but she was good. I remember the first time I stayed the night, she cooked and after we ate she made oatmeal cookies then let us stay up and play games until we fell asleep. That's when I realized she wasn't as strict as she tired to act. I remember sleeping over another night and her making liver, onions and gravy on top of rice. Before that day, I hated liver and onions. But when Ms. Tina made it, she put her foot in them. Afterwards, she heated up what she called apple turnovers. Up until that day, I didn't know what that was, but mixed with ice cream, that stuff was good.

Back then the educational system was a lot different than it is now. People really seemed to care more about education. For example, all the little kids in my neighborhood attended elementary school out in Grosse

Pointe; an affluent suburb of Detroit. They actually bused us from the hood to high society. It was mainly white children, but half the teachers were black, so we underprivileged blacks did have teachers that could relate to us and we to them.

Nico and I shared all our classes together. Usually the class you started the day with, was your homeroom and that was the class you ended up in for dismissal. Nico was my best friend. We even shared a few ass whippings together. One ass whipping in particular came at my house after my grandpa had warned us about making too much noise. As silly as it sounds, the argument was over a graham cracker, and who would eat the last one. At the time, all we had to do was break the thing in half and share, but hell, we were 7. I guess we weren't arguing quiet enough 'cause next thing I know Grandpa Isaac came storming out that back door like a bat out of hell. He grabbed me by one arm and her by the other. Then took us both down the basement and tore our asses up. He only wacked us four times a piece but you would have thought we were runaway slaves the way we were hollering. His whippings hurt.

Whippings weren't just limited to Grandpa Isaac. The whole block chipped in to raise us. That old saying, "it takes a village to raise a child," is true. Had we been across the street, Ms. Tina would have done the same thing.

That was not the only time me and Nico got in trouble together. It happened when were about nine. The year was 1982. I remember the year, because it was one of the coldest days ever recorded. On top of it being cold, it also snowed about five or six inches, which made the weather even worse. Anyway, every day we would take the bus to school, but on this particular day, when me and Nico got to the bus stop, we waited, but the bus never came. So after about twenty minutes, we started walking. Hell, I figured our grandparents did it, so why not us. As we walked, I could hear grandma sharing stories about being my age, and walking miles to school. So I figured, if she could do it, so could we.

It took an hour and a half to reach the school, but we finally made it. When we got there, we were cold as ice, but also excited that we had walked. We rang the bell, waited, and about a minute later five teachers came rushing outside to greet us. Come to find out, Ms. Tina and my grandmother had spent the last hour looking for us. It had been announced that school was closed for the day and when they went to the bus stop to get us, we were no where to be found. When the principal, Mr. McMichael's pulled us into his office, we were like ice sickles. My feet were frozen. Still, and in spite of the cold, I just knew he was going to pull out his paddle and whip our butts. Teachers back then didn't play. They were strict. So I had no reason to believe otherwise. But this time, it was not to be. This time, he was saving us for our families, and they didn't let him down. We got our asses tore up.

For the most part, Hanstein elementary was a great experience. My primary focus during this time was music. I loved it. Ms. Chandler was the vocal teacher. Vocals were mandatory, but I also played an instrument. I played the snare drum. Both me and my friend Anthony Stallings played it. Another boy, Kirk, played the big bass drum and together the three of us were a team. I remember my first concert. It took place in the gym. Me and Anthony lived around the corner from each other, so every day, in preparation, we would practice with our drum sticks and pads. Leading up to the concert, our band teacher, Mr. Elmyer said he didn't want to use us, because we weren't ready. But we proved him wrong. Every day after school the three of us would get together and practice. And the plan worked. A few days before the concert, we played what we had practiced and he was impressed. We were a hell of a combination. We looked so good that my team ended up closing the show. It was a proud moment in my life. My father didn't make it but my mother was there. She was so proud of me. It was a great day.

In my opinion, the teachers at Hanstein were really good. What made them so was their patience. It was rare to see a teacher lose their cool. One exception was my vocal coach, Ms. Chandler. We use to drive her crazy. An elderly black woman, she had all but reached retirement age, and we took full advantage. We would intentionally sing off key just to irritate her. It would take the teacher in the next class, Mrs. Strong, to come in and demand us to be quiet.

Another teacher that really stands out in my mind was my first grade teacher, Mrs. Gordon. She was the best. She would break down words in such a way, that by the time she finished explaining how to properly pronounce a word, everybody understood. I also remember my math teacher, Mrs. Rush, and the shop teacher Mr. Ropa. They were both really good also.

I remember next door to the shop class was the L.D. room. Kids with learning disabilities. When you're real young and you first experience kids like that, they kind of throw you for a loop. However, once you get use to them, some of them are actually pretty cool. My friend Jimmie was one of those people. He was really cool. Jimmie was like six feet tall and 180lbs in the fourth grade. And he had this one hand that didn't have feeling, and he was always banging it on something to try and impress me. For whatever reason, Jimmy considered himself my boyfriend. After school he would come over to my street and hang out on the block. While visiting, he would stand in front of my house and bang his hand on the truck of our tree. When the kids would tease him about being my boyfriend, that only made him more excited. At that point he would bang harder. I was amazed that he never ripped his hand right off his arm.

Again, I really liked Jimmy. I mean, how many boys gone bang them- selves up for ya. I hoped when I got older that men would do things to impress me. Maybe not bang their hands on trees, but you know, Diamond rings, pearl earrings, gold watches. That would be nice.

Another major part of my life as a child, was my Uncle Ronald. He was Grandma Erma's only son. In addition to Ronald, she had four girls. Ronald was a very handsome man; dark complected, smooth skin and straight black hair. He was also a good fighter. He actually boxed in the amateur ranks for awhile and won a few belts.

For most of my childhood I thought my uncle was a superstar. This was because I thought he lived in this huge mansion. Whenever we would visit I was always in awe. We'd pull up to the guard station, tell the guard who we'd come to see and he would let us through the gate. Driving toward his house reminded me of a castle. Upon entering, grandma would have to sign this guest book and then we would sit and wait in this big lobby until one of his body guards would come and get us. After the body guard acknowledged us he would then check our bags and then lead us through a set of bars down to a huge dining room filled with vending machines. I would always be so impressed that they would check our bags before entering to see my uncle. I remembered thinking how much they must really care about him.

It wasn't until I got older that I found out that my uncle was actually a career criminal, and that mansion was actually Jackson State Prison. But for a time, I thought he was rich.

The year I graduated elementary school, my uncle's daughter, Cassandra came to live with us. When she moved in she was about sixteen. She was pretty, dark, and also had that long black hair and smooth skin. In addition to her good looks, she was also thick. Thick just like the boys liked. From what I could gather she and her mother didn't get along. I guess Cassandra was ready to be grown but her mother wasn't having it. On top of that, she'd already had a baby, who her mother was raising. To make a long story short, Cassandra was ready to be 'bout grown. In the hood when teenagers start feeling that way they generally head to grandma's house, where they usually get a little bit more understanding than they got at home.

After Cassandra moved in, I could see where her mother might have a problem. Cassandra was fast, within a week, she'd already had sex with my neighbors, Cedric and Big Willie, both at the same time.

## Chapter 3

## CHURCH

Grandma did what she could to keep us righteous and grounded. We attended church every Sunday; New Testament Holy Baptist Church. Rev. Kerris was the pastor. Rev. Kerris was unique, in that he only had one arm, therefore leaving him with only one hand. On top of that, the one hand he did have only had two fingers. But he was good with those two fingers. He could paint pictures like Michelangelo. He made beautiful paintings, which he would hang around the church. Some of his paintings were even featured in national magazines.

The church itself was an old converted house. It wasn't big but when the pastor would get up and get to shoutin' you'd think there were a thousand people in there. In fact, the church held about 50 people. Each Sunday me and grandma would get there early to help set up. We would set up seven rolls of wooden folding chairs with each roll having seven chairs each.

I loved listening to Rev. Kerris, preach. When it came to church, I guess I had an old soul, because I loved it as much as the elders. Each Sunday when the pastor finished preaching, I would sneak up to the Alter and do my rendition of a Baptist pastor. "The lord is my Shepard, ha, I shall not want, ha, he makes me to lie down in green pastors, ha, he leads me beside the still waters ha, he restores my soul." When I'd get going good, grandma would come around and grab my arm and snatch me down. She would always scold me about playing with God's word, but what she didn't understand was I wasn't playing. I was serious when I was up there, ha.

Pastor Kerris served two functions for his membership. During tax season he was also a tax preparer. During this time of the year he would hire me to help around the church. My job was to clean and help move items that the pastor couldn't. I would be there all day and get paid four dollars an hour for my services. It was a job so I can't complain, but I sure didn't like getting paid four dollars an hour. I thought I should get at least eight. Nevertheless, I learned the value of a dollar at an early age and was taught to be grateful for whatever amount of money I made, so I'll just leave it at that.

**Diary entry:**

***July 19, 2006- It is 8:30pm and me and my boo is broke as hell. Still we're on our way to Chene Park for the summer jazz explosion. We're not actually going into the venue; we're going to lounge out on the grass. From there we can hear everything. It's a nice little spot right off of the water where a lot of people set up. Tonight we gone be parking lot pimps. My boo say's he got some steaks, some scrimp, as we call them in the hood, some baked potatoes, and we're setting up our lawn chairs along with a little tent I bought from CVS last summer. I really loved that tent because it was regularly priced at $20.00 and I got it on sale for just $4.00. My son was pissed before we left because he asked for some money and I told him to take some bottles to the store. But what else is new.***

You know, in hindsight that was an old country church. Located next to the Alter there was an old stove and grandma and the other mothers use to cook meals on it after church. There was a kitchen; too, it was located in the back. That's where we would eat. The church also had a back yard, however there was so much junk back there that us kids weren't allowed to play back there.

There was also an apartment back there which had these old rickety stairs that looked like they would fall apart with the slightest wind. I couldn't imagine anyone ever using them, in fact, my Aunt Mona and her man

Robert later moved into the apartment and started using them every day.

Robert was a story in and of himself. He was a mess. He was best friends with Aunt Juanita's man before he hooked up with Aunt Mona. And was intent on making it into the family.

One thing I can give him credit for was he carried himself real nice. He was what you'd call a slick dresser. He wore his hair slicked to the back, always wore a dress shirt, nice pleated slacks and kept him on a nice pair of paten leather shoes. At the time they moved in together Mona was pregnant. She also had a 1-year-old child at the time name Christine. I loved Christine, but I despised her at the same time, because up until she was born, Aunt Mona treated me like her own. I always felt like Mona was my mother and Christine took her away from me. I can remember dropping Christine on a few occasions when I babysat. They were mistakes, but I dropped her nonetheless.

In spite of where the apartment was located, it wasn't too bad. It was a nice two-bedroom unit. After awhile I got use to her having her own family. I would visit every Sunday, and sometimes visit through the week. Things with Robert were good at first, but after a few months' things seemed to change. Aunt Mona went from her bubbly, happy self too aloof. Especially around Robert. Whenever he would come into the room, and make any sudden movement, she would jump. I was too young to figure it out, but I knew something wasn't right. Then one-night grandma received a call telling us that we needed to get to Mona's house right away. That there was a problem. Come to find out, this nigga over there beaten her upside the head. When she called it was like somebody had blown a bugle because everybody assembled like soldiers. Our family didn't play that shit.

So me, Victor, Travon, Nana, grandma, and Juanita, who was pregnant, all piled into grandma's car and headed over to Mona's. It must have been about eleven o'clock, because the news was on, and I had already gone to bed. The ride there was tense. I wondered if Robert was going to die. After about ten minutes we skidded to a stop and everybody jumped out. When Mona walked down the steps to let us in, we brushed her aside and rushed up the stairs. When we got to the apartment Robert was sitting on the couch like he didn't have a care in the world. Meanwhile my aunt had bruises all over her face, arms, legs, and back. This nigga had gone to town. So anyway, he's sitting on the couch, pissy drunk. Then he gone look up and have the audacity to ask us what the hell we wanted. As soon as he said that, grandma and Aunt Juanita went to wailing on his ass. My grandma swung first. She busted him dead in the mouth and after that, everybody else just went to swinging. Victor was holding on to Aunt Juanita, and I was holding on to Victor and Trevon was holding on to me. Everybody trying to get in a lick. All I remember is just kicking. I think I must have kicked him about 20 times.

When we were finished beating his ass half to death, we stood in front of Aunt Mona and told his ass to leave and we weren't leaving until he got the fuck on. After he left, we stayed for a few more hours, hugging and consoling Mona then we left and went home. It was strange to come back a few days later and see him there like nothing happened. He was lumped up but he was there.

My dad was good about taking me around his side of the family. Whenever he would call I knew there was a good chance I would see them. He would take me to visit his Aunt Hattie a lot, I use to love visiting her. Her husband was Uncle Gordon. He died back in 1982. I remember him vaguely because my dad would drop me off over there a lot during the summers. I still don't know how he died, Auntie Hattie simply said he got sick and died. Auntie was cool, but she was strict, and could cook her but off. Her specialty was home made collard greens. I also use to enjoy her homemade rolls. Everything with her was home made. She had no problems hooking up stuff from scratch.

Auntie was very religious. She was a firm believer that everything in life happened for a reason. She stood by the motto that God did not make mistakes. She also liked to travel and kept herself busy. She was active in numerous organizations. She made sure that whenever any of the organizations had any major functions that could include kids, that me, and my cousins Robin and Jason were a part of it. She even took us to Toronto one summer. She always tried to expose us to something better. That was my Auntie Hattie. I love her to death.

During the hot summer days, one of our best past times was playing outside under the fire hydrant. We would get a tool, crack it open, and before you knew it, the entire block would be out there getting sprayed with water. That water felt like heaven. Our street was located on a dead end so there wasn't much traffic and we took full advantage. We would stay out there for four or five hours, or until one of the neighbors would complain about their water pressure.

I also use to enjoy the free lunches that the social service agency near our house would pass out. We would always plan our day around those lunches. Each day about eight of us would head the few blocks to the agency and pick up a lunch. As a matter of fact, we never started any serious games until we had first picked up our lunch.

My crew during this time included my friends Tanisha, Travon, Victor, Leonard, and a few other kids. Among this group I was the oldest, so I pretty much picked most of the games. On most days our game of choice was stick ball; an alternative game of baseball. The difference was instead of a bat we used whatever piece of wood we could find. We would head over to the lot located next door to Ms. Peet's , gather up cardboard boxes for bases and then ask our neighbor Big Cory, who played semi pro ball, if we could use one of his balls and bats. Stick ball was our sport. We would stay out there all day...until the street lights came on.

I grew up with a great bunch of kids, we would get into fights from time to time, but for the most part, we stuck together. Nobody from the outside could come on our block and start shit, unless of course they were from the projects. The project kids had a free pass to a lot of shit. Those kids kept an attitude. They were always fighting and bullying kids. They would take shoes, coats, whatever. It didn't matter. If you had it, they took it. The project kids also never fought one on one. They traveled in packs. If you fought one you would have to fight the whole damn projects. Whenever we would hear them yell, "choo wooo!" that meant they were coming and we would scatter. They would be coming out the wood works. Jumping off buildings, coming out of windows, it's like they were possessed...like zombies. If you were not a fast runner, you could forget it. You was gettin' your ass beat.

***Diary entry:***

*July 20, 2006- I had a full ass day. Hell I had a full ass few days. Well you know last night me and my Boo went to Chene park and I swear it was like our first date. I had on this sexy light blue sun dress that fit my newly developed body, meaning I gained a whopping 25lbs. Which put me at 154 lbs. Big baby! And I have tits and ass now. The dress has dark blue flowers with little green leaves and I wore a light blue scarf that I wrapped around my shoulders. I also wore my light blue Enzo Angelinii flat sandals. I was looking oh so sexy. We had the small pit and like I said my boo brought some steaks which he had already seasoned and some scrimp kabobs. I set the little tent up by this tree facing the river with a great view of Canada. It was so romantic. He baked the potatoes before we left. Then he surprised me with this lunch bag full of condiments. When he opened it there was sour cream, cheese, baby rays bar b que sauce, worcestershire sauce, A 1 steak sauce, everything our fat asses needed for a good meal. Afterwards he made him a jail house pillow. That's where you take your shoes off and wrap a shirt around them and your straight. I lay next to him with my head in his arms and we just gazed at the stars until there was no more music, no more people and no more boats. When we got home I went straight to sleep.*

*July 21, 2006- Today was a long stretch but it was cool. I got off work and took a little nap before I got the girls from day care. On the way home we stopped at the park for about ½ hour. Denise played on the slide while Alexis played on the swing. Meanwhile I perched myself on a bench and chilled. I took the opportunity to write a little and pretty much just cooled out. A piece of mind was rare in my life, so at every opportunity I welcomed the serenity. It seems like in my line of work that the devil is always busy. I'm in customer service so I see it as early as 7:00am. How you gone wake up with an attitude. I don't understand it. How you gone have the mitigated gaul to need something from me and you can't even say good morning or hello. That is just rude. That ain't nothing but the devil and sometimes it can last all day, just people acting ugly and it is always your cousin and them. Pooky and Big bro'. You know who I'm talking about. So that ½ hour of peace was a blessing. The lord is the only one that can keep the devil at bay for that long.*

*When we got home Alexis bugged me for something to drink, then could she ride her bike, then that she was hungry, then Denise joined in, she wanted to watch me cook. Sometimes I just want peace. Yes, yes, and no. Go play. Its Thursday, pay day tomorrow and ain't shit in the fridge. It takes Alexis to say we need to go to the store and get some milk and bread cause we don't have none like I didn't know that. They are item number 1 and 2 on my grocery list. After just pointing out what we don't have she ask if she could make them a sandwich. I say in a calm voice, don't you see*

***me cooking, please go sit down. Meanwhile, I commence to work my magic. That is when you don't have shit but you make a meal that deserves to be in somebody's low budget cook book. I browned some hamburger with some onions and green peppers, I made some gravy... put some mushrooms in it... made some rice and mixed vegetables on the side and some little mini loaf rolls and dinner is served.***

***Its late, and I still have to give the girls their bath and answer all the questions they have about their pocket books and other personal issues. But my night is not finished yet. Mister still got to climb on top of me and do his business then after that, I'm out for the count.***

It is the summer of 1983. It's hot as hell and summer vacation has finally arrived. All the kids on the block are outside and we're geeked because we're practicing for our upcoming video. None of our families had much money and it seemed like all of us were being raised by our grandparents. Grandparents who encouraged us to be creative with our time.

After practicing the routine to the thriller video for a week, we were ready. Cory was Michael Jackson and I played the girlfriend. Everybody else were the zombies. When we performed, everybody came, including the adults. Everybody was use to us giving shows, but the actual performance was always a surprise. The week prior we had break danced for everybody and the neighbors loved it.

After a few final touches, we were ready. Aunt Juanita brought her speakers on the porch, turned on the music and we went to town. We tore it up. We had a few hatters from a few blocks over and from the project kids that didn't want to participate, but when we finished, everybody clapped and gave us a standing ovation. You would have thought they were watching Michael Jackson himself.

## Chapter 4

## FAMILY

My cousin Travon was a trip. He was so spoiled. I don't know how but he had it all. In fact, he was the only one on our block with a video game. As a result, everybody would try and go next door to Aunt Juanita's. Aunt Juanita didn't play everybody coming in though, so on most days we, including me, would have to beg her to let us play with the game. It had to be a real good day though because she wasn't having a bunch of kids coming in the house. Most of the time we stayed on the porch and peeked through the door and watched Travon play, that is, until somebody would suggest something better and we would go and do that. Then after we would get to laughing and having such a good time Travon would pop up and want to join in on the fun.

We played all kinds of games. Red light, green light, hide go get em', and two square, which was my favorite. Two square was my joint. That was my favorite game. All you needed to play this game was a big round ball and a sidewalk. The object to this game was to stand face to face, with each person standing in their own square. One person then bounces the ball into the next person's square and each time the ball bounces into the crack that separates the squares that's a point for the other person. It's a simple game, but one that you could play for hours. And for hours we played. Deep into the night we played. Many nights well after the street lights had gone off and we could barely see the ball, we played.

On weekends my father was always pretty good at picking me up. However, whenever he didn't pick me up, it was always very disappointing. I remember this one particular weekend, how I had gotten all pretty, had ironed and packed my clothes, Aunt Mona had done my hair real nice and my father didn't show up. Every ten minutes I would run in the house to see if he had called and each time the answer was no. I ran back and forth in the house so many times that my grandma told me if I ran in the house one more time that even if he did show up that I would not be able to go. After so much time passed and he didn't come or call, my excitement turned to depression. It was one of the worst feelings of my life. I simply couldn't understand why he hadn't called. I began to make excuses for him. I conjured up all kinds of reasons as to why he didn't show up. I remember falling asleep in my clothes still waiting.

As disappointed as I was, I knew I could not jump to conclusions. I knew my father loved me and I also knew that if he didn't pick me up it probably had something to do with his music. As a musician anything could come up that could cause him not to call, so I tried to be understanding. This was before every one had cell phones, so it wasn't as easy to just stop what you were doing. At least that's the way I thought. All in all though, my father not picking me up was rare. If he said he was coming, nine times out of ten he came. Hey, some kids father never picked them up. Would tell them they were coming and never show up. My brother's father never came around, and when he finally showed up, never came back.

When my father came the following week, he showed up in a brand new Maximum. It was nice; the kind of car that talked. It would say things like, "the door is ajar," or "please fasten your seatbelts." It was triple white, had a sun roof and it had buttons on the side that allowed you to punch in a code when unlocking the door. What an exciting day. To get a new car in the hood was a big deal. It didn't matter that my father didn't live with me, the fact that he was my father and had a new car was good enough. *We* had a new car. That's the way kids look at it. Whatever belongs to your parents belong to you. That's the way it is, right? So anyway, before we left, my father came in the house and spoke to everybody. He had a pretty good relationship with my mother's side of the family. Being that they were young when they met my father had had plenty of time to get to know my mom's family. They actually got along really well. That always made me feel good. Things were the same for my mother with my dad's family. She knew the whole family and they also got along well.

Whenever I was with my dad I always felt safe. Like no harm could come my way. When I was little, he took good care of me. He would wash me, feed me, and even do my hair. The lines would be crooked, nothing like how Aunt Mona did it, but he did his best. He would also take me to his band rehearsals with him. Now that was fun. It was also unique. I mean, how many fathers are in a band. When we arrived, I would take a seat and watch the band set up. Meanwhile, the band members would then give me candy, chips, pop, and other junk and then I would watch them perform. To them what they were doing was rehearsing, but to me, they were performing. Each time I went I had a ball. Everybody would tell me how cute I was, tell me how good I was for being so patient, and give me money. You could tell that some of the band members didn't have kids because when I came around they really lit up. You know how grownups do who don't have kids. You could always tell.

My favorite instrument was the one I played in school, the drums. I loved the drums. In between sessions I would ask the drummer if I could play and he would always let me. He would even give me tips and show me a few things. I remember him showing me a combination from one of Sade's songs called the Sweetest Taboo. I caught on fast, too. After playing it on my own, Sticks, the drummer, said I was a natural.

Another thing I remember about the rehearsals was there were always a lot of women around. But you know, I never once saw my father act inappropriate. He was always focused. I was always impressed by that. I mean what man in Detroit would act right in such an environment. Hell what man in America.

After rehearsal, we would go back to Pam's house, eat and then sit up and watch TV. Sometimes I felt like we were one happy family. By this time my father and Pam had already married. They had a beautiful wedding. My dad went all out. He even rented out a Mansion. It was like something out of a fairy tale. Of course, I would have preferred that it was my mother in that white wedding dress, but that's another story. I was happy for them, though. When I was around, Pam treated me like one of her own. She never made me feel like a step child.

The best part about them being married, was now I had two mothers. That meant Christmas presents from two households. Pam even went out of her way for me because she was a Jehovah Witness, and they didn't even celebrate Christmas. But for me, she did. She understood how important

Christmas was to kids, so when it came to that, she allowed us the pleasure of the holiday.

I knew a little bit about Jehovah Witnesses' because there were a few people in my class who were members. Whenever we would celebrate birthdays they would always inform the teacher that they couldn't participate. Back then, I thought that their parents were so cruel. No holidays, or birthdays. I'm glad Pam wasn't like that.

Whenever I'd visit my dad, I would always dread Sunday's. That's the day I had to go back home. Every Sunday, on the ride home, like clock-work, once we hit the freeway, my dad would get all sentimental and start preaching. He would talk about real life issues; like my future, and setting goals. A lot of the things he discussed I didn't understand because I was too young. But the more we talked and the older I got the more I understood. Every week, I would find my self crying. Emotions would get heavy and the tears would start flowing. A lot of the tears came from anger at the fact that I couldn't live with him. Don't get me wrong, living with my grandmother was not bad, grandma took good care of me and my mother and my aunts loved me, but that wasn't enough. I needed my dad. And I needed his lifestyle. I needed peace.

I brought my thoughts up to my mother a few times however she refused to let me go. I don't know if it was because she was receiving

ADC or the fact that she resented my father getting married to Pam. I loved them both and at times I hated that they weren't together and that I was left to choose. I hated that. Why should I have to go through that? At this time in my life I really started to question why they were not together. I couldn't understand it. As a result, I began to resent Pamela. One summer I stayed with them, and it got to the point where I actually stopped talking to her. This went on for months. It wasn't until summer was over and it was time for me to go home, that she decided to call a meeting. We met on the porch. I had so much anger built up that I'd gotten to the point where I was being flat out disrespectful.

As I walked to the porch, I drug my feet like the disrespectful brat I had become. I then flopped down on the seat, like I could care less about talking to her. As far as I was concerned she was the cause for my parents not being together so at that point I had no reason to like her. In my mind she was the devil. When you're a kid you think you have all the answers. You think every solution is simple, but Pam was there to help. She sat me down, and told me how much she loved me. She explained that my mom was a wonderful woman and she was doing a beautiful job raising me and the way she knew that was because of the kind of child I was. She also let me know that my mom and dad were not together when she met my dad. She also let me know that all the ideas about us going to the zoo, Greenfield village, to the show etc., were not all of my dad's ideas. A lot of those ideas were hers. She explained that she enjoyed taking me places as much as my dad. That she was not trying to take the place of my mother, but intended on treating me like a mother whenever I came to visit. She said that she didn't understand why I was so angry, but in hindsight, I think she understood, she just wanted me to understand why I was feeling the way I was. After we finished talking we hugged. She made everything make sense. After that, I understood that in life, shit happens.

It was during this time that I began to really notice my mother's extra curricular activities. Every day it got to the point where she would call her doctor to fill her prescription. I don't even think the Doctor had a name. All I know is when she left out and came back she would have all types of pills. Tylenol 4's, emprums, uppers , downers, whatever you needed she had. After awhile she would have so many different types of pills that I stopped trying to keep up with the names.

***July 24, 2006 -My little cousin Marie did my hair. Afterwards I just chilled over there with the family. I can always count on my Aunt Juanita to have some kind of mixed alcoholic beverage. It's not that she is a lush or anything, I think more than anything else, she just loves trying out her new gadgets. Me and Aunt Juanita don't talk much, but when we do get the opportunity, we catch each other up on things over a small drinky poo. I***

*love being over there. We laugh and joke and have a good time. My cousin had me looking like a super model, so along with the drink, I was really feeling good.*

*After leaving Aunt Juanita's, I headed over to Aunt Mona's. She lives in the house that I grew up in. Being back in the house drums up a lot of memories. I always have fun when I go over there. No matter what we're going through we always take out the time to laugh and crack jokes. We always look at life like there is always gold at the end of the rainbow, so we never let ourselves get too down when times are tough. I couldn't help tripping out over my cousin Christine because she's with this guy and they've been together for a minute. So I asked them about their plans for marriage. Both need to get back in school and do something with their lives because time is not going to wait on no one. I was laughing and joking when I was talking to them but at the same time I was serious. After the jokes died down, me, Aunt Mona and Christine sat out on the porch and started talking about the past. It felt like everything just happened yesterday, but in fact it had been 20 years since I lived there. Unlike me, Aunt Mona never smoked weed a day in her life, so all her brain cells are intact and she likes to talk about the past. While sitting there, she cracked jokes about her childhood. By looking at the old pictures, I can see why. She and her sisters had it rough. She also revealed a few secrets to me, however I wish she would have kept them to*

***herself. Some of the things she told me answered age old questions about things that went on in the family. She also clarified the situation that led my mother to taking pills. It started when she was about 15 or 16. She was coming home from school one day and this boy tried to rape my mother. He was a big guy. They tussled, he threw her to the ground and she ended up injuring her back. The pills started off serving a purpose then gradually turned into a habit. I also found out that my mother was molested by my grandmother's husband. Maybe if I had known that bit of information years ago, maybe I could have been a little more patient with my mother.***

I remember my mother dating this white man named Andrew. Whenever he would come by he would always give me and my brother these candy coffee nips. I know, kids remember the damndest things. But Andrew was not just any white man, to us he was our ticket out the hood. He lived in a big house in Grosse Point and had asked my mother to marry him. Of course me and my brother was all for it. He was an older man and really seemed to adore my mother. In fact, during this time, my mother was a nice looking woman. She had beautiful legs and men loved her. Andrew took us to his house a few times. He even had rooms already picked out for me and Victor. We begged Nana to marry this man.

***July 26,2006- Its Darshawn's birthday. That knuckle head is 17 years old. Time sure***

***does fly. I'm running around like a chicken with my head cut off because Chavez wants to go to this special school for 9th grade, and he is trying to get a job, all in the same day, and I'm trying to make it all happen on my lunch break. He just filled out the application... he wants this job so bad. After he filled out the application the manager had him stay and take a test. She was so impressed with how Chavez carried himself. I hope they call him back. They said he should call them if he doesn't hear from them in the next couple weeks.***

I remember on my 11th birthday, Andrew pulling up with my mother in the car. He came up to the door and asked if we could come out and help my mother in the house. So we get out to the car and Nana in the car going in and out of consciousness. She's drooling at the mouth and the music is blaring. She was obviously high off pills. I couldn't believe what I was seeing because I had once caught her friend Ruby shooting up in the basement and my mother had promised me that she would never get like that. Now here she was, high as hell. So me, and Victor who was 9, proceeded to lift her up and carry her into the house. I was embarrassed as hell. All my friends were outside and here we were staggering into the house with my mother. A few people even came over to help; Cory and his friends among them. Cory had her arm and the other kids got in where they fit in. The grown ups just watched. She didn't weigh that much; I would say about 135lbs but to us she was heavy as hell. We struggled up the stairs, into the front door and into the living room where she fell out on the couch.

You know, as disappointed as I was in my mother, as I watched her laid out on the couch I couldn't get mad. I mean what good would it do. She'd wake up the next day and forget everything that happened so what's the point. So me and my friends went on in the dining room and finished eating cake and ice cream. Of course for the rest of the day I had to hear about my mother being a dope fiend, but other than that, I had a good 11$^{th}$ birthday.

The next day when my mother woke up she was as good as new. She hugged and kissed me like nothing ever happened. She had no clue that I'd become the brunt of jokes during my party. In fact, she didn't even remember the party. But it didn't matter what she remembered, after that day we become known as Dana's kids. Remember how I talked about hard headed kids, etc. Wep, now we were Dana's kids. Whenever people would see us, they wouldn't call us by our names, from that day forward we were only known, as "Dana's Kids." That meant that your mother was either a dope fiend, a crack head, a drunk or a prostitute.

To be honest I got used to it. Being singled out like that. But don't get me wrong, I stayed angry. But I got use to being called one of Dana's kids. I think over the years the anger just fueled me to want to achieve something in life. To want to be different. Hell, that same summer Victor was so intent on making something of himself that his little ass even got a job. He started disappearing on the weekends for a few hours, so one day I finally asked him where the hell he was disappearing to? That's when he admitted that he'd gotten a job at this bar around the corner. They'd hired him to clean, take out the trash and rinse out the beer can and beer bottles. He even helped me get employed there. They would feed us these colossal ass chicken wings and whenever I was there, it always seemed like the same song would be playing on the jukebox. "I be stroking," was the song. It went something, like. " I stroke it to the east and I stroke it to the west and I stroke it to the woman that I love the best... I be stroking", I didn't quite know what it meant but I liked it.

Like my brother I kept my employment a secret. We didn't tell anybody about our new found jack pot. Then one day, one of our neighbors, this boy named Shawn noticed us coming out of the back door and questioned us about it. Shawn was fucked up in the head. He was crazy. He used to talk to himself and growl at people for no reason. Then he would just start laughing. Of course you had to really be careful around him because you never knew what he might do. He used to beat people up for no apparent reason and out of all the girls in the neighborhood, why did this fool have to have a crush on me.

One day he seen us coming from the bar and ran over to me trying to hug and kiss all over me. Then he started questioning me about coming out the bar and threatening to tell that we were in the bar. He didn't know what we were doing there just the fact that he had ammunition was enough for him. After I wouldn't kiss him he got mad and started growling at us like he was gone kick me and my brother's ass, so we took off running. After we got half way home my brother had the nerve to ask me why I didn't kiss that fool. Yea, whatever.

After about a month, Nana became suspicious. She noticed that we no longer asked for money for candy, chips or ice cream and that we always seemed to have burger king. So she drilled us until we admitted to having a job. We knew it would only be a matter of time before she found out, so we were prepared. We thought we gonna get our asses kicked for being at the bar, however when she found out that we were making money, she was kinda glad. Now, after we got paid, the first person to hit us up for money was Nana. And she wouldn't wait on us to get home and hand her money, oh, no. As soon as we walked in the house, she ran our pockets. She'd then take what she wanted, and give us what she wanted us to have. Each time she took money she would always say that she would give it back, however you can about imagine how that went. She would always say when Thomas come, I'll give it back to you.

Thomas was her latest boyfriend. He was an older guy with one hand. He used to wear a hook sometimes and other times he would wear his artificial hand. I don't know what the hand was made of, but I remember, it would tear, and he would place it in a bag, and want Nana to sew it up. He was always ripping it doing something and he would never give it directly to my mother, he would always give it to me and ask me to give it to her to sew. Anyway, whenever he came by, we would beat Nana out to the car. Sometimes she gave us our money, and sometimes she didn't.

That next summer when we went back to work, we lied about having a job. Hell, my grandmother always said if we did wrong and asked the lord to forgive us, he would, so we ran with that... I guess calling ourselves being smart. Anyway this one time we lied and was therefore able to keep the money without our mother knowing.

Relatives were always just popping up at grandma's house to live. One day I looked up and my cousin Edmond was walking down the street headed to the house. Edmond was my Aunt Eleanor's son. Aunt Eleanor was my Grandma Erma's younger sister. He was from a part of the family that you only saw during special events like family reunion or funerals. I knew he was coming to stay because he had these two big bags hanging over his shoulders. The thing about Edmond was that he was also crazy. He use to take medication and in between his medication he use to stay in and out of mental institutions. I remember when he was perfectly fine though. I don't know what happened. Maybe somebody put something in his drink. All I know is now he was crazy and he was coming to live with us.

Although Edmond was crazy, he still had a girlfriend. One day while grandma and Aunt Mona were at the spa, his girlfriend stopped by. I'll never forget it. The two of them went down in the basement and like the little rascals we were, we waited good until they got comfortable, then me, Travon, Victor, Cory, Tanisha, and Leonard snuck down just to see what they were doing. We were all packed close together but stayed quiet, as we tip toed toward the back room. As we got closer, that's when we heard the noises. To me, his girlfriend sounded like she was in pain. She was moaning and groining... for a minute I thought he was killing her. We tip toed to the curtain, peeked through, and boy, Edmond was going to town. He had her ass up like two dogs and he was tearing it up. He was doing the crouching tiger, hidden dragon on her ass. Edmond black ass was moving up and down side to side... I was getting dizzy just looking. Then because people started giggling and shit, he heard us. Without taking his thing out, he turned around and yelled for us to get back up stairs. So we all turned and ran. We ran and acted like we were going upstairs but we turned around and came back. Shit, I didn't know Edmond had it in him.

Edmond and his sister Karen were the only ones on my grandmother's sister's side that we maintained contact with. Karen and Aunt Mona had come up together and were fierce competitors. Karen had a daughter the same age as me named Lameka. Lameka was beautiful; pretty skin, and long pretty wavy hair. Karen would take her daughter's hair down and Aunt Mona would take my hair down to compete as to whose hair was the longest. Lameka would win every time.

When Lameka would visit we would play two square together. She never wanted to play the other games with my friends but that was o.k. I liked playing two square. Lameka was shapely even when we were young; you knew when she got older she was going to stop traffic. But the boy's on my block could care less about the future. They wanted her now. When she came over they forgot all about me, they would converge on my house like zombies from, "Night of the Living Dead."

But I didn't mind too much, because true to form, whenever she would leave, they would get right back to chasing me.

Lameka was real cool but when she turned about 12 or 13 she started really acting out. She started getting into fights in school, started running away from home and pretty much took my cousin Karen through hell. It all started when a few of my cousins got killed. From what I recall they were 5, 7, and 8. From what I can remember, Karen's brother Gary, and his wife, divorced, and her boyfriend at the time got mad, came over to their house and beat and drowned two of the girls and my cousin's ex-wife. He left their bodies in a tub of water laying on top of each other. The baby girl hid and when my cousin came to get them for the weekend he found them like that. The baby was hiding but saw everything. It was the biggest family tragedy of my childhood.

The few times I saw them they were happy kids. Very well mannered. Walking up to those little closed caskets looking at their pictures I couldn't imagine why someone would do such a thing. I believe at that point I realized just how ugly the world could be. It was during this time that I learned to appreciate the phrase: "God will not give you more than you can bear." I held on to those words whenever the pain grew too much.

Aunt Juanita saved the clippings from the newspaper. From time to time we go back and dig up the article and reflect on what a terrible time that was for our family.

During this time in my life I was a television fanatic. I woke up every day to the television. I couldn't leave the house without getting in at least Gilligan's Island. Grandma would be outside blowing the horn and I'd have to tear myself away from the television. Then when I got home it was, "Good Times," then "Happy Days," then "Mork and Mindy".

I organized my time around television shows. I could tell time by what was on T.V. Two of my favorite shows were "Benny Hill" and "Cell Block H". "Benny Hill," was so funny. The show was about a little foreign man known for patting women on the but. But he also did movie skits, where they sung and danced. I found it very entertaining, but my mom didn't like it. Whenever she saw me watching it she would make me turn it off. I would have to wait until she fell asleep or passed out, which ever came first, and I would turn it back to the channel and turn it down. When that went off, "Cell Block H," came on. This show was about women in prison. They used to fight and curse and every week somebody had a situation going on. I found this to be very educational as well. I knew if nothing else, I did not want to go to prison.

My mother hated me watching these shows just as bad as my daddy didn't want me listening to Prince. It got to the point that when the kids would come get me to go outside, I wouldn't go. So they would sit down with me for a few shows then get bored and leave. I guess I was fascinated by other people's lives. When you came to visit, I would give you the overview of what was about to come on and you could decide from there if you wanted to stay.

I loved "The Night Rider," with David Hasselhoff. Now that was a fine white man. And the men from Miami vice now that was the dynamic dual, and they were fine too. On Saturdays there was, "Welcome Back Carter," then on Saturday mornings it was "Tom & Jerry," "Bugs Bunny, and Friends," and "The Power Rangers," which became the new crave. I loved being a kid and being able to escape into television.

Chapter 5

## Middle School

I went into Middle School with the excitement of a wide eyed little girl ready to take my life to the next level. However, before I could get going good, one of my classmates gave me another rude smack of reality. He committed suicide. His name was Alex Morgan.

Alex, was a quite kid who kept to himself. He never gave anyone a clue that he would do something like that. But he did and it affected everyone. One day we're happy go lucky, excited about middle school, and the next day, one of our classmates is dead.

The next morning after it happened, we came to class and the teacher announced he had killed himself. Like clockwork everybody gazed at his empty chair and paused. For one second, it was like the world had stopped turning. I wondered what could have been going on with this kid that would cause him to take his life. I mean life was hard for everybody, but then who am I to determine what's good for one and bad for another.

Later that day, I rallied up some folks from class as well as a few people from the hood, and went to his house to express our sorrow. Only five people were part of the group; however, his mother was glad to see us. His mom told us he had hung himself.

It's interesting how kids deal with death, because the next day, we were back in class as if nothing happened.

My classes were cool; my only problem was I talked a lot. My English Teacher Mr. Purdue caught hell. I ran my mouth like water. He would call home to tell my mom and since she worked for the government she was always home to get the call. After school, I would dread going home. Nana was quick to put my ass on punishment, too. A few of those days he faked me out. He had me going home acting like the perfect angel waiting on her to say something and the next day he would stress how he had given me a second chance.

Middle School was exciting. It wasn't long before I had put a little click together and we were creating havoc. It included me, my friend Aaron, my girl Aretha and my girl Nancy. The four of us had nearly every class together.

I had one class that I loved; swimming. It was my favorite. I also had a fascination with dance and tried out for the dance team.

Just when I was really starting to get into the feel of Middle School, I met someone who would try and make my life pure hell. Her name was Big Joann, the bully of Jackson Middle. Joann was this big two-hundred-pound chick who met her prey everyday at the candy store. I would have to deal with her the entire time at Jackson. I mean this girl never took a break from bullying; it was a full time occupation.

Each day, in order to survive, you had to have a method in how to avoid her if you wanted candy. What I would do is after we got out of school, I would wait behind a little I'd wait for her to attack one of the other kids and then move in and then out real quick. Many times my ploy didn't work. She would spot me, and I would try and act real friendly, but it never worked. She would give me that mean look, snatch my bag then dare me to say something. She wouldn't take everything out the bag, just what she wanted, then give me what was left. Every day was the same thing. I'd get near the store and there was Big Joann, heaving somebody off the ground, swinging them in circles, then tossing them in the air like rag dolls.

All in all, walking home from school gave me a freedom I never had. It gave me the opportunity to observe the neighborhood. One of the things I took notice of was the Kingdom Hall. My girl Chrstina lived right next door to the hall. They were half black and half Hawaiian and she had the cutest brothers. There were three of them and they were all fine. They had that thick curly hair and they were also Jehovah Witness. The Sanders who stayed next door to them were also Jehovah Witness. I had a crush on both the oldest Sander's boy and Christina's older brother. They both were a few years older than me but I didn't care; I had a thing for older men.

I also had to pass this boy Booky's house on the way home. Now Booky was also fine, but he wasn't Jehovah Witness. Matter of fact he was the most popular boy in school. All the girls loved him, and from what I heard, he already had a girl pregnant in the 8th grade. And I could see why. He would cause my heart to flutter every time I saw him and I would break my neck to speak.

I also had to pass Ms. Flower's house on the way home. Now her daughter was friends with Nana, so I had to be real careful how I carried myself. Ms. Flower's was also the first person in our neighborhood to get HBO. The summer before I had got my ass beat because me and a few friends had disappeared into Ms. Flowers's house to watch HBO without getting permission. I told dumb and dumber Victor and Travon to tell Nana where we were going, but they didn't. So we're sitting there, the movie almost over and the next thing I know, somebody's banging at the door. So Ms. Flower's went to the door, opened it, and the first thing I saw was this large group of people with about a hundred torches raised in the air. I couldn't believe it. It was "Eye On the Prize" live and in living color. The 1960's all over again. I looked in front of the crowd expecting to see leaders of the civil rights movement; but instead I saw my mother, grandmother, Aunt Mona and others. From what I could gather, they had been looking for us for hours. On the way home I tried to plead our case, but Aunt Mona for one, wasn't hearing it. The more I talked the louder she became. Well, to make a long story short, me, Travon and Victor got the whipping of our lives. It would be the last time that I ever trusted either of them to deliver information that could determine my fate.

Every day, our house was always full of people. Out of those, you could always find my mother's friends, Ruby and Carol. Carol stayed across the street in a two family flat with her mother, her twin sister, her sister's husband and her boyfriend. Carol and her boyfriend stayed in the basement and her sister and her husband stayed upstairs on the second level. Carol was a pretty brown skinned young lady with a nice shape and big pretty legs. She and my mother grew up together and boy when they were young, they were both beautiful. Men would ride down our street just to see them walk. They both had walks to die for.

Ruby was not as pretty as the two of them, but she was Nana's girl just the same. Ruby was tall and skinny, I'll say about 6ft and she always looked like she was high. In fact, one day I went downstairs to get something off the clothes line and when I got down there I heard a noise. So I crept back to where the sound was coming from and there was Ruby, standing there with a needle sticking out her arm. When she saw me, you would have thought she would have tried to hide it, but she didn't. She just stood there pushing the needle into her arm until the heroin had disappeared into her veins.

When she looked up and saw me, she rolled her head around a little and then told me to never do drugs. That it was bad for you. That I should never be like her. I was stunned. I had never seen anybody doing drugs before, and to see it first in my home was even more shocking. Without saying a word, I turned, went back upstairs and told my mother what I had just saw. Me and my mother was close in that regards. She made me feel like I could talk to her about anything, and as long as I didn't think the talk would get me in trouble, I usually did.

After I told her what I saw, she told me that she would talk to her about doing drugs in our house. I then asked her if she did drugs and she said no, that she didn't. She then said that she popped a few pills and smoked a 51 every now and then, but that was about it. I just looked at her. If I wasn't mistaken a 51 was weed mixed with cocaine, just what was she talking about when she said no. I guess she figured since she wasn't sticking needles in her veins that nothing else counted. To me, however, it was all the same. Drugs were drugs. At the time, I was glad that she had been honest, or at least I thought. Because it wasn't long after this that we were pulling her out of Andrew's car, herself, high as hell.

After discussing drugs, I asked my mother if she could give me some tips on dance, being that I was going to try out for the dance team at our school. When she was younger my mother had been a dancer and was still pretty good at it. So she got up and started showing me a few steps. She then told me that I needed to learn proper warm ups first and started showing me a few of those. I loved the way my mom moved. She moved nothing like me, she was very graceful.

Well, in spite of my mother's help, I didn't make the team. I remember coming home and as soon as I walked in the door she knew what had happened. She immediately pulled me to her, gave me and hug and a kiss and told me if I practiced that I would do better the next time. My problem was, I was so tomboyish. It was going to take a miracle for me to do splits and leaps in the air. Now I had no problems doing backward flips and swan dives off the back porch, but this was going to be a challenge.

After that day, I decided to put my heart into getting better. I practiced every day after school and I would also sneak into the auditorium and watch the girls there. Ms. Jones, the dance teacher was cool, after seeing how interested I was she would let me sit in and watch. I really admired the girls on the team.

They were all popular, pretty and each year during the annual spring fling would be the stars of the show. I'd never seen the show in person, but I had heard a lot about it. Just watching them practice gave me enough to know, that on stage is where I wanted to be.

After much practice, observation and a little luck, the next time around I made the team. Deep down inside, I think Ms. Jones just let me on the team because she felt sorry for me. But I accepted my position and worked hard every day. I did have nice legs, and Ms. Jones said I had great potential, whatever that meant.

My best friend during this time was a girl on the team named Melanie. She was tall, pretty and shapely. The boy's loved her. The thing I liked most about her was that she was grounded. She knew she had it going on but she never let that affect the way she carried herself. In school, she hung with all the popular kids but when we'd walk home, she acted like I was just as important as anyone else. She, like me, also lived with her grandmother, along with other relatives that lived in the house.

After awhile I learned to love her family like my own. They too were a bit dysfunctional, but they were nice. I didn't see her mother much, and her father never came around. But I saw her grandmother and aunts a lot. They all had good jobs working at the plant. As a result,

Melanie didn't want for nothing. She stayed fresh.

I would go over her house every day after school to practice. Her house wasn't as active as mine so we would have a lot of quite time to focus on our craft. I would stay over each evening until right before the street lights came on then I would hurry home.

Sometimes on the way home I would run into Booky. One day I was walking home and I saw him but it was getting late so I tried to ignore him. The street lights were already flickering and if it was one thing that Nana didn't play, that was coming home after the street lights came on. So now I'm almost at a trot. So I pass the camper, but he sees me, runs out and jumps right in front of me. Now keep in mind I was not the cutest girl, I looked alright, I had acne, was skinny, no titties and no ass. So when he jumped in front of me I was shocked. I had to admit, that at that moment he made me feel worthy. Like I was pretty. So I was flattered. So anyway, this fool jumps in front of me and blocks my path. When I tried to walk around him, he would block my path. I have to admit that doing this made my heart flutter. He could probably see that I was blushing but in my mind, the street lights were still flickering and if I didn't get my but home it was my momma I was gonna have to answer to, not Booky. Before I knew it though, he was no longer just trying to block my path, he now had his arms around me preventing me from going anywhere. I didn't know what to think at this point. I tried to wiggle and wrestle out of the hold, but he was too strong. As I struggled, I could feel his thing on the back of my butt and each time I'd wiggle it would get bigger....and bigger...and bigger. By this time, he had me in a bear hug that was impossible for me to get out of. Nevertheless, as visions of my mother meeting me at the door came over me, a superpower shot through my body thus allowing me to break away. As I ran off, he yelled that the next time I would not be so lucky.

When I got home, I ran through the door just as the street lights were coming on. As I ran toward the bathroom too ready my bath, Nana cut her eyes in my direction to let me know how close I was to getting my ass on punishment, and I responded with a head gesture just to let her know that it wouldn't happen again.

Unlike some of the kid's parent's in my neighborhood, my mother trusted me. She had no reason not to because I was a good kid. I had never been a liar, plus I wasn't good at it anyway. I realized at an early age, that if you told one lie, you would have to tell another one to back that one up and so I figured why not just come clean the first time.

When my bath was ready, I took off my clothes, but when I got to my panties they were wet. It was the first time I had ever experienced being wet as a result of a boy. When my mom came in to use the bathroom I told her what happened with Booky, then told her about my panties. She then teased me and asked if I'd peed on myself, then seeing my face said that I had gotten that way in response to Booky. I had kinda figured that but her telling me help to relax any fears I may have had that it was something else. Before leaving the bathroom, she told me to be careful. That I was getting older and the last thing I wanted was to end up getting pregnant while still in middle school.

The next day I couldn't wait to tell my friends at school what happened with Booky. The older girls were already screwing so they weren't impressed and left as I started talking, but the younger girls were all in. All we did was wrestle and tussle for about 15 minutes, but when you almost 13, and a virgin, hell that was a lot.

Just as I was finishing my story, Ms. Jones walked in to help us with dress rehearsal. We were having what would be my first concert the following day, so I along with all the other girls were very excited. Although I wasn't a part of the main group, I was to participate in four different dances and costume changes. One of Ms. Jones's old students, a young lady who was currently dancing on the television dance show "The Scene," came in and helped us with our dance moves. Everybody knew her from the show, so we were also excited about her being there. She was like the Debbie Allen of Detroit.

Between Ms. Jones and the girl from The Scene, we were ready. Ms. Jones was a natural. She was brilliant. She knew how to run a show. We practiced so much that if I heard Family Reunion by The Ojays or Pink Cadillac by Aretha Franklin one more time I was going to die.

The following day the concert was set for 4:30. I went to class as usual, but everybody and I mean the whole school was excited about the concert; everybody from the teachers to the students. I felt like a star. Everybody either wanted to be around me, or wanted to be my friend.

This was also the day that I would meet the girl who would later become my best friend in life. Her name was Naomi. She was much smaller than all the other girls in our grade and as she sat in the back of the room, I couldn't help but notice her because of the way she was dressed. From the rings on her fingers, to the fresh clothes she had on, I knew it was something special about her. When class ended I found myself intrigued enough by her to follow her into the hall. When she got out in the hall, two big burly girls, known for kicking ass, were out there waiting to escort her to her next class. At that point I was really curious. Who the hell was this girl?

When I got to lunch, I discovered I was about the only person in the school who didn't know Naomi. As it turned out, she was a bad ass who'd been transferred to Jackson after getting kicked out for fighting. Everybody in the lunch room seemed to have a story about her. I mean this girl was maybe 4ft'3" and at best 60 or 70 pounds' soak and wet. So to say the least, I was impressed.

When 4:30 came, I was a nervous wreck. My heart was pounding. The best part about it though was I didn't show it. As I stood behind the curtain watching the crowd, I watched my mother, grandmother and Aunt Mona walk in and take a seat. Then Ms. Jones went onto the stage and prepared everyone for what was about to come. Soon, the first act was on stage doing their thing. They tore it. The crowd went crazy. When my turn came we did an African routine to the song, "Wade in the Water." When we finished my mother acted a fool. You could hear her voice on top of everybody else in the crowd. I felt wonderful. It was the best feeling of my life.

My dad wasn't able to make it, but he did pick me up later to spend the weekend with him. That evening he took me to his sister's, Aunt Jackie's. Usually when we'd stop over it would turn into an all nighter for me because she had a daughter, Robin, and we would get together and convince my father to let me stay. Aunt Jackie was a real sweet and hard working person. Every time I saw her she was always doing the same thing; folding clothes, cleaning the house or cooking. And boy could she cook. I loved going over there. As nice as she appeared though, Aunt Jackie also didn't take no mess. She was as mean and strict as they came. Robin also had an older brother named Jason and she kept those kids in line. There was no back talking in that house.

Her husband Larry was also stern. He didn't talk much but he didn't have to. When he gave you that look, you knew it was time to stop whatever you were doing and sit down somewhere. Also, unlike my house, they ate dinner together. There was no walking around the house with plates and sitting where ever and then leaving your plate all over the house after you finished eating. They ate at the dinner table, and when you finished, the scraps went into the garbage and the plate into the sink.

My dad's side of the family was very family oriented. When he would take me home on Sundays I would always beg him to stop at my great grandparent's house. They lived on Lilliebridge. Grandma Missy and her husband Lester were my grandmother's parents on my father's side. Grandma Missy was a beautiful high yellow woman. She was half black, half Cherokee, and had that long black Indian hair. And boy could she cuss. She would cuss you out at the drop of a hat. With her, I was the exception. She never had to curse at me because I never gave her reason to. I generally only saw the softer side; the funnier side. I remember her as always being comical; forever making light of a situation. She was also a good piano player and would play and sing for me whenever I came by.

I loved to just sit on Grandma Missy's porch and look through the screen at the cars going by and listen to her tell stories about the old days. She had a very colorful personality. I loved her so much.

## Chapter 6

## THE BEST MOMMY

Back home, when Nana wasn't high, she ran a tight ship. She made sure I went to bed on time each night, and woke up ready for school the next morning. Each new day started with grandma hooking up a nice breakfast. It usually started with farina, which was the poe version of cream of wheat. She would get it from Focus Hope along with our usual block of cheese, canned meat, and powdered milk. That powdered milk was some nasty stuff. Grandma would mix it with water, fill up an old regular carton and try and pass it off as real milk. When she first started doing it I would taste the milk and knew something wasn't right. I would then look at the expiration date and see that the carton was some two months old. After that, I quickly figured out what she was doing. With grandma, whatever came out of the kitchen, we had to eat. I remember once pouring some of that milk into my cereal and then protesting about it. Well protest or no protest, I had to eat it. After that I learned to take my time before rushing into the kitchen and just plopping anything down on my plate without first checking what I was getting myself into.

My grandmother was a great cook though. She could hook up anything. By Friday of each week, she would take the leftovers from the previous days and hook up a gourmet meal. Along with her famous cornbread, she was no joke. Thanks to my grandma's rules about eating, hunger was never an issue in our house.

Many of you have probably heard the saying, "jack of all trades, and master of none," well that was my grandma. As a matter of fact, the first time I heard the phrase the person was referring to her. I didn't quite know what it meant the first time I heard it, but like most sayings, I knew at some point, I would understand its meaning. One thing I did know about her though, was there wasn't anything that she couldn't do or anything that she didn't know. I figured that must have had something to do with the saying.

Around about this time in my life, my grandpa Isaac came to live with us. He was my mom's father. When he moved in he really seemed to uplift my grandmother's spirits. I don't know why he'd moved out in the past, I was too small to remember, but I do know that having him around really made her happy. Grandpa was a man's, man. About 6',2", light complected and strict. Even though, like my grandma he was known as a man who could practically do anything, this time when he moved in he was somewhat sickly. He didn't look it at first, but I remember grandma saying that he had emphysema and for all intents and purposes, had come to stay with us so grandma could help make his life easier during his remaining years.

I didn't know much about grandpa other than he had moved back to Detroit from Milwaukee and was the father of my grandmother's last three children, which were Nana, Aunt Juanita and Aunt Mona. He and grandma had never married.

Like I said grandpa was very strict. He didn't take any crap off of anybody; especially my mom. I remember how my mom use to sit with her legs open and he would constantly tell her that ladies didn't sit with their legs open, but of course Nana had a hard head and really didn't listen to anybody about anything. Well one day she was sitting with her legs open and the next thing I know a shoe was flying through the air headed dead for her head.

Another day, she was lying around nodding off, legs wide open, with food hanging out of her mouth and he came in fussing about her taking pills and how tired he was of her popping them damn pills. So I'm sitting there, and I'm thinking to myself, if he was so damn tired of her taking pills, where was he all those years before she got to that point. Would you believe that he walked over to her, grabbed her up by her arm, drug her downstairs and commenced to whipping this grown woman's ass with a belt. I'll never forget it. You could hear her crying all throughout the house. Grandpa was crazy. He was also a walking contradiction. Only a week before this incident, I had gotten sick and grandma was in the kitchen trying to get me to take a couple of pills for my headache. Well grandpa heard what was going on and came storming in the kitchen. He asked why I was making all that racket, and grandma said because I was sick but didn't want to take this pill. I admit I was in there crying and acting a fool, but it was my first time taking a pill and I just couldn't swallow it. I wasted three pills before he came in there. When he saw what was going on, he walked over to me, stuffed a pill into my mouth, then grabbed me by the face so tight that I had no choice except to swallow the pill or die.

I also can thank grandpa for turning me against professional baseball. That happened as a result of a rule of his that included no slamming doors and no running in and out the house. Well, one day after being guilty of this rule, he grabbed me and made me sit on the floor next to him while he watched the entire game. He made me sit right next to his spit can, so all afternoon as I sat, he would spit tobacco into that can then sit it back down right next to me. So thanks to grandpa, I hate watching baseball, hate chewing tobacco and I know how to swallow a pill.

My Uncle Ronald's daughter, Cassandra couldn't stand my grandfather. And I don't think he cared too much for her either. Her favorite words to him whenever he would threaten to whip her was; he was not her grandfather and therefore couldn't tell her what to do. One day he asked Cassandra of all people to bring him a cup of butter milk and why did he want to do that. To get back at him, she poured some red pepper in his milk, then stirred it up real good and gave it to him.  I saw her doing it but I didn't feel it was my place to but in so I didn't. The next thing I knew she was running out the door yelling and grandpa was right behind her threatening to kill her.

Like I said before, Grandma loved having Grandpa around. So if she was happy, hell, so was I. Their favorite past time together was fishing. Every chance they'd get they would go up on Alter Road right at the edge of Jefferson and fish. Sometimes they would take me and the boys with them. We all had fishing poles. It was rare that I ever caught anything, but grandma and grandpa did. They were good. When we got home, Grandpa would gut the fish and Grandma would cook it. They made a great team.

In March of 82', Grandpa's health started getting worse. It got to the point where he could barely walk from room to room without being out of breath and had to resort to using an oxygen machine just to get around.

***August 14, 2006- I am frustrated as hell. I have been working on this carnival and I don't think it is going to happen this year. It would have been a nice fundraiser for my program. There's always next year, but I'm still***

***holding out for a miracle. I couldn't get anybody to come, partly because I'm new on the block and because I only know half of what I'm doing. Most carnivals have standing contracts; like the State Fair for example. It wasn't a total waste though, I did get three donations: the science center donated a family pack of 4, the Tigers donated an autographed picture of Craig Monroe and the Red Wings donated a signed hockey punk.***

It got to the point to where my grandfather stayed in and out of the hospital. Then one day after one of those visits, we got the call. My grandmother had been in her room praying all day and I remember falling asleep in her bed and waking up seeing her door open by itself. When the door opened both me and grandma sat up. When she sat up though she started talking, and nodding like she was talking to somebody. But I didn't see anybody, so I asked her who she was talking to and she said grandpa. She said he had come to tell her that he had passed on. Right after she said that, the phone rang. It was the hospital calling to tell us that grandpa Isaac had died.

When it came to school, I'll be the first to admit that I wasn't very smart. Whereas some kids could pick up things the first time around, I would have to really concentrate and have to ask questions before understanding the material. I had to work hard just to maintain a C average. As a result, whereas a lot of my friends ended up getting accepted to Cass and King, I was headed to Finney.

Dance and beat boxing were my two favorite things to do in school. I was the queen of beat boxing. Like elementary school, I still couldn't be touched. Both boys and girls would try and come at me but I would always send 'em back with their tails between their legs. I also loved math, but that was before I was introduced to Algebra and Calculus.

I officially met Naomi for the first time in dance. Ms. Jones called me over one day and introduced us. At the time Naomi was not in our class, but use to come watch us practice, just as I had the year before. I could tell that Ms. Jones was fascinated by Naomi. She would constantly refer to her size, but in the same breath say that she was going to be one of the best on the team.

From the time I met her, me and Naomi hit it off. She would sit in on our practices and before long, found ourselves spending a lot of time talking as well as walking home after school together. Naomi was unlike any girl that I had ever known. First of all, she knew everybody, and secondly, for her size, she had the heart of a lion. She wasn't afraid of anybody. If you wanted to fight, I don't care who you were, she was ready. Her house was closer to the school than mine, and when we'd walk home, I noticed that she knew everybody. We'd stop at the store and she even knew the

Arabs. Matter of fact she knew them so well that they would allow us behind the glass, and give us chips, pop or whatever else we wanted.

I later found out that the two body guards that I would see her with in school were sisters. They lived on her block. When she first introduced us they didn't even speak. They just looked at me like I was nothing. I mean, I didn't want any type of standing ovation or nothing, but damn they could have at least spoke. As time passed, things never really got any better with them. They were consistent from the rip. They didn't like me and I didn't care too much for them.

The first time I went to Naomie's house, it was pretty interesting. Her grandmother, like mine spent most of her time in the kitchen, her mother spent most of hers primping, and then it got kinda crazy. She had one uncle who was demented and on medication, and another one who was a pimp.

From day one, I knew things would be different with her. Unlike most kids who watched television, Naomi wasn't interested in regular sitcoms. I get there, and we sit down to watch T.V., and this chick turns on a porno. I'm thinking we're about to watch Mork and I look and the next thing I know we're watching asses, tits, and dicks. I was in shock. I mean grownups were walking around, coming in and out the room, and we're in there watching an X rated flick.

After watching the porno for about an hour or so, I told her that I was kinda uncomfortable so she turned it off and we went outside. As soon as we walked out on the porch I see this black beautiful woman walking towards us draped in gold. She also had on Diamond earrings, a Diamond necklace, Diamond bracelets and Diamond anklets adoring both ankles. I looked over at Naomi and before she could respond, the lady, who turned out to be her mother, introduced herself, then reached in her purse and handed Naomi a wad of money.

Before that day I had only heard about her mother. The gossip was that she was a hoe, didn't wear panties and made a lot of money. So when her mother turned to walk to her car, my dumb ass was staring trying to see if the no panty rumor was really true. I didn't know if the rumor was true or not, but I knew that I was definitely in no position to be judging nobody's momma. Like Aunt Mona always said, people in glass houses should not throw stones.

After that first day of hanging with Naomi, we were stuck like glue. We did everything together. You didn't see one without the other. Naomi even made the dance team. Ms. Jones said that I needed more instruction so she sent me over to this church in Indian Village to work on routines. I went there from Monday thru Thursday's. I guess she still believed in me but she knew that without a lot of special attention that I would never become good enough to be one of the best. In other words, I could dance with the company, but I was still not officially a member.

Like her mother, Naomi was also a sharp dresser. She stayed fresh. Levis was her thing. She had every color. And she always had money. We were only 12 when we met, but she kept a hundred-dollar bill. I couldn't understand why she ever needed that much money. I surely didn't. I started each day with a warm breakfast, I got free lunch, and grandma would have dinner ready when I got home. The penny candy store was about the only thing I ever needed money for and everything in there was like 20 cents. So you do the math.

Naomi and Nana hit it off from day one. After awhile, they even had their own little language. It was one that I didn't understand, but one I also didn't care to. I knew if my mom had anything to do with anything secret that it was best to try and act like I didn't know. Grandma on the other hand didn't like Naomi. I guess she was a little too slick for her taste. She told me more on more than one occasion that she didn't like me hanging out with her.

I remember the first time Naomi showed up at my house driving a car. She called and said that she was on her way. I figured that her mom's was dropping her off, so I get fresh, she gets there and I go out on the porch and I see this little head sticking up over the steering wheel. I couldn't believe it. She was 12. The closest I had ever got to driving was sitting on my dad's lap as we drove around Palmer Park a few times.

Hanging with her was a brand new experience. As we rode out of the neighborhood and headed to the west side, I felt like a bird flying from its nest for the first time. Now the car wasn't the best, it was old, rusted and had a radiator that leaked, and we had to stop every few miles to fill it up, but we were free.

Our first stop was to Sinai hospital to visit one her friends. When we got there, like the body guards, this girl also had an attitude problem. Come to find, she was fast as hell. She was already dating this fine chocolate dude about 15, who was in the streets, and had spent all kinds of money on her and had bought her all kinds of expensive Liz Claiborne shoes. The crazy part about the whole thing was she was wearing a cast on her foot because she had shot herself with a 12 gauge shot gun after getting mad at him for not buying her some other shit. Would you believe while we were there, he showed up with another bag full of shoes, I couldn't help but laugh to myself. And I thought people from my hood were strange.

The next person that we stopped to see was a mutual friend from my hood named, Rita. I had attended elementary school with Rita and Naomi had known her from the neighborhood. She was one of those girls with a real strict momma. Every Sunday was church. Then Monday was prayer night, Wednesday bible class, Thursday women's meeting and Saturday choir rehearsal. She was locked down. When she stayed in the hood she rarely even came outside.

Around 7th grade her, her brother, and their mother moved close to the airport so she switched schools, but we still kept in touch. She kept in touch more so with Naomi than me but it was all good. When we got over their things still hadn't changed. Her mother came to the door like we were there to kidnap her daughter, then without letting us in, sent Rita out on the porch to greet us.

This time though, I guess after realizing that we had traveled so far to visit her daughter, she went on ahead and let us in the house. When we got up to Rita's room, Rita took off her coat and as soon as she did, we could immediately see she was pregnant. She said she was hiding the pregnancy from her mother and had stayed up in her room most of the time and whenever she did come down she would always make sure that she was covered up. She was knocked up by this dude that lived around the corner from her named Jonah. How funny was that; the girl with the strictest momma on the planet was pregnant? She said she had gotten pregnant her first time out. That information alone was enough for me to put off sex for another few years.

***August 17, 2006 – What is wrong with kids nowadays. Chavez giving me lip because I asked him to wash the dishes and sweep the floor. I can't understand why he thinks I should come home from working all day and wash the dishes. He doesn't pay no bills. When I was his age the things he says I'm messing with him about was called chores. I don't understand, I didn't raise him like that. When dinner was ready I had to stop and catch myself. Edward was gone, Denise was sleep and Alexis wasn't hungry. So I figured I could make my plate while the food was still hot, and not have to worry about making anybody else's plate. But who do I hear from across the kitchen complaining? Chavez. asking why I couldn't fix his plate. I couldn't believe it. I told him hell nol. I couldn't believe that the same person that I'd asked to clean the kitchen was now complaining because I wouldn't fix his plate. But I didn't care how much he complained, I wasn't fixing it. His thing was that I fixed everybody else's plate every day, so what was my problem. Yea, right. After he realized that I wasn't gonna do it, he had the nerve to say "yea alright," as if he was gone beat my ass or something for not doing it. I think that boy smoking crack.***

My childhood came with many adventures, along with many firsts; my first kiss, my first fight and my first period. I remember it like yesterday. We were outside playing baseball, and I was up to bat. Like most tomboys, I was ready to smack the ball over to the next street when all a sudden, I felt this wetness between my legs. It felt something like the wetness I experienced with Booky, but this time, there was no Booky. So I called time out, told everybody to give me a minute, then ran home like a bat out of hell. When I got home, I burst through the door, sped past Nana and ran straight to the bathroom. When I pulled my shorts down, I almost passed out. Blood was every where. I sat down on the toilet just as my mother started beating frantically on the door. "What's wrong," she asked as she turned the knob and walked in without waiting on a response. When she walked in I pointed to my shorts and I could see the relief on her face when she saw the blood. In the end, the funny part about the whole thing was after I got myself together, I wasn't upset about the blood, I was upset about not being able to finish the game.

As my mother instructed me about my situation, I thought about the conversations we'd had about when this day would come and how she and Aunt Mona had schooled me about which method of protection was best. I laughed to myself as I recalled Aunt Mona describing their early days and how she had once gotten a tampon stuck up her coochie and how my mother had to come to her rescue to help pull it out.

The next six days after the initial onset was miserable. I was so uncomfortable. I had really bad cramps and I bled from the time I got up to the time I went to bed, and the smell was unbelievable...it was unbearable. No one had prepared me for the smell. I stayed in the house that whole weekend. I remember asking my mother for some pills that could relieve the pain, and her bringing out every kind known to man. She had Tylenols, emprems, Motrin, pink pills, yellow pills, she had 'em all. Of course I knew not to take any of those, but the way I was feeling, I was tempted. Instead my mom went and got the big red water bottle hanging up in the bathroom and filled it with hot water. She then wrapped it with a towel, and placed it on my stomach. Then she poured me a half glass of Night Train, and baby, after that wine finished doing its thing, that was all she wrote. I was out like a light. Later that evening, when I woke up, I felt so much better. The night train had done the trick.

It took a few months before I got use to my period. After that first time it actually wasn't that bad. The main thing was that I was now at a greater risk for getting pregnant, so if I thought I had any inclinations before, now I was sure I didn't.

When school started back that September, everybody who wasn't developed when school let out, was now in full bloom. Naomi was even wearing a training bra. I was also not the first one to get on my period during the summer. Naomi had also started hers. And not only had she started, she had chosen tampons over pads. After the story about Aunt

Mona, I hadn't even considered tampons. However, knowing that I would have to fail swimming unless I tried them, I gave them a shot. So me and Naomi went into the bathroom and she gave me the step by step instructions. The whole thing was so funny because she couldn't possibly know too much more than me. Anyway, after about three attempts, and a big mess, I finally got it in.

Wearing a tampon was nothing like wearing a pad. By the end of the day I was in extreme pain. As a matter of fact, I was limping. Everybody kept asking me if I had hurt my leg, but what could I say? To tell you the truth, it felt like somebody had shoved a foreign object up my coochie, and was making me walk with it as a method of torture. I couldn't understand how Naomi could stand it.

When I got home, I explained to my mom what was going on, and she said that I must have put it in wrong, or maybe was tense because that would also cause discomfort. So I went into the bathroom and this time relaxed and placed another tampon up my coochie. She was right. This time, other than the pain from earlier I didn't have a problem. That was a relief.

***August 18, 2006 - I'm stressed to no end. Mainly I'm tired of feeling like I won three hundred billion dollars in a lottery sweepstakes and the only option of payment is fifty dollars a week. I still haven't closed on the house.***

*Everything I'm trying to do right now consists of me pulling the rest of the money out of this house. The program that I'm trying to put together is getting a little frustrating only because I'm not up and running like I would like to be. I'm making progress though. I am in the process of assembling my board. Everything that I want to happen I know eventually will happen. It's just a matter of time. When I pray for something hard enough it might not happen right then and there but it happens. It happens when I least expect it. Don't get me wrong, I have gotten an instant response from the heavenly father on a few occasions. For instance, I was broke as hell Monday. I'm sitting at the desk and I'm plotting on how I'm going to eat breakfast... lunch, something. Not less then 10 minutes into my stomach growling one of the directors gave me a meal ticket for going over and above my job description. I got my ass up and went to the cafeteria so fast it wasn't funny. As I walked to get the food all I could say was "God is good."*

*Aug.21, 2006 - It is 8:30am. I'm at work and who walks in but Mrs. Ruth, my old English teacher from middle school. She was at the hospital visiting somebody. She was still as pretty as she was back in the day. It was nice to see her. She acted like she remembered me but I know she didn't. When I first saw her I tried to hide my face because I don't think I was a prized student in her class. I got put out of her class a few times for running my mouth.*

*Till this day I don't know what was so important to where I had to talk so much that I got put out.*

*Aug. 22, 2006- I was late as hell today. I caught a damn flat on Davidson right before the exit to get on 75. It was 6:45am. I pulled over to the side and got out to change the tire. I had just put my make up on and combed my weave when the car started shaking uncontrollably. I had just replaced the passenger side tire on Friday. I also need the control arm replaced, the tire rod fixed, a wheel alignment, you name it, it needs to be repaired. What a way to start my freaking morning. Davidson is no joke. Cars were flying like they on a race track and I'm out there, makeup flawless, weave flowing and can you believe no one stopped to check to see if I needed any help. Hell, I'm a woman with a flat on the side of the road with a jack in my hand. HHEEELLLOOOO HHHHEEEELLLLPPP. I told myself that once I started breaking the lugs someone would stop and help. Nope. Still nobody. After I broke the lugs still nothing. So I pent my weave up, jacked the car up, took the lugs off, removed the old tire and put on the spare. Would you believe as soon as I started tightening the lugs this white gentleman came out of nowhere and asked if I was okay. He then took the four- way out of my hands and tightened the lugs the rest of the way then jacked the car down. It's good to know that there are still good people out there. Anyway I*

***thanked him for his help, then headed to work. I got there at 7:15 am. Not bad for a girl, huh.***

By the time I reached 13 years of age, there seemed to be at least one pregnant girl in every class. Well, maybe not every class but there was a lot. Also generally when they would leave to have the baby many never returned. The one's that did return seemed to only stay a short period before they also dropped out. It was like monkey see monkey do. I was willing to bet if you asked one of them if one of their friends jumped out of a window would they jump the majority of them would probably say yes.

Anyway, the first day back was cool. It always is. The only problem was that most of my friends were put in separate classes. And for some reason, it seemed like the teachers had spent their entire summers preparing for the fall. They were ready. In each class the teachers gave us supplies and a stack of work to go along with it. You could tell they had worked hard making sure that they were ready when the semester started because each teacher had assignments set aside for weeks.

When I got home, my intention was to set time aside and start on some of my homework, but no sooner than I finished the dishes, Naomi called. She said she was on her way to pick me up so I ran through a few math problems right quick and waited for her arrival.

When she arrived we decided to go visit Rita because she'd had her baby. When we got there, the baby was so cute. The baby daddy was also there. The whole time, the only thing I could think was how different Rita's life was going to be. I couldn't imagine waking up in the middle of the night to feed and change a baby. I'd stopped playing with my dolls two years before because they were too much maintenance. I wondered how she would attend school and who would watch the baby. I also wondered if her momma had told her about protection. Mine had told me long ago that if I ever got the urge to give up my precious jewel to let her know so we could go to the doctor and get some protection. She reminded me that it only took a drop of sperm on the tip of a dick to get you pregnant. Need I say again, Rita got pregnant her first time.

I'm not gone say that my mama was so honest to where she never lied to me, but a lot of the things she told me was true and something always happened to me or somebody that I knew to confirm it. The day after I told her about the panty wetting situation she told me about the urge. I guess she knew sex was coming next or at least the curiosity of it. I was always reminded that the adults in my family were also children at some point and that they had been through some of the things that I would go through. I would talk to my mother, aunts, father, grand parents, and they would answer my questions. I know it's a lot easier said then done, but I can't name anybody in my immediate family that wasn't patient with me and not willing to help me along the way. Even if it was to just get rid of me.

On the other hand, I would be visiting friends and after the first question their parents would get frustrated and hostile. In my house it took an average of about six questions before I got hollered at or told to go play. I could never understand how parents could not have patience with their kids. They are the first teachers and other relatives and adults are the substitute teachers. Their job is to teach, and the job of children is to learn.

***Aug 22, 2006- Oh my God, Denise is going to be such a liar. We stopped by the park and while there I asked Denise about a little scratch on her face. I knew it was from the cat, Gracie, but I get a kick out of her answers. When I asked her about it, she said the cat had scratched her on Saturday. But it was now Tuesday and I hadn't seen it before. The problem was that she would always be up in the cat's face, pulling on its tail, etc. and the cat would end up scratching her. So instead of telling me the truth because I know that's what happened, she would act like the innocent party and make up stories.***

***Edward brought this little cat home a few months ago and I don't mind having a cat because they keep mice out of the house.***

***Since Gracie has been in the house I have not seen one mouse. She is definitely on her job.***

Well, for all things considered, things seemed to be going pretty well for my mother. Then one night about twelve midnight grandma gets a call from a Ms. Betty Jones, telling her that a lady has shown up at her door, who says grandma is her mother, and it looks like she needs medical attention. The woman has been brutally raped and beaten. Ms. Jones said the lady didn't want her to call an ambulance, but instead wanted grandma to come pick her up. So we all got up, put on our clothes and headed to a street near Kettering High School called Townsend. Grandma didn't like driving at night so I drove. The weather was terrible. It was pouring down raining. As I lacked the experience to drive in such weather, it took us a while to get there. Cars were blowing their horns, but I didn't care. I couldn't even see the white lines in the road.

When we got there, I was really afraid. I didn't know what to expect. I was scared out of my mind. I didn't know whether she was near death or what. When we pulled up, I told grandma to stay in the car while I went in. When the lady came to the door, the first thing she did was look at me and ask how old I was. I told her 13. She then looked passed me to see if anybody else was with me. I then told her my grandmother was in the car so she relaxed and let me on in the house. When I saw my mother I was shocked. She was wrapped in a blanket, didn't have on a stitch of clothing, and her face looked like she'd been dropped face first from a five story window. It was swollen so bad you could barely tell it was her. As she rocked back and forth, all she kept saying was she just wanted to go home.

The lady was just as shocked as me. She said she'd heard her knocking on her back door, and it had appeared that somebody had rapped her and takin' all of her clothes.

Walking mom back to the car was a chore. It wasn't enough that she could barely walk, she also had the blanket covering her and she seemed more concerned about covering her face, than she was about walking up right. When we got to the car, she crawled into the back seat and laid down so she could rest. Meanwhile grandma was doing all she could to see her face, but because it was dark, in addition to the blanket, she couldn't.

As we headed home, the rain had let up just enough where I could now do the speed limit. I whispered to my grandmother that Nana needed to go to the hospital, but Nana heard me and demanded that I take her home but I didn't. I went straight to the hospital. When we arrived at emergency, they took one look at her and rushed her right in. I gave the white lady at the front desk my mother's name then told her my grandmother would come in and give the rest of the information. As I was leaving, the lady called out and asked how old I was, but I acted like I didn't hear her and kept walking. At 13 years of age, the last thing I needed was an investigation. That's how white people are. Don't get me wrong, I don't have anything against white people, but they like to do things by the book, so I knew better and kept walking. Especially in view of the fact that my mom was obviously a crack head, who'd gotten caught up in a wayward trick gone bad.

As my grandmother sat outside my mother's hospital room, you could tell that the stress of dealing with Nana was starting to take its toll. Only a few months before we were at the hospital getting Nana's stomach pumped after a near death pill overdose. When I walked in the room, I walked over to Nana and gave her a kiss. I asked if she was angry because I'd brought her to the hospital and she said no. She said she would be okay but still wanted to go home. When the doctor came in he asked her a few questions, then told her that the police were there, and that they wanted to talk to her. However, before talking to the police he wanted to do a rape test, check for infections, then asked me to leave. But before I could turn to go, Nana grabbed me by the hand and asked me to stay. As much as I loved my mom, I was not ready to be all up in her coochie. But it was too late, before I knew what was happening the doctor had spread open her legs, placed them in stirrups, and was scraping this white stuff from in between them. After a minute or so the doctor asked her what the white stuff was and with tears rolling down her face, said Elmer's glue. I couldn't believe it. This mothfuckin' rapist was crazy. I mean I had seen some sick shit but this shit cut the cake. But that's what I get for staying in the room. Meanwhile grandma was still outside of the room rocking back and forth and praying.

For the next several weeks, while everybody waited on her, hand and foot, Nana stayed home. It took a while for her to heal, but the minute she did, she was back out in the streets. She'd leave and always come back late at night with a new friend. She'd always had company before, but nothing like this. Now she never came back unless there were two or three people with her. At first I couldn't figure it out. They would go in the room and close the door, and there was always this funny smell coming from under the door. It wasn't weed, so I didn't know what it was.

It was through my own friend that I found out that my momma was smoking more than weed. When I asked Naomi what she was doing in my mother's room whenever she came over, she told me; selling crack. When Naomi told me that she was selling that shit to my mother I got mad as hell. I didn't let her know how upset I was though because the way I figured it, it wasn't her fault that Nana was on crack. But Naomi was in just as deep as my mother, she had no mercy.

That whole day, as me and Naomi drove the streets of the Detroit, I couldn't stop thinking about my mother being a crack head. I wondered how long she had been addicted. At that point she didn't look like she was on crack. To make things worse, my own friend had to tell me and on top of that, made me promise not to tell my mother she had told me. This was terrible. I couldn't tell anybody. I couldn't tell grandma, or Aunt Mona because number one, they wouldn't believe me. In their eyes Nana would never do something like that. I couldn't tell Victor because he would tell anybody willing to listen. The only person I could probably tell was Aunt Juanita. However, that wasn't a good idea, that would just be one more thing for her to hold over my mother's head.

You know, even though my own friend had sold the stuff to my mother, I was still somewhat in denial. I tried to rationalize that she had bought it for some of her friends. After all they were bonafide crack heads and were always around. It took a few weeks before I mustered the courage to ask if she was smoking. I went into her room one day while she was alone, and asked her why was it that everybody who came into her room was on crack. I then asked if she was smoking too. Her answer was no, that she smoked 51's from time to time but that was about it. She then called herself getting mad and asking me who did I think I was coming in her room questioning her about what she did. She told me that I was no better than her. But I didn't care how upset she got. I knew it was only a matter of time before every one on the block found out, and when that happened, that would be all she wrote. Our reputation as a family would be destroyed.

After I left her room, I called Naomi and told her that I needed to talk to her. I needed her to come right over. When she got there, we drove over to Chandler Park and chilled. Everybody was out but we were not there to socialize. I needed to know from Naomi face to face, if she was sure that my mother was a crack head. I told her what Nana had said about smoking 51's, and Naomi looked at me like, "what's the difference, that's cocaine mixed with weed." And I totally agreed, but it still wasn't crack. Nevertheless, Naomi said that that was even a lie. That my mother still owed her money for crack, and that she intended to pick that up on Friday. She joked about my mother and how she better have her money, but of course I didn't see anything funny. She then went on about how much money she was missing by hanging out in the park, so we wrapped up our conversation, and she dropped me back off at the crib.

During this period of time, I became somewhat rebellious, and destructive. If I wasn't up in some boy's house kissing and humping, I was fighting, falling on my face, or simply being accident prone. One incident involved the time I was riding on my friend Cory's handle bars, and my foot got caught in the spokes, almost chopping it off. At least that's what I thought. Grandma on the other hand thought different. Yea, an entire layer of skin had been ripped off, but to grandma, those were injuries all consistent with being a kid. She took one look at the injury, told me to sit down and relax then said that everything would be alright. She then retrieved a bowl out of the kitchen, went and got a bottle of peroxide out the bathroom, then told me to hold my foot over the bowl while she poured the peroxide over my foot to get all the dirt out. She then patted it dry, pulled the loose skin back, then rubbed ointment all around the injury. After that, she wrapped it in gauze. Over the next several days, she repeated these steps. After about a week or so, I was as good as new.

There wasn't anything that grandma couldn't fix. I got into a fight once, and after the fight was over, I was walking home and one of the little boys I was fighting threw a rock and hit me square center in the head. Once again I went running in the house, thinking that we were headed to the hospital. Instead, after getting me calm, grandma took a look, got her famous peroxide, her ointment, placed a spider web in the cut, bandaged it real good, and again, a week later I was good. She did the same thing after my ice skating accident when I fell and my top front teeth cut into my bottom lip almost ripping it off.

You would have thought grandma got money back at the end of the year for not using her medical insurance. I came to believe that the only reason she might use it was if we had lost a leg or an arm. Now in terms of our immunizations, and routine exams, she stayed on top of those. We were always up to date when it came to such things. Even when all of us caught the ringworm after playing in the alley with dirty mattresses; she did take us to the family doctor, Dr. Spike. Then, even though he prescribed her enough medicine for everybody we all had to share the same tube of ointment so she could save the rest for later. Dr. Spike cared for all of us from grandma to my aunts. To this day my aunt goes to the same office. Today his son has now taken over the practice.

My grandmother was something else. The only time I can remember any of us going to the hospital for an emergency was when Victor got hit by a car, and because of the severity of his injuries, we had to take him to the hospital. Grandma was from the old school. She made sure that we were taking care of. Grandma didn't just fix ailments, she made sure we ate fruits and vegetables, ate salads, baked foods...she was serious about our health. The days that she did fry something, which was rare, she made sure that she was baking something the following day.

In terms of my mother, things seemed to start going from bad too worse. Every time we looked up, it was something different. I remember one-night grandma answering the phone, and it was the police. Come to find out Nana was in jail for trying to cash stolen checks. We didn't have the money to get her out, so she had to stay in jail for a few months. It wasn't until right before Christmas that the judge decided to feel merciful and let her out. Grandma still had to pay a few fines before she could come home, so unfortunately that was one Christmas cancelled in our house. I tried to convince grandma to let her stay another month and finish out her 90 days so we could have Christmas, but she wasn't having it.

When we picked up Nana from jail, she spent the whole ride home talking about cleaning herself up. This was only the beginning of many such speeches, but with each conversation came hope that she would do as promised.

***Aug 25, 2006- I'm stressed out and mad because I owe my school $500.00. I don't have it and I'm supposed to start school in a few days. I'm trying to close on the house but I still haven't done that. That money is supposed to be for school, my program, the janitorial service, helping Edward get his ice cream truck up and running, and to fix the house. So until I close, I can't do too much of nothing. The roof is leaking so bad to where if we don't repair it soon the damage to the inside is going to be unrepairable. Social service said they would pay $1,500.00 which is half the roof, so that's cool. I will make arraignments after I get my taxes or the closing to fix the other side. I've been waiting on them since April, 06'. Hopefully they will be out Friday. I still got so much on my plate though. It would be different***

*if Edward was bringing in extra money or even being more supportive. I'm hoping when we close that I can look out so he can start where he left off on his business ventures. He contributes financially but it only covers the bills. Thank God for that, but that's all he does. I did request to manage the money so that helped. I do all the running around, if I have four errands I will ask him to do one and do you know somewhere down the line I have to hear about it, or he will just say no. Last week we beefed all week because he said he got in trouble at work for being late after taking Chavez to his new school. His job was to help him through the application process, and get the necessary paper work to go with it; birth certificate, shot records and things of that nature. To make a long story short, I ended up having to leave on my lunch break to finish the process because when it came down to getting the job done, Edward came up with an excuse. He said he had a meeting and therefore couldn't make it. It was always something with Edward. I told him I couldn't possibly do it because I had two people on vacation. That was the only reason why I asked him to do it. I am very independent so I try to do everything myself. I've been told that I have to learn how to delegate responsibility, especially now that I have a, quote on quote, help mate.*

*I have to be at work at 7:00am so it is physically impossible for me to do things in the morning. Edward's job is a little more flexible and he doesn't have to be in as early as me.*

***But that doesn't seem to matter. No matter what I ask him to do, he always make it seem like he has to go so far out his way to do it.***

When my mother got home from jail, grandma decided to enter her into a rehab center. Even though grandma didn't know about the crack, Nana did so many other things, that she knew she needed to be committed. She was to be gone for up to six months. Like grandma, I was all for getting Nana help. It didn't matter that the facilities never seemed to help, we just believed that one day they would. So, I helped my mother pack her bags, hugged her goodbye, and wished her luck. I didn't take the ride. The facility was two hours away so I opted to stay home.

After about a week, all her friends started asking about her whereabouts. Ordinarily, I didn't like to lie, but I told them she had gone out of town to visit relatives. Her friends were a trip; it was strange seeing them act like they couldn't get high without her. They would come by every day... as if I hadn't just told them the day before that she was out of town.

By this time, I was reaching my 14$^{th}$ birthday. When the day came, all the kids from the block came over and celebrated. Afterward, Naomi called and then came through. By this time, she was always picking me up in someone's late model vehicle. By now, she was making money, so it was nothing for her to throw somebody a few dollars to rent their car. You could bet, that whatever year it was, that that was the year car she was driving.

When she got to my house, we made a few stops and then picked up a few of her girls, Tae and Lena. When they got in the car, Tae took out a bag of weed and handed it to me. I took it from her, looked at it really good, then asked what else was in it. It wasn't like I was an expert or anything, hell I didn't even smoke weed, but I wasn't taking any chances. I was looking for anything white. Shit, in my mind, you could never trust a drug dealer when it came to getting high. I mean, I was all for smoking a few joints, you know, to me, weed was a harmless high, so I didn't have a problem with it. But that's all I was willing to smoke.

In response to my question, Naomi turned and looked at me like I was crazy. I told her that my mom had started off smoking, "normal looking weed," and after doing 51's, was now a crack head. So I needed to make sure nothing else was in it. She then called me a few not so nice names, and told me to roll up the shit, that there was no way that she was about to mix cocaine in any weed that we were about to smoke. So I rolled it up.

After I hit the joint, I was fucked up. Nothing else seemed to matter. I felt good... and free. I was high than a motha. We stopped at the store and Lena scored some Bartles and James coolers and that only added to the high.

During my next go around, I hit the joint a little harder than the last few times and went into choke mode. It got to where Naomi had to pull over so I could get out and get some air. When I got out, the other girls were yelling for me to pass the joint, and to me the shit was funny, because there I was, all bent over, choking, still holding the joint.

After that day, my life was never again the same. Whenever Naomi would pick me up, the first thing we would do was light up a joint. Now, whenever I would visit my Aunt Jackie and Uncle Larry's, when he'd light up a joint, or funny cigarette as I was still suppose to think, he would have to tell me at least five times to go outside and play.

None of my other friends knew I smoked weed. I didn't smoke at home, and I definitely didn't smoke when over my dads. He would have killed me had he found out. Nobody ever knew. I became a functional weed head. I went to school, I did my chores, still played like a kid, but I would smoke weed three to four times a week. I hid it from my friends like Aaron, Nancy, Aretha, Melanie, and Janice. Nobody on the block knew and nobody else my age smoked weed. This actually worked out to my advantage because had they also smoked, I probably would have been smoking every day.

During this time, I was dating this boy named Steve. He lived near my Aunt Mona, so I started spending a lot of time over there. Like I said before, I wasn't really doing anything at this point, a lot of humping and grinding, but for me that was saying a lot.

Not long after I started hanging out with Steve, my cousin Cassandra moved downstairs from Aunt Mona, so that gave me another place to crash. I didn't care too much for Cassandra's new boyfriend though. Whenever I would visit, he would always break his neck to speak. So whenever he was down there I made it a point to stay upstairs. But that didn't work. After awhile he started coming upstairs when I was there. Aunt Mona never thought anything of it, but I knew better. All that laughing and joking didn't fool me.

Steve and I spent all of our free time together. If we weren't on the phone, we were meeting half way and walking the other back to either his house or Aunt Mona's. I didn't go in his house, though, I would sit on the porch. His mom was a real funny type person, so I didn't go over much. After she moved out the projects, I guess she thought she was some what better than other people. At least that's the vibe I picked up.

After watching her she taught me a lesson. To keep it real. I made a promise to never change once I moved out the hood. To never forget where I came from.

When we were at Aunt Mona's, she was a bit conservative. She would let him come in, but she kept a close eye on us. That was good too, because my little coochie was hot. I think I would have given it up to Steve. But it was not to be. I don't know if it was fate, the stars, or what, but that summer he ended up going to Texas. Well, so much for that. Now, I would have to hold off a little longer. But I knew going all the way was coming, I just didn't know when.

***Sept 5, 2006-It is back to school for the kiddies. Alexis is going to the 2nd grade, Chavez in the 9th grade, and Denise is going to head start. The cost of day care is killing us. I had to go to the 2nd hand store to get Chavez a few pair of pants and a couple shirts. Right now he's in California with his uncle on vacation. A vacation from us being broke. I know it's hard on him, hell it is hard on all of us. But we make do. Bush in office and ever since he been in office it has been tight out here. He even cut the time allowed for unemployment. It use to be a time where you could receive unemployment for 26 weeks and if you hadn't found a job during that time you could get an extension for up to one year.***

When my mother arrived home from rehab, once again she was hell bent on getting back to her old ways. This time, I looked up, and whereas before she only had people running in and out of her room, now she had a group of young boys hanging around the house. Come to find out, and I had to find this out from Naomi, these niggas were selling drugs from our house. We had stepped to an all time low. Their boss was this man named Damon. He would show up every other day to pick up the money.

During this time, Nana was constantly putting me on punishment for, as she says it, my smart mouth. But how could I not run my mouth. I disapproved of everything going on. Naomi was my savior. I was generally ordered not to leave the house, so she would come over and spend the punishments with me. When she was over, I would flirt with Damon and she would flirt with one of the boys named Wayne. Shit after them being over so much, after awhile we got cool.

Now even though I had my eyes on Damon, one of the other boys, this dude named Tray liked me. He was always skinning and grinning in my face. So, you know, we was cool. Or so we thought.

One day the boys asked us if we wanted to go to a room to hang out and party with them, and of course we said yes. We were always up for a good party. So we get to the motel. The first time we went everything was cool. We drank, smoked weed, then went home. None of the boys tried anything. They were just cool. Well a few months went by, and again, they asked if we wanted to go get a room. So again, we said yes. This time when we get there, its ten niggas in the room. Some of them looked familiar, and some of them didn't. Still I thought everything was cool. There was like six guys sitting around me and I'll admit, I liked the attention. After awhile though, Naomi started bugging. At first I thought she was paranoid from the weed, but then I saw one of the boys whispering in her ear and her get up and announce that we needed more ice. Well, everybody was so high that one of the boys told her to get it herself, so she looked at me, motioned for me to come on, and we headed out the door.

Now mind you, I trusted most of those dudes. I mean they were practically living with us, so I had no reason not to. However, Naomi knew different. When we got outside and neared the ice machine, she started walking fast and told me to come on because the boy whispering in her ear had told her that the boys were planning to run a train on us. They were planning to rape us. Come to find out, Nana had gotten paid for them taking us to the motel. She had sold us for a total of five rocks. I'm not gone say that I was surprised, shit Nana would stoop to anything at this point. But to sell her own baby for a rock. I mean, I was a virgin.

Well, now here we were way out on 15 Mile, too far to walk, so we were stuck. I didn't know what to do. The only person I knew with a reliable car was my Aunt Juanita, and trust me, she was the last person I wanted to call. Aunt Juanita was going to have a fit if she found out I was at a motel with a bunch of boys. But I had to call her. I had no choice. Naomi wasn't about to call her mom. So I had to call. Well, I called, got cussed out, then prayed and waited that she would show up. I told her this horrendous story about Di's cousin visiting from out of town and how she had left and not returned in time for us to get home. But Aunt Juanita was not our only concern. Now we had a group of niggas riding around looking for us. The desk clerk seemed to sense what was going on and told us that we could wait with him. So we waited. And waited.

Just when we were about to give up hope, Aunt Juanita pulled up. We peeked out the door to make sure the coast was clear, then ran and jumped in the back seat. Even before I could shut the door, Aunt Juanita was burning rubber. I started off about Di's cousin, but she didn't want to hear it. She wasn't stupid. From that day on, whenever she saw Naomi she would look at her like she was crazy then act like she wasn't even in the room. We never told Juanita the truth about what happened. We were just thankful we were able to leave with our coochies in tact; I shutter every time I think about how many dicks we would have had to entertain. I get sick just thinking about it.

After that night the boys didn't come back. Even though Nana had played it off and acted like she didn't know anything about the arrangement, I guess she felt guilty enough not to allow them back in the house. It's really crazy when I think about my age during this time in my life, but the fact is I was still only in the $8^{th}$ grade.

## Chapter 7

## THE DRUG DEALER

When it was time for my senior 8th grade trip, I was very excited. Like most kids, I looked forward to going to the Cedar Point amusement park. Problem was, my father and grandmother had given me money to pay for the trip, but I had no spending money.

I didn't want to ask my daddy because he gave me what he had to go and grandma had given me her last. All she had left was food stamps. I would be all day buying candy to break as many of those as I needed for spending money. I knew Nana didn't have it, because her check wasn't due until after the trip.

Anyway, Booky heard me telling a friend that I didn't have spending money, so he came back around and asked if I was interested in selling a few rocks. He said that he'd noticed that many of my mother's friends were on crack and he could give me a few sacks to sell. That way I could have money to spend at Cedar Point. I told him I would think about it. So I thought long and hard for about 20 minutes. Then I went back outside and discussed it with him. I asked obvious questions. Like if I could go to jail. Would I be killing my own people and would I be considered a drug dealer. Then we discussed that somebody was gonna sell it to them, that it would only be temporary, and if I didn't do it, then I wouldn't have money for the trip. So I agreed to do it. He then went and got a hundred-dollar sack, which contained 10 rocks, then told me that I could get thirty dollars per sack. So I went in the house and told Nana that I had a sack and to let her friends know when they came by. Within 5 minutes she was knocking at my door. Within I'll say...three hours the bag was gone and Booky was bringing me another bag. I didn't get any sleep that night. Every hour on the hour Nana was knocking at my door to cop. At one point she told me that there were 5 people in her room and she bought 5 at one time.

By 4:00 am I was paging him to get another sack. Granted, my mother still had not admitted to smoking crack, however, I knew better. I tried to also be in denial, because I didn't want to admit to myself that I was selling her crack- to smoke. After a few days the guilt started getting to me. I asked her again if she was smoking crack and again she said no. She said by me charging her 10, she was charging them 12 and keeping the two dollars for herself. She assured me that that was it. But it didn't take a rocket scientist to see that she was smoking the rocks, too. Shit, even if she wasn't smoking, she may as well have been because with the amount of smoke in that room, anybody would have gotten high.

After a week, 15 sacks and $450.00 dollars, I threw in the towel. My conscious would not allow me to sell another rock. I just couldn't come to grips with selling drugs to my own mama. I was helping her kill herself. She looked normal and healthy, but she had a sickness and I knew it, so that was it. I quit.

During this same period, Naomi started having problems with her mother. She would stay at my house for days at a time. Her mother would call, and I would deny knowing where she was. She even came to the school once and called me out of class. Again, I lied and said I hadn't seen her. I hated lying to her, but I didn't have a choice. I couldn't turn my friend in. But I didn't have to. Her mother finally caught up with her, and when she did, had her committed. She turned her in to the authorities and the next thing I knew I was getting a letter from a boot camp somewhere in Ohio. The letter went as follows:

*Hey chic, my mama turned my ass in to juvenile. She says I'm out of control and she can't handle me so I'm in this place for at least 6 months to a year depending on how I act. All these hoes up in here either gay as hell, crack heads, or prostitutes with pimps and shit. This place is wild. The butchy bitches love me. I guess they can tell I aint taking no shit, it ain't so bad. Drop me a line or two. Love Naomi.*

After reading her letter I went in my room, closed the door and plopped down on the bed. Naomi's birthday was coming up and I felt bad for her. I couldn't imagine spending my birthday locked up in a six by six-foot cell. So I sat down and wrote a response.

*Hey girl I got your letter. You know I ain't no good when it comes to writing letters. I miss you, don't let them girls get your pie. Nothing going on out here, same o same, o Nana home she been doing well but you know she always do well for the first few months. So far so good. I can't wait until you come home. Try to have a Happy Birthday write back. Love Kiikii.* I also sent her a few recent pictures of everybody to help cope with the loneliness.

After Naomi went to camp, I started spending more time with my father. I had a few friends in his neighborhood so I would spend a lot of time over there. My best friend on the west, was my girl Shawnda. She was real cool. My father lived in a nice area, so things were a lot different over there. On the east side, there was always something going on. From the crack heads, to the projects. On the west side, things were a lot more peaceful. Same with Shawnda. We didn't have to worry about who we were gonna fight and all that nonsense. We played together like teenage girls. Matter of fact, she was the one who showed me how to properly apply makeup. Those are the kinds of things we would do. I loved Shawnda like a sister.

My favorite part about being with my dad was watching him rehearse. He played guitar. When he'd rehearse with his band, he would plug in his guitar, put on his headphones, close his eyes, and get to plucking. He also rehearsed alone. I'd stand in the room and for the first 10 to 15 minutes he wouldn't even know I was in the room. Nothing else existed. Nothing else mattered. When he had that guitar in his hand it was just him and his audience. I didn't realize how passionate he was about his guitar until one day me and my cousin came into the living room while my dad was rehearsing. We were sitting on the floor and he had his eyes closed doing a serious performance. I mean he was really into it. We thought it was funny. You know, we were young. So when he finished we started imitating his moves and laughing thinking he would find us funny. But I learned something that day. I learned that what my father did was not a joke. He asked us what the hell was so funny and it only took a fraction of a second for me to see that he was serious. At that point we got quiet. He asked if what he did was funny. Because if so he wanted to know what was funny about it. He said that he didn't see anything funny about playing the guitar. That this was how he made his living.

I had seen him practice many times with his bands, but that was the first time I'd seen him practice alone. So even though it was entertaining, and funny, it wasn't funny to him. What he did was serious and from that point on that's the same way I looked at it. Dad was on a mission. His goal was to be very successful and so for us to laugh was out of place. And I agree. It was out of place. But we were young. Everything to us was funny. But I realized from that day on that there was nothing funny about working hard to achieve your goals.

Dad played in a mixed band. He and the other guitarist were the only blacks in the band. The band was really good. They played both pop and R&B. My dad sung when they did R&B songs. You could tell that everybody enjoyed each other and enjoyed what they did. I didn't hear many disagreements between them so their communication amongst each other was pretty good. The leader of the band lived out in the suburbs and I would go out there with dad a lot. Back then the area was all white. I remember when I was about 6, one of his band members invited me to his daughter's birthday party. I was the only black kid there. It was a lot different from the parties back in the hood, this little girl had a clown.

My dad did other odd jobs in between gigs. He was never shy about doing what he had to do. His wife Pam made the bulk of the money though. She worked at a hospital as a lab tech.

Each weekend, when it was time for my dad to drive me home, he would start with the lectures. He'd talk from the time we got in the car, till the time we got to my house. The talks mainly covered boys as well as the importance of education. He would remind me that all boys wanted was one thing and how much of a distraction they could be from focusing on my school. And I listened. I understood that he just wanted the best for me. He would be so passionate when he spoke. I guess that's why by the time we reached my house I'd have tears in my eyes. It was like he was looking through me when he spoke.

Each time he dropped me off, you could hear the hurt in his voice and see the pain in his eyes. He always stressed how he wished I could live with him, but Nana would never agree. Therefore, he would have to sum up all life's lessons on those long rides home. God forbid we missed a weekend, then we would have to take the street, just to make sure he didn't leave anything out.

***September 16 2006- I finally met someone who can help bring my visions to life. He talks good and he is not going to charge me an arm and a leg. Mr. Light tries and he is very good with words but it is so hard to get him to see my vision and it gets frustrating. On top of everything I'm dealing with, Edward still hasn't found a way to deal with his temper, so we argue about the smallest things. Tonight we arguing because I simply asked about a particular young lady that called a few days ago. True enough he might not be doing***

*anything, but the way he handles situations such as this drives me crazy. He said he didn't know who she was. Okay, but she called the house and all he can say is I don't know, next time she calls, ask who she is. As far as I'm concerned he's too cocky with his answers. In a marriage you can't be cocky. Leave that shit in the streets. Why the fuck do I have to investigate and solve the case of the bitch that called my house looking for my husband. It would be different if we had a trusting past but Edward has not made me feel like he trusted me from the beginning of our marriage, which makes me think he might not be as true as he would like for me to believe. Usually when someone is always accusing you of something it is because they doing something that they have no business doing. Just two weeks ago he went through my phone and started calling numbers back. It's a good thing I wasn't fucking around. What the fuck… and I can't ask if he found out who the girl was- so we start arguing more and I go into the basement to keep the girls from hearing what we're talking about and he follows me and starts talking about every problem that we've ever had. My thing is tell me something. Tell me the girl was a bill collector; something. I can't take this shit, the devil's busy. I'm trying to build an empire so I can provide jobs and take care of my whole family so we can come up together and the last thing I need is a motherfucker I go to sleep with and wake up with arguing with me all the time over little stuff. And if we ain't arguing he tearing up the house, punching holes in the very walls I'm trying to fix. I'm still patching holes he put in the wall down stairs a few months back. The devil uses the closest to you. I find as long as they have an ounce of anything... evil, jealousy, envy, insecurity he molds it into something so major that sometimes it's hard to just let it go. The lord is the only one that can get me through this. I'm gone let go and let God. He has brought me thus far. If I stop now I would not only be letting my family and friends down, I would be letting myself down too.*

*September 25, 2006- I had a rough week but I'm feeling good. Still haven't closed yet, but we getting close. Last week the whole house was in an uproar. As long as you here on earth you will continue to have problems. Life ain't easy so you solve your problems and keep moving. Its just the revisiting of the same problems that I have a problem with. Arcyle baby mama bought a few things for the house. I told her last week I couldn't afford to feed her any more, so we would have to limit her visits to just staying over the weekend, so the next day I get home its 3 gallons of milk, cheese and 3 boxes of cereal. So I'm cool. She used her WIC coupons. Chavez whispered to me that he asked Arcyle if he could have some cereal and he said Arcyle supposedly said no. When Chavez came in to relay this to me I had just finished with the dishes so I asked Chavez why he didn't wash the dishes. They had been sitting all day. I also asked why he didn't have*

*Arcyle and his baby momma to wash them. To be honest it wasn't that many, plus its his job to do the dishes and take out the trash. Chaves wanted to argue about why I was fussing at him and not Arcyle and I told him this was not about Arcyle, it was about him. I don't take care of Arcyle the same way that I do Chavez. Chavez is my son. Arcyle, my brother. So don't worry about him.*

*As soon as I saw Arcyle I went off on him about not letting Chavez eat any of his cereal. Of course Arcyle denied that he'd said no and insisted that the real problem was Chavez wearing his clothes. That Chavez had gone through his hamper and taken a shirt out of it and was now wearing it. So now Arcyle getting mad and hollering because he said he didn't say anything about cereal. As we're going back and forth Edward walks in and all he had to hear is anything about Chavez being picked on and he immediately jumped in the argument. He immediately takes Chavez's side because he can't understand how Arcyle could be home all day and not do any work. My argument is that he has a point, but that has nothing to do with Chavez doing his chores. His job is to wash dishes and take out the trash. Yea, Arcyle should be doing something if he's home all day. So now that Chavez feels he has back up, he's in the background saying that I always take up for Arcyle and always takes his side whenever anything comes up. Edward then goes on to say that I act like I don't care how he and Chavez feels. I told him I do know how he feels. I understand that It kills him to pay the bills and buy groceries and that Arcyle should be in college somewhere instead of sitting around here. Then Edward goes on to say that that's the first time that I've said anything about Arcyle grown ass being here and not contributing. I understood how he felt however I don't see why I have to say what I feel everyday. So I ask him if I have to bring up my disappointment in Arcyle everyday and he said no, so I asked him... then what did he want me to do. To prevent this same thing from happening again what did he want me to do. My whole marriage seems to be about revisiting problems that never gets solved. When everybody left the kitchen I took the pork chops, corn bread, and macaroni and cheese out of the oven and sat it on the counter. I turned the mixed vegetables off and dinner is fuckin' served. I got my keys and left.*

*I drove to the eastside to see my girl Mody Woowoo. The way I was feeling with all the turmoil in my house Mody or Aunt Mona were the only ones that could bring my spirits up. I met Mody a while back through someone I once dated, who was her man at the time He introduced us and I loved her from day one. I loved her so much to where when they broke up me and her still remained friends. I think the last time I spoke to him was when I was in Alabama and at the time she lived in Alabama and I couldn't find her number so I called him to try to get in touch with her. Anyway, I get to her house and wake her pregnant ass up. It's 8:00p.m. on a Wednesday. I'm usually home during the week. I used to get my ballroom on, on Wednesday or Thursday's, but for the last 3 ½ years I been at the crib. When she opened the door I noticed her stomach had gotten bigger since the last time I saw her. You have to understand with rocks in her pocket. Mody Woowoo weighed in at maybe 110 soak and wet. Now I have seen pictures when she was younger and she used to be thick but I have known her for about 7 years and as long as I have known her she has always been light in the ass. Now that she is pregnant she got a little weight. Her tidies, ass, and legs are bigger.*

*She looks so pretty to me pregnant. I came in the door asking if her old man had a bottle of something to take my mind off things. Hell, I can use a smoke the way I'm feeling. She said she had some pink lemonade and I told her that's not what I had in mind. I was straight. So I immediately starting airing out all my problems and she was tripping because she knew me when, and now I had put all of my eggs in one basket and to hear that I was now just depended on one man made her tickled pink. I was always so hard on men and one of my mottos was what you won't do, another man will. But this was my husband, it was different. So after I released all that tension we talked about her pregnancy. She already has one child, he's 15, so she scared as hell. It took her so long to have another child because she almost died having her son. He ripped her so bad to where you couldn't see where her coochie began and her asshole ended. I'm looking at her like, hell nol. She says she gets jealous when hoes say they only had 2 and 3 stitches. She said she was stitched from the inside out. As I listened to her I couldn't help but visualize her ass wide open and blood all over the place. I'm like that's what I get for waking her pregnant ass up and loading off all my stress on her. She said when she looked up, there was ten more people in the room. She said she should have charged admission. I laughed so hard those few hours with her, bout time I got home I was cool.*

*I still didn't have much to say to anybody, but I was cool. Come Friday its Edward's pay week. I told him I wanted to pay the light bill and I had to pay day care. Now I know he had to pay his car note and I had to get Chavez some shoes for school so I'm looking for at least $450.00 to $500.00. Instead this nigga gives me $275.00. I didn't count it right away, so when I sat down and counted it I called him and asked him what I was suppose to do with $275.00. Lights was $200.00. Carlee $75.00. That's not including gas for me and what about groceries. He then says he can give me some gas but since I got all those people living with me that I should figure it out. Ain't this a bitch. On top of everything I'm dealing with, you gone make money an issue like I'm not already struggling to make ends meet. It would be one thing if he gave me the heads up* *like at the beginning of the week that he will only be able to give me such and such, that way I will have time to make other arraignments. But he waits until the day of with no explanation. Since I've been with him I've been doing nothing but pulling off miracles. Compared to before I met Edward, I took a pay cut with no benefits. I suggested we think about separate living arrangements 'cause he can do that at his mama's. He said ok, but nothing happened. Then he goes to tell Chavez over the phone... yo mama don't want me to buy you no shoes so I call him back and ask him why is he telling my son I didn't want him to buy him some new shoes. What I said was don't buy you no new shoes. Just wait for the closing. I told him it seems like you going out of your way to turn my son against me and tear my family apart. You want me to put Arcyle out and the whole time I'm talking he on the other end of the phone sounding like he had a few drinks. He said he was playing some game so between me yelling and him playing I just hung up the phone. The next day before he left the house he gave me another 100 dollars like it supposed to be extra money. I didn't say a word. It's hard 'cause I don't want to be ungrateful, but damn, I'm trying to be patient because I know its going to get better, but I feel he shouldn't make it harder in the process.*

*I went from a glamour girl to a broke down drag queen. I can't tell you when the last time I been to the shop to get my hair done. Now don't get me wrong, I'm not a superficial person. Aunt Mona and Marie hooks me up for free, but I don't try to go to them every week, because I don't want them to feel as if I'm taking advantage. So lately I have been wearing my hair slicked to the side and a clip on bun. And let's not talk about nails. I have had my nails done maybe 3 times this year. And lashes... please, don't speak of it. Now even with the 100 dollars I still don't have enough to do nothing with. I get paid next Friday and I know my whole check gone be gone to make up for what he didn't give me this week and make it so bad he knew my check was going to be short so since he gave me 375 and not the 500 I was looking for, we not gone have any money to get through next week, and I can't borrow another quarter from no one. So anyway, he took Chavez and got his shoes and a few items and I still don't know what all he bought for his self... but I found a few tags to show he bought more than just one shirt. He also bought Alexis some tights and he bought me some Victoria secret lotion and spray.*

*I'm glad he thought of us in that way but everything he bought he could have waited until we got a hold to some more money. Rather it be the closing taxes, hell, that is only a few months away. Don't take it out the bill money! How could he think about buying shit and we in debt.*

***So we got through the weekend just to fall back out first thing Monday. When he called my job, like normal, we were talking and at first he was sounding nice. But then someone called on my other line for me. It was a friend and she wanted to talk about her evening. She and her booboo was beefing so me, befriending my husband, I start discussing her situation and the advice that I gave her. Mind you, we straight, we good right. So it shouldn't matter what other people are going through. My advice to her was" FUCK THAT NIGGA." He aint right. Me, her and a few coworkers went out this past Friday and just so happen she ran into an old friend and he invited her to dinner and I let her know if she wanted to go out with him, hell, he could pick her up at my house. I have to listen to her complain about this nigga and my thing is she ain't married, so she could do what ever she wants with whoever she wants. Why did Edward ask out of nowhere, "where do I meet my boyfriends," and I said, "boyfriends, I'm married or did you forget." I told him I didn't want to start anything but that he was always calling me out about my mouth. So let me back track so he can see why I say some of the things I say to him. First, you just asked me where do I meet my boyfriends. That is no question to ask a married woman. If I had a boyfriend I wouldn't be fussing about having no money. He goes on to say, "that with the kind of advice you giving, why not?" Well the advice that I gave I gave to a woman who is***

*not married for one, and she found text messages from another bitch on her man's phone that she has been devoted to for the last five years and this aint the first time it has happened. So my advice to her is, "FUCK THAT NIGGA!" I'm thinking to myself why is he so mad. So now all I hear is silence. So I asked for an apology from him for asking me a dumb ass question like that. I felt this was a good time to let him know that he does it all the time so by me bringing it to his attention now maybe it will stop. His response was that he had done nothing wrong. But asking me where I meet my boyfriends is wrong as hell. Then he gave me the driest apology I have ever heard.*

*Well, we have a new security guard at the job. He tried to holler at my girl Hershey when we went out a few months ago. We met him through one of our boys. This was before he got hired in. So he walks up to the desk at the same time as I'm talking to Edward. So I speak to Edward and all I get is this dry ass, hey, back. The new guy goes, (without knowing I'm talking to my husband) that Peanut told him to give me his number. O.k, I'm thinking to myself, what the fuck for now. When Peanut was working here we flirted a little, and kissed a few times. I'm not one to fool around with co-workers but he was fine as hell and he had a body, ok. Shortly after we started, it ended. We never got past first base cause I met Edward and it was a wrap. I'm just gone keep it real... Edward fucked the shit out of me and the next day I was calling my applicants and letting them know that I had filled the position for life partner and if anything, changed, I would consider their application.*

*Now Peanut and Edward had their own little rivalry for the bitches at the work place. Apparently they have been going after the same girls. So after me and Edward hooked up, Peanut hooked up with somebody and shortly after they became a couple. When me and Edward started talking, Peanut made some remarks letting me know about the hoes Edward had and the ones who brought him food, but it didn't matter. Once my mind was made up it takes a whole lot of convincing to change it. About 2 months later Peanut left and I ran into him once since, at his new job. I'll say it was about 10 months since he'd left. When I saw him, I gave him a hug. His girl was pregnant, I had my baby and me and Edward were married. We had a 10-minute chat, then I went my way and he went his. I had nothing but good things to say to him about my husband. Even if we were beefing that day, Peanut wasn't gone know. I'll be damned if I give him any ammunition to hate on my boo. But that's it. It has now been almost four years since I seen him. Now some chick that work at the hospital hating on me and makes it seem like I just seen this motherfucker yesterday and not a few years ago. So now me and Edward beefed out. He already has trust issues with me to start, so anything else is extra. This shit is hell. Can you believe Edward believed that nigga over me. Me and Peanut never fucked, he never took me out, we never did anything that was worth remembering, definitely nothing for Edward to be intimidated by, but yet now I have to deal with this bullshit.*

*I've been flown 1st class to Atlanta and took shopping by someone I liked and fucked. Why in the hell is he so intimidated by someone that meant nothing to me and did nothing for me. So I did what any woman in a fucked up situation would do. I flipped the new guys badge over because I forgot his name. Then I said Gene, this is my husband Edward. Edward this the new guy Gene. Mind you Edward ear hustling so I say it loud enough for him to hear.*

*Then I continued talking, again so Edward can hear. "So he still at the mall, oh yea, what shift. Afternoons, O.k." I then handed the new guy a piece of paper and told him to write down the number. The first thing out of Edward's mouth after that was, who number did I get. I told him Peanut's. Since I didn't have a reason or a clue for why he gave me the number I had to make one up. I told Edward I was working on putting a team together for my boot camp. So that's why I needed the number.*

*In fact, because of Edward, Peanut was not even in the running for the team. But it's not like Peanut wasn't qualified, so I went on to talk about his military background trying to sell this shit. When I saw that wasn't working I added that his girl had asked about me and I saw that wasn't working. The whole thing was basically fucked up because I don't normally lie. Especially when you're dealing with someone who is jealous and insecure and not to mention has trust issues.*

*I hate that I had to lie 'cause it is so easy to tell the truth. But Edward, being the type of person, he is, was not going to leave empty handed. I wish that I had the kind of relationship with my husband where I could have just asked the guy why Peanut wanted the number in the first place.*

*After trying to explain myself, I just put it out there where Peanut was and what shift he worked, so if Edward wanted to know why he was asking for my number he could just go ask him himself. It's situations like this that cause Edward to say he doesn't trust me. We've had a few other situations like this. Nothing that ever turned into anything. So me and Edward get past this. A week passes and we're half way back too normal. Whatever normal is. You know I still don't know why Peanut wanted to give me his number.*

Unless I was with Naomi, or my dad, I didn't get a chance to travel much. My grandma would only leave the house if she needed to go to the grocery store, or run some other type of errand. And when she did Aunt Mona would drive her. Nevertheless, I saw each occasion as an opportunity to get out. Of course I had no interest in following her to the doctor's office, or other such appointments; however, I was always desperate to get out of the house so was willing to go almost anywhere else, except Focus Hope. I hated going to Focus Hope. I remember one time when I was tricked, and ended up going anyway.

It happened one day after I'd arrived from school and saw the two of them sneaking to the car. I say sneaking because Aunt Mona knew that if I saw them leaving, I would ask to go. So they get outside, and they're walking to the car like there's some sort of emergency, but I spot them, run out and beat them to the car and block the door. So, like always, we go back and forth a little bit, and before you know it I'm in the back seat, buckling up for the ride. So I'm in the back chilling, takin' in the sites and the next thing I know, we're pulling up in the Focus Hope lot. That's what I get. Focus Hope was so depressing to me. When you walk in you have to wait on one side of the wall for awhile, and then they finally call your name. At that point you get your grocery list. After that, your buggy, and once you have your list and your buggy; you walk from bend to bend to pick up your items. All of this was fun when I was little, because I use to ride on the buggy then jump off and get the stuff out of the bends. But those days were long gone. I was way too big for that now.

So I'm pouting and dragging my feet and Aunt Mona loving it. She's laughing and acting like she gone hit me with the buggy while dictating to me at the same time to hand her the bag of mashed potatoes, can of chicken, and government cheese. It took everything I had not to tell her to get the stuff herself. The only thing is, if I'd told her that, she would have jumped on my back and wrestled me to the ground right there in front of everybody in the store. She had no problem tossing me around regardless of where we were.

I hate to say it but that Focus Hope, Farina (Cream of Wheat) was good as hell in the morning, and when grandma would make that canned chicken, she would season it, cut up some green peppers and onions, then she would make her special gravy, then take that and place it on a piece of toast, and baby, that was some good eating.

The workers at Focus Hope were pretty strict about getting more than you were supposed to also. However, the lady at the register loved my grandma. She always let her get an extra juice or something. She stayed in the hood and knew my mama was a fiend and that grandma took care of a lot of people so she always made sure grandma got just a little extra.

Whenever we'd get back to the car, my grandmother was always very appreciative. She'd always say, bless her heart, and I'll tease her and say, oooh grandma, you stole that juice. Grandma is a thief. And she'd scold me and tell me to be quiet before someone hears me and takes me serious, then we'd all break out laughing. Right in the middle of laughing though, Aunt Mona would stop and get serious, and tell me to stop talking about her momma, or else.

But by then I would be on a roll...it was hard to stop. I reminded my grandma about the time we went to this, all you can eat restaurant, called the Sweden house and how she had stole some chicken wings. Ah... Mona really got mad then. She looked back at me and was like, "yea, but who ate them. You and your rock head brother, that's who." Then she leaned over the seat and tried to grab me but I was too fast. Aunt Mona didn't like me picking on her momma, but grandma didn't care, we laughed all the way home.

Six months came and went fast. Before I knew it, it was almost time for Naomi to come home. I considered myself a terrible friend because I had written her maybe twice. I hoped she would understand but I just couldn't write.

My Uncle Ronald also went back to jail during this time. After awhile, I concluded that he was probably just better off in jail. Hell, he been to jail so many times that he actually had more connects and more respect at Jackson than he did in the streets. Meanwhile, Sandra and her kids were still in the house. I wondered over and over when they were going home. I mean its not like Ronald was there, and it's not like they were married. I knew I never attended no ceremony.

Since Naomi wasn't around, when I was home, I use to hang out around the corner at my friend Rachel's house. I liked kicking it with her. She helped remind me that I was still a kid. Whenever I went around there she would always be playing with her dolls and her little brothers would be running around tearing shit up. Rachel was cute, too. She wore glasses and looked a little nerdy but you could tell when she got older she would grow into her looks.

I remember one time going around there, and her telling me that my brother had just walked passed her house. That he'd gone up on Forrest, so I decided to go and see if I could find him. At that age my brother was part of my responsibility and going too far from the house could get us all in trouble. I told her I would come back after I found him.

So I walked up Forrest and I see the Grant brothers all standing on their porch. Its about four of them and they all real nice looking. They have a nice pretty house and they're one of the few families in the neighborhood where the mother and father still lives in the home.

As I walked passed their house I asked if they'd seen my brother. They said they'd seen him and another little boy go in this weird white man's house that lived across the street from them. So I head over there and before I could knock on the door, the door opens and the two of them walked out. As soon as I got close enough to Victor I immediately popped him upside his head and proceeded to tell him about leaving the block and going into people's houses without anybody knowing where he was. Would you believe after I popped him he had the nerve to get mad. But I didn't care, he knew better than that. That man could have killed them and nobody would have ever known what happened. Could have chopped them up into little pieces and buried both of them in the back yard.

As we walked home Victor told me that the reason he went to the man's house was because he let them clean up around the place. That the man was somewhat handicapped and needed help lifting things. I asked him if the man ever tried to touch them and he said no. That he had a lot of different kinds of motors in the yard, including mini pads and the man said if they helped him around the house they could earn enough to buy one of the bikes.

That may have been fine and dandy, but at this point, nobody knew him and it was dangerous being somewhere and nobody knew where he was.

***October 10, 2006- I got a lot done today. Denise stayed with Edward's aunt.***

*Chavez went with Victor, this the third weekend in a row since they got back from California. Alexis is home, but I got her busy taking all her French braids down. Edward is finally finishing up the painting in the hallway that I asked him almost 2 months ago to finish and it is looking good. I cleaned both of the girls' rooms, washed two of my comforters, now I'm at Belle tire waiting to finally get my wheel alignment. I have gone through a whole set of tires in a month. In a pleasant voice the clerk says it is going to be a 2 1/2 hour wait. I'm like, hell no! . But it's Saturday and most people are off work. When I initially drove by and looked in the place it was empty, however before I could turn around and get back to the place, just that fast when I got in and looked behind the wall people were lying on top of each other. I can't do anything today; I have to get the car fixed. The car drives so raggedy and I can't afford to buy any more tires. What the hell, ok so after having a ten-minute conversation with myself in front of the clerk, I give him my keys. Again, hell no!. When I get to the waiting area, I have to wake people up for them to scoot over. I asked one girl, who had her pillow out, and her pajamas on, how long she had been waiting, and she said she had been waiting since 8:00am. It was now 1:00 Hopefully when they finish I can still get out and enjoy this beautiful day. Saturday and Sunday are the only days I can get the house in order so I rarely get out. Usually, once I'm*

***finished cleaning I be so tired I usually lay my ass down and go to sleep.***

***My Aunt Jackie got a new car two days ago. Thank God 'cause she needed and deserved one. She stays on the west side and between running to the east side to take grandma to her doctor's appointments and things she has to do, she really need that new car. I hope I don't be in this tire shop all day because I want to go see her car. They don't even have any coffee left in this place. Now that's some bullshit. I see the restaurant across the street is open and I am hungry as hell. Since I put on this little weight I can't stop eating. I think I'll kill some time and this hunger pain at the same time.***

After that first day, Victor and his little friend started to spend more and more time at the white man's house. They assured me that no monkey business was going on so I agreed to let him go. I felt comfortable that Victor would have told me if there was a problem because he liked to see me go off on people and act a fool. I would kill somebody over Victor and Travon and everybody knew that. I didn't like to fight but I would if I had to. The thing is it had to be for a good reason. I didn't just beat people up for the fun of it.

Well, after a few weeks of helping the man out, sure enough, Victor and his friend, each came flying up the street on their new mini bikes. The only thing they needed now was helmets.

One thing I can say about him is when that boy sets his mind on something he'd get it done. Come to find out, the man wasn't so creepy after all. He was a retired mechanic who also took care of his ailing mother. Actually, Victor being over there working was not unusual in terms of his skills because he was known around the neighborhood for fixing lawnmowers. He was skilled in that way. Grandma called him her little fix it man.

When Victor finally slowed down and stopped at the house, he let me take the bike for a ride. Damn it was fast. I flew to the corner in no time at all. I didn't see any cars coming so I kept going across the intersection then turned back around. I knew if I'd gone any further that boy would have broke down crying. As a result, grandma would have surely given me two to three weeks of hard labor. One thing my grandma and Nana didn't play was messing with Victor. They both loved him to death. You can best believe if the house was burning down, Victor would be the first one they'd wake up. They'd woken me up, but they would have wrapped his little yellow ass up, and carried him out in a blanket.

I guess they treated him that way because his father wasn't around. That was there way of making up for his absence. I understood, but at the same time it hurt that they treated him so much better than me. But, anyway, as I'm riding the bike, I'm flying. I ride up to the alley, turn around and then fly back down the street to the house. When I get there Victor face red as hell. As soon as I stopped he demanded that I get off. But I didn't just yet. I revved up the motor like I was about to take another ride. Then when I saw he was about to burst into tears I went ahead and got off. Those little bikes are fun!

Before I could turn to see what else I could get myself into, Nana came to the door and yelled for me to get the phone. When I got to the phone it was my girl, Naomi. She had gotten home the night before. Her mother and Naomi's boyfriend had picked her up. I told her I had gone over her house a few days before and that it was vacant. I asked her where they had moved and she said on Cadillac. She said their ex landlord had started tripping because of the amount of traffic at the house, but that the new house was cool. It was located on the corner, which made it easier for people to come and go.

Although I was eager to see her, we agreed to hook up the following day because her grandmother was taking her shopping and then to Mr. Little's to get her hair done. Back then, I had yet to here of the legendary Mr. Little. He was just getting started, but being the person she was, Naomi was always a step ahead of the game. Back then he was still working out of his momma's house, but he was good.

Back in the day I wasn't real hard to find. Like I said I was a walking TV guide and when certain shows came on I could always be found in front of the television. So when Naomi stated that she might stop by later if her mom wasn't too busy I told her that the Karate flick, The Five Deadly Venoms was coming on so I wasn't going anywhere. At times, I would stay in the house all day. While the other kids would be outside playing, I'd be in the house watching television. Travon would always tease me about staying in the house all day. He thought only grownups should stay in the house like me. At times, I wouldn't even come out to play baseball. That's how glued to the television I was. But I liked it, also because it was peaceful. It gave me time to be alone. Nana would be in the streets, grandma somewhere doing chores, and Sandra and her clan would be over her mom's.

The next day Naomi was ready to hang. She asked if I was dressed and I said no, but I would be ready when she got there. She said she had her cousin's car and would be over in an hour. So I said cool. When she got to my house my boo boo was looking good. She was fresh as hell. She had on a black, white and gray Adidas track suit, with matching Adidas gym shoes and her hair was fresh as hell. I wasn't looking too bad myself. I had on some tight nice looking jeans, a cute shirt, some new gym shoes my dad had bought and my hair was still fresh from when I'd gotten it done the week before.

We were looking good and riding good so you know she had to make her rounds. We hit the hood first to see some of her old crew. We stopped and kicked it with them for awhile then rode passed the school to see how many people were out. Along the way we ran into this boy named Michael Johnson. He was another popular fine ass boy from school who all the ladies wanted. He and Naomi were real cool though. He loved her like a sister. As we stood hanging with him, Mani, Naomi's ex before she went to juvie came walking down the street looking like he could be her brother. He walked over to her, hugged her, then continued on his way. Seeing the two of them together reminded me of the munchkins on the Wizard of Oz.

After we finished talking with Michael, we headed down Wayburn. Wayburn was right around the corner from the skating rink and that's where a lot of people hung out. So we ran into a lot of old friends from school. After Wayburn we hit the freeway. I told Naomi that since we were headed to the west side that I wanted to stop and see my girl Melanie, but Naomi said this was her day and that Melanie was my friend and not hers. That she wanted to visit her friends. So we headed over her girl's house and when we got there she wasn't there. So Naomi gave her mother a hug and left a message that she'd stopped by.

Naomi's aunt also stayed on the west side, so we also stopped over there. Naomi's aunt had done very well for herself. She had a good job at the plant and lived in a beautiful home. Naomi was kind of iffy about her because she thought her aunt felt like she was better than others in the family. She was actually probably the most successful of her grandmother's clan and I guess Naomi didn't feel that comfortable being around her. She respected her though, enough to visit and come around. Her name is Dine, which is also Naomi's middle name. Naomi actually said that she wanted to change her first name to Dine and ironically, the day before, had asked me to start calling her Dine. So that's what I did. It was hard though and at first I kept forgetting and kept calling her Naomi. But I didn't mind the change, I thought the name was cool. It would just take me awhile to get use to.

Anyway, when we got to her aunt's house, she seemed mean as hell so we didn't stay long. We didn't have time for that shit. We were on a mission.

After we left her aunt's we decided to stop by my father's house. So we headed down Livernois, then hit 7 mile, rode a few blocks and reached my dad's house. I got out, knocked on the door and when my father answered you could tell he was shocked. I had never been to his house without him. He looked over to the car to see who was driving and when he saw Naomi's little ass jump out the car, his mouth dropped. She then walked up to him like a little lady and introduced her self. She said that it was a pleasure meeting him and that she had heard so much about him. He told her that he'd also heard a lot about her and then as he was about to start questioning her about driving I put my hand up to his mouth, gave him a kiss on the cheek and whispered in his ear not to worry. That we would drive safe and that we were on our way back home. I told him to tell Pam and Nannie that I said hello and to kiss little Rodrick for me.

When I turned to walk back to the car, my friend Shawnda was walking up. When I saw her we both screamed and ran toward one another. After we hugged, she told me that this boy Timothy had been asking about me. I asked what he'd said and she said just that every time he sees her he asked about me. He said he'd lost my number so I told her she could give it to him. I then told her to come meet my girl Dine. So we walked back toward my father's car and I introduced her to Di. After a brief greeting, I said goodbye and told her that I would come back and visit the following week. After we drove off, Di said that Shawnda was pretty. That she was skinny as hell, but really pretty.

On the way home, Di decided to make yet another stop. She wanted to stop on Burns to see her girls, Lena and Tae. Tae was her dog, they both dark as hell and both had the same fucked up attitude; always ready to fight. Unlike them, my yellow ass had to have a reason to scrap, so to them I was chicken. But I didn't care; they could think what they wanted. Whenever they started talking about fighting, I'd stand there and get quiet. That fighting shit was for the birds.

After we left Tae, we made one last stop. We stopped by to see our girl Rita; the one with the baby. When Rita came to the door she looked tired as hell. Her baby was getting big though, and was real cute. Looking drained, she said that taking care of a baby was no joke. And dealing with baby daddies, didn't make things easier. That she'd just finished arguing with her baby daddy about diapers.

After we were there for awhile, the baby started crying, and we took that as our cue to get outta there. Plus, it was getting late and Di had to get the car back. So we said our goodbyes and left.

On the way home I asked Di what she was planning to be for Halloween, which was only a few days away. She looked at me like I was crazy and asked if I still went trick or treating. I said yea, of course. That Aunt Mona was taking us. She then started teasing me and asked if I also believed in Santa. At that we both started laughing. Of course I didn't still believe in Santa, but dressing up for Halloween was fun. Not to mention all that candy, I would be straight for a month.

When I asked if she wanted to go with us, she said no, so I told her to make sure she didn't ask for any of my candy. Because I knew, Halloween or not, she'd want some candy.

When I got in the house, Grandma had already been to the ten cent store and bought Victor a Dracula costume. It had the black plastic cape and came with makeup. They didn't have anything for me. She said by her getting there so late all the costumes were already gone. But that was alright, my family was good at being creative and I knew they would come up with something. Being poor allowed us to use our imaginations and sure enough, Aunt Mona and grandma went to work. They pulled out one of grandma's old dresses, slapped me on some makeup and a wig, made me some big ol titties, and bam...I was good to go.

When it came to Halloween, Aunt Mona was real cool. She allowed as many of my friends that could fit in the car to go. The car was so packed; people were sitting on top of each another. In the car was Aunt Mona, me, Tanisha, Leonard, Cory, Victor and Travon. We didn't ride around the hood; we went straight to the suburbs. Unlike our neighborhood, out there, they give out money, fruit and two or three hands full of candy. Aunt Mona brought extra pillow cases and bags in case we needed them, and we would. After only two blocks our bags were already half full.

When it came to candy, we were all very competitive. We hated for one to have more than the other. At the end of the night we would compare and see who had the most. This time however, since we all went together, we all had a lot, so that kept down the drama. And that was good, because the weather was cold and after two hours of walking, I was in no mood for drama. As soon as we walked through the door I hid my candy and went right to bed. I had to be careful though, because if I got caught slipping, and didn't find a good hiding spot, Victor and Travon would wipe me out. They wouldn't take all my candy, but would take all the good stuff, like the candy bars, chips, etc.

***October 15, 2006- It's 11:00am. I'm laying up watching the Sanford and Son marathon. I forgot how funny this shit was. Della Reese was on one of the shows. She's grandma's 1st cousin. I never met her, but she and grandma grew up together and played together as kids. Their fathers were brothers. It's funny how people grow up and then grow apart. But I guess that's life.***

The next day at school everybody had candy falling out of their pockets. We were not supposed to bring candy to school but everybody did. My friend Anthony, with his hustling ass was the only one who didn't bring candy. He was the type who would wait on everybody else to eat theirs, then would bring his to school and sell it. I loved that about him, he was a hustler.

This was also Di's first day back since coming come. That girl really use to get on my nerves. She was too, smart. When she got back, she didn't skip a beat, it was like she never left. I was just the opposite; I would sit there trying to figure out the assignment, especially Algebra, and by the time I figured out a problem, she was already done, and chit chatting around the room. It was the same in all her classes. Then after school, while I had tons of homework, she was always ready to hang.

It wasn't soon before I began looking forward to the next holiday, which was Christmas. Like most kids, I lived for holidays. Especially the one's geared around kids. It wasn't like I was looking forward to a lot of presents; in fact, the only present that I knew I could count on for sure was a Good fellow box. And even that was about to end. Because of my age, this year would be the last year that I would get the outfit, t-shirt, panties, coloring book, socks and candy that came in the box. I really appreciated the Good fellows. The only drawback was the first day back after Christmas vacation, everybody would be dressed alike. We'd point each other out in the hallway and laugh and call each other poe. But hey, I guess we were.

***October 22, 2006- I had a beautiful week. I partied what seemed like everyday. On Wednesday a coworker convinced me to come to yesterdays and she came and got me. I am having so many problems with the***

*Intrepid. I only drive it to work, school, to pick up the girls and back home. We got there around 8:00pm and we left around 11:30pm. I was home before 12:00am which was cool. I got my ballroom and Latin hustle on and she introduced me to everybody. Can you believe I knew every bit of 4 people. As long as I been hanging I felt like the new kid on the block. Thursday I went to the hospital appreciation dinner to honor the employees who have been working for at least 5 years. Certificates are given out in honor of every five years of service. For example, 5,10,15 years etc. This year three of my co-workers were honored. I was honored last year so I wanted to be there to support them. Not to mention getting a chance to eat good and dress up in my after five attire. The place was elegant. Every year they hold it at the Rooster Tail.. Everyone was dressed to impress. You get so use to seeing people in scrubs and lab coats so when they come out to play I'm always curious to see what people are gonna wear. Everybody was beautiful. Friday was cool, but I got another flat so I left the car at the job in the underground garage so Edward came and took me to pick up Alexis. On the way home, I didn't even complain, I'm just glad it didn't blow on my way to work. I have been praying for a new whip; preferably a truck, but at this point I would be grateful for anything that runs well.*

*Edward cooked breakfast and dinner on Saturday, which was great. In between that, he and his uncle fixed my car and brought it home. After that we chilled together for most of the day. We were broke as hell but the mortgage was paid so it was alright. Sunday, I got up and cooked a little breakfast; my aunts famous sausage and egg recipe. As Di would say, it's just a sausage omelets scrambled, but it's not. You crumble up Bob Evans sausage and cook it until its brown. Then you add green peppers, onions and mushrooms. After that I crack a few eggs and scramble it all together and you serve it with rice on the side. Talking 'bout some good eating. The rest of the day I washed and folded a few loads then after that I began to look for old pictures of me and Di and our life together. I got pissed because I couldn't find the pictures we took a few months ago when we went to Connecticut. We was balling. We were with some of her peeps; a gang of niggas... but they were cool. We went shopping in New York and later that night went to a cabaret. When we got there everybody was suited and booted and popping Crystal. They were not ready for us... we had a ball. So that's why I'm pissed, because I wanted to gather all the pictures, put them in a book and send them to Di. I know I put those pictures in my album, but now I can't find them. I got all our pictures as kids, but not those. I took the pictures to work and my co-workers found them so funny. They clowned me for the rest of the day.*

*On my way to pick up Denise from school, I ran into Ms. Petal's...Di's mom. I looked up and she was yelling my name out of*

***her car window. I was so happy to see her. I haven't seen her since all the drama. She say's Di getting out in Dec. Cool... I'm still gone send her the book though. Damn, God is good all the time. I'm glad she's coming home soon. That's good; hopefully she will be out for Christmas.***

When I got home from school, my crazy ass Uncle Edmond, who was back living with us, had flipped out. He would stay with us from time to time until my grandmother would get mad and put him out. After he would get put out, no matter what he always found his way back to our house. I remember this particular night so well because it was really cold and Edmond was in the house talking about how God was coming to get him. That in his last life I was his wife and that they were coming to get him tonight. When he started talking that way, me and my brother and cousin would urge him on because to us it was funny. He would start pacing back and forth and if he was standing in front of you he would start bobbing up and down while he was talking. He was hilarious. On this given night after pacing back and forth and doing the bobbing thing he took his shirt off and walked outside in the freezing cold and started chanting. It took grandma to go outside and convince him to come back in the house. Grandma had a way with crazy people. After putting his clothes back on he started rocking and singing, Lou Rawl's song; you'll never find... as long as you live... someone who cares about you, the way I do...

Every day after Di came home from camp, either I was at her house or she was at mine. It got to the point where whenever I would go someplace by myself, people would ask about Di. People started calling us Ebony and Ivory. When she first came back and saw Edmond, she looked at him and then at me, like, what the... and I told her he was crazy. She just looked at me and started laughing. That girl didn't have no sense.

***November 29, 2006- That damn Victor has done it again. That boy really knows how to work my nerves and bubble my gut at the same time. Everything else seemed to be going as perfect as can be expected. Me and Edward been extra lovey dovey, and the girls are great. Chavez went to California with Victor for Thanksgiving. They left Tuesday and got back Sunday. He dropped Chavez off then called me Monday. We kicked it for a minute and he said he would come visit me at my job Tuesday. Come Tuesday morning, my first day back from vacation, he started my morning with a dreadful phone call saying he had been robbed. So now I'm glad it was him calling me and not the hospital or the police. I knew this shit was gone happen sooner or later, I just hoped it was later or not at all. Victor doing good for himself, and when he got home Monday at least three men were in his house waiting on him. They duct taped his girl and her autistic son then they pistol whipped Victor, taped his arms and legs and took whatever money and jewelry he had in the***

***house. As I'm listening to him tell the story I'm seeing it like a movie playing out. I almost lost this boy a few times. I think he is the bionic man or something. It ain't nothing but the lord keeping that boy alive. I'm convinced he has a greater purpose... we are still trying to figure out what it is but I can honestly say with every near death experience, it has transformed him into somebody different. In a good way. He acts differently and talks differently. Nothing drastic but definitely a difference for the better. I am so glad that he was ok. But all I can think of is what if Chavez was with him.***

Thanksgiving seemed to come and go real fast this year. It just flew by. We ate over Aunt Jackie's as usual. Christmas was coming soon and I was looking forward to spending Christmas with my dad. Me and my cousin Robin were also looking forward to meeting up at Grandma Sheryl's. We'd already plotted and agreed to meet there. Me and her have so much fun over there. The year before she gave us some cold duck and we dressed up and performed. It was only a half of cup but that was all it took. I put on a wig and some powder on my face and acted like I was Marilyn Monroe. It was so funny.

Meanwhile, Nana had started acting strange. I didn't know if it was because of the drugs, but all of a sudden her face started getting fact and she started acting moody and sending me to the store to buy pickled pig feet. When she first told me to buy them, I couldn't believe what she was asking. I mean, who eats pickled pig feet. In addition to her mood swings, the traffic in the house also began to slow down. I asked her if she was alright and was there anything she wanted to talk about and she said, no, she was fine.

After awhile, I figured out what I thought was the problem. She and that damn Leon had been hanging tight. He was there every night. I think that's part of the reason why the traffic slowed down. Whenever I asked if she was pregnant, she always said, no. But I figured, if she was, that time would tell. She wouldn't be able to hide that shit forever. After awhile, I even got up the nerve to taste the pickled pig feet; and you know, it wasn't as bad as I thought.

During this time, I would just sit and think about how good grownups had it. In spite of my beliefs though, my grandmother would tell me that I needed to stay a child as long as I could. But to me that was bull. To me adults had it made. They got to come and go as they pleased, and do whatever they wanted. So to me that's what I looked forward to.

In the meantime, hangin' with Di was close enough. I felt reckless when we were together. Sure we weren't grown, but we thought we were. That was until it started to get dark. That's when the street lights came on and I had to have my butt home. To avoid these rules, it got to the point where some weekends instead of going to my father's, I would spend the night at Di's. I remember one weekend staying with Di and her getting her cousin's car and us going the Ju Joint. That was a club where everybody hung out. It was a hole in the wall, but it was always off the hook. That night, we picked up some of the girls, smoked a few joints then got there around 11:00 and hung out until it closed at 4a.m. When we first walked in, I was tripping, because I knew if Nana ever found out, she would lose her mind. And let's not talk about walking out at 4a.m. That woman would have killed me!

The next day after I got home, it was back to reality. When Di dropped me off, I couldn't get in the door good before Aunt Mona was handing me a bucket, some pine sol and a rag and announcing that we were washing walls. I ran back to the door to see if I could catch Di, but it was too, late. She was gone. I looked at Aunt Mona and asked her why she was at our house trying to wash walls. That she stayed on Nottingham. But all she did was tell me that I had jokes and that as long as her mama stayed there, that that was also her home and today her Momma needed her walls cleaned. I looked around for Victor and spotted him under the dining room table cleaning the legs with pledge. So I took off my coat, sat down my bag and commenced to washing walls. It took me five hours to wash all the walls in the house. My arms were sore as hell, but that didn't stop me from wanting to go outside. I walked to the front door to see who was on the block, and although it was cold, everybody was out. As I stood, planning my next move, excitement turned to disappointment, as Cassandra ass pulled up in front of the house and started removing bags. Hell nol, I couldn't believe it. All I could think was...she back.

She must have gotten tired of living in that jail her mother called a home. I don't know why her mama kept trying to start over with her. She was now grown and trying to live in a house with a bunch of rules would never work. Her mother should have laid down rules before she got grown and out of control. At this point Cassandra was in her twenties and wasn't about to change for nobody.

I turned and yelled to my grandma that Cassandra was back, then opened the door and helped her with her bags. I asked her about the person who'd dropped her off and if he was coming in, and she said no, that he was just somebody she'd met at the bus stop and had offered to give her a ride. Hell, I wasn't mad at her. I guess a girl got ta do what a girl gotta do. But I'll tell you, our house was always full. As soon as we would get rid of one person, another was always right there to take their place.

***December 11, 2006- God is good, everything is everything. Di will be home tomorrow. I made her a photo album filled with pictures of us since age 12, as well as***

*pictures that we took out of town. She so materialistic so I hope she appreciates the thought.*

*Paying off everything on my credit report didn't really help as far as the house. My credit still wasn't strong enough. We gone try again in about 8 months. In the meantime, I did get approved for a 05 Buick Rendezvous. Its not bad, it has everything I wanted; leather seats, wood grain on the wheel and around the radio, 3rd row seats and last but not least, a DVD player to keep the kids quiet on those long trips.*

*I felt good so I took my butt to church Sunday. One or two even three miracles, I say a few thank you Jesus' and keep it moving but when he get to doing things like sparing my brother's life again, keeping peace in my home longer then a few days and to top it off taking me out of a 97 intrepid and putting me into an 05, oh yes, time to go to church and give praise. I wanted the whole family to go but you know the devil stay busy. I knew something was going to prevent all of us from going, and sho nuff, Edward said he was going to get up at 10:00am to get ready, but can you believe at 10:00am his mama called for him to take her to the emergency. I swear he planned that. Please lord forgive me for thinking like that but with Edward ass and his mama you can never tell. From what I gather she got her hair done Friday and afterwards started having an allergic reaction Saturday. Why she*

***didn't go Saturday? Who knows why she didn't ask one of the many people that live in her house to take her. Who knows? I know that's his mom but I stressed how important it was for us as a family to go to church. We all had a lot to be thankful for. We don't go every Sunday so I was a little disappointed he didn't come. His dad came though, so that was good. I have to try harder to put church into our routine every Sunday. I feel as long as we put the lord into our everyday life, and try and live Christ like... until we find a church home we should be alright.***

When Christmas came, just like I thought, it was a little skimpy, but for some reason I was still happy. My grandmother stayed up half the night cooking and first thing in the morning got up and continued where she left off. Every holiday I could count on her to do it big. As I headed toward the kitchen I could smell the ham, dressing, chitterlings and turkey. Then when I saw the dough for the sweet potato pie I walked over and gave her a big hug.

After I left the kitchen I got on the phone and called all my peeps on the west side to wish them a Merry Christmas. Like I said Christmas wasn't the best that year but I knew my father would be picking me up so I knew I would be getting additional gifts when I got over there. Again it wouldn't be much because Rodrick who was now three, and then there was the new baby Mathew who was about to turn one. Also since I'd started hanging with Di, I'd stopped going over there every week, so I felt that probably made a difference. I now only went over there about once a month.

I remember when my father first told me Pam was pregnant. It seemed like before I knew it Mathew was born. Pam was raised different than me, and she raised her kids accordingly. I'm not saying that the difference was either good or bad, however her methods of discipline were different. In my house a lot of the stuff that Roderick did, I would have gotten my ass whipped for. Pam believed in time out and would yell, stop it, a lot. In my house after the first stop... and you kept doing what you were doing, you best believe you'd find yourself on the floor. But the flip side was, Pam was heavy into education. She taught her kids everything. They even fell asleep to classical music. I knew from an early age that private schooling and college would be in their future.

***December21, 2006- Four more days until Christmas. I'm doing my traditional breakfast. I usually have a good turn out. I started about 7 years ago with basically my moms side, because we rarely get together for anything since grandma gone. No matter what, I can always count on Marie, Christine, Tooky, Shannon, Mathew, and Rodrick to come through. They've been coming for the past few years. Last year they even brought Pam, so***

*now its whoever come. Moma side, daddy side, whoever side. Just come eat. It brings me pleasure seeing everybody enjoying the food I have prepared.*

*This Christmas gone be a little skimpy but I'm gone pull a trick out of my hat and make it happen. The girls gone be easy, it's that dam Chavez, he so materialistic I can barely afford to keep him. The tree looks nice. I bought a live one this year. I put the Charlie Brown tree we had last year upstairs. I decorated it with Denise's decorations she made at school. Victor usually come after all the food is gone, but this year he is spending the holidays in California with his girl's family.*

*January 2, 2007- The new year is upon us. Christmas was beautiful. Marie brought everyone she could. I love her. I made Aunt Jackie's egg and sausage recipe and Arcyle and his family came. They rode with Marie. We didn't have much to say to one another but as much as we been through, nothing needed to be said. When he walked in he handed me his baby; Little Chocolate and that was that. Rodrick, Mathew, and Shannon stopped in and ate. Everyone came around the same time and they all left about the same time. That's always good. It gets easier and easier every year. I cleaned up as I went along. Shortly after everybody left Victor brought his tall yellow ass in cussing me out for not calling him. Hell, I thought he had left for California but it was nice to see him. He was leaving out*

***that next morning and of course he was taking Chavez with him. This little dude done been to California 3 times this year...he just bawling.***

***After he packed his stuff and they left I had the girls secluded in their room playing with some of the goodies Santa brought. Then me and Edward, who were both tired as hell, went to bed. Although we were both tired, it was a very pleasing tired, a feeling of accomplishment that every task on our need to do list was achieved.***

When my father picked me up later that afternoon, Grandma Sheryl's was our first stop. As soon as I walked in, I gave her a big hug and a kiss. My dad's side was very affectionate. They really made you feel loved. As soon as you walk through the door, there is always an embrace and when you leave out a goodbye hug. Every year my grandmother would get me something. This particular year she gave me fifty dollars. I was so happy I almost knocked her out her chair hugging her. As I was hugging her, she whispered not to tell anybody about the money. Grandma Sheryl always had a way of making me feel special; like I was her only grand child. I knew she didn't actually favor me over everybody else, it was more about her making up for the time that I wasn't around. You see, my cousins Robin and Jason had that luxury. They saw her whenever they wanted. My Aunt Jackie was always over making sure grandma had what she needed, she acted like she was the mama and grandma was the child.

After we left grandma's, we went next to my father's. When we got there my Uncle Charles was there and Nanie was in the kitchen finishing up. There was also a spread laid out similar to the one at my house. As soon as saw the food, I got me a plate and filled it up. I got me some turkey, dressing, ham, yams, and cornbread. There was other stuff, but I had already eaten, so that's all I wanted for the time being.

As I was getting my food, Roderick was running around being bad as hell; and throwing his toys at everybody. I don't just mean little light toys, but hard ass toys that hurt when they landed. Meanwhile, Pam was upstairs breast feeding Mathew, so before I started eating I went up to speak to her. While I was up there I thanked her for the new outfit and coat they'd gotten me for Christmas. She smiled and said not to thank her, that I should thank Santa. Whoever, I was just glad I got the stuff. I then watched her breast feed for a few minutes and then went back downstairs where my food was waiting.

When I got downstairs my dad had gone to the basement to his recording studio, so I got my plate and went down there. My dad was good at constructing things and had built the studio himself. It was really nice. It looked just like a real sound studio. I was so proud of him. I told him that he would be rich and famous one day and I believed it.

After kicking it with my dad for a few minutes I went back upstairs to finish eating. I stopped by the kitchen to get a piece of pie before it disappeared then found me a quite place to sit and eat.

The next day, when I got home, Cassandra was still there. Since it was the holiday, I was hoping she had left. Meanwhile, Nana was still walking around the house sick as hell still tryna tell people that it was probably something she ate. It took Aunt Mona to finally tell me the truth.

As soon as I found out, I went looking for Victor. I finally located him next door at Aunt Juanita's. When I told him, he looked at me surprised and then asked who the father was. I told him Leon, the man who'd been spending all his time in the room. He kind of shrugged his shoulders then went back to playing videos.

After that I went home and called Di. Di took the news in stride. When I told her I asked her if she could believe my mother was pregnant and she was like, why not. She was fucking wasn't she. She then asked how far along she was and I told her, then she asked if she was still popping pills. When I told her she was, she said that the baby was probably gonna be retarded. I told her I hoped the baby would be born healthy, but she was convinced it would be born fucked up. Between the crack and whatever other drugs, she was using, she just couldn't see it. I told her thanks for her support, but she said that she was just keeping it real, then told me she would call me back after she finished counting her money. Then hung up.

After hanging up from Di, I went in the living room and sat down to watch the Dukes of Hazard. I needed an escape. But as soon as I sat down, Aunt Mona came in and flopped down on the couch. She asked how I felt about my mother being pregnant and me having another brother or sister and I told her I didn't know. So she held up her fist, emulating a microphone, and asked again. "We have Kiikii here from the Nana clan and we just have a few questions for you. How do you feel about your mother smoking crack and bringing another baby in this already cruel world? "I don't know," I answered. "How do I feel, I don't care."

"You don't care," she said. "That's going to be your brother or sister." At this point I was frustrated. I didn't want to play this game with her. So I started pushing the make believe microphone out of my face. Boy...why did I do that. Like some crazed woman, she grabbed me, put me into a head lock and started tossing me around like a rag doll. When I managed to squeeze out of the head lock she snatched me up and pinned me down onto the couch. That's when I started hollering for help. But that didn't work. That only got her more riled up and she started pouncing up and down on me. I was begging by this time, for her to please get up.

This was child abuse. I'd done nothing to deserve what she was doing, not to mention all the pouncing was killing me. I had to stop and catch my breath just to get any words out. I was hollering to my grandmother for help but she just yelled back from her room for Aunt Mona to stop. So at this point I started begging for her to get up. Finally, she looked down, so I was about to pass out and got up. But not before she got in one last pounce.

Aunt Mona wasn't all bad though. She was the one in the family that tried to keep everybody together. She knew everybody on both grandma's side as well as my grand father's. She also taught me how to crochet. I really enjoyed her a lot. That is when she was not penning me to the floor.

1986 went by fast. While everybody else was either planning which party to attend, or coming up with New Year's Resolutions, I was just looking forward to the New Year.

***January11, 2007- God is good. I started school last night and it almost killed me. But my old ass got through it. My instructor is amazing. Although the course is very demanding he makes it interesting. He's a retired lieutenant and very knowledgeable about the law. I took Chavez and his friend to the library before class. When it closed, they walked over and waited in the car. They were out there for two hours. My class didn't let out until 10:00p.m. Why them little niggas run my***

*battery down, so when it was time to go we were stuck. Of course, I didn't have any cables, so my teacher came out and although he didn't have any cables he drove across the lot and brought somebody back that did, and then waited until we were good.*

*The next day, me and Edward dipped on our lunch breaks and came home and fucked real good. It was a quickie but it was good as hell. Lately, thoughts of having another child has been dancing in my head. I stopped taking my pills yesterday, I feel like we ready. Denise will be four in a few months and all the kids are very helpful. Edward sent me an email a few weeks ago of us at the hospital's black tie affair and we look so happy. He sent it in a PowerPoint presentation and the caption read, "Can I knock you up again." What a romantic.*

*January 14, 2007- Another dream flushed down the drain. I want another baby, another boy but I will take a girl by my husband. I told Edward that in the beginning but I don't want to do it alone, been there, done that. We both have to want it and we both have to be ready at the same time. I don't feel it now. He changes his mind which ever way the wind blows. He fooled me once. Fool me once shame on you… fool me twice shame on me. Me and Edward were coming from somewhere and we pulled into the McDonalds drive thru and the young lady taking the money was pregnant. When I saw her I just started crying. He reached over to wipe the tears and I'm thinking to myself, you the reason why -at the rate we going- I will never have that sense of joy and all the feelings that goes along with a pregnancy. I don't want another baby daddy. I got married to solve that problem. Well at least I thought I did. Hell, I'm not getting any younger.*

*We beefed out because I asked him on his day off if he could pick Alexis up so I can catch Marie and get my hair done and be back home in time to get the girls ready and myself ready to be at Robin's house by 8:00pm so we can surprise her for her birthday. Yes, I have asked Edward to do little things on his day off. One day, in order to keep me from driving all the way from my job on the east side and then back, I needed him to ride six blocks from the house to give me the exact cross streets for this church because I was writing a proposal asking permission to use the property for a carnival. His response was that I didn't respect his days off. That he has things to do on his days off. Another time I made the mistake of asking him to drop some papers off at the social service office by the house since I have to be at work at 7:00am and they don't open till 8:00am. He had to come up to the job anyway to get some money for gas and go back west so I didn't feel that it was a problem. You are my husband... I'm thinking to myself- you are suppose to be my right hand man, who else can I call to do these simple tasks, especially since the paperwork was to help us get the roof repaired because we couldn't afford to fix it. I also asked him to pick up Alexis because sense he was already on that side of town it would be easier for him to get her than me. He said no because he had to go to the Secretary of State. I couldn't believe it. I should be his first priority. If this is what I need him to do just do it. I have already made a way to get my hair done for free cause we cannot afford to get it done at a salon. Just yesterday we came home on our lunch break and had a little quickie. You mean I'm coming home for lunch to satisfy my husband, something that not many wives are doing nowadays, and you can't pause your day for a minute for me. What did he have to do that was so important or where did he have to go that his step-daughter couldn't go. She's a big girl, she don't jump on furniture. She knows how to act. He called back around 3:00pm after I done changed my whole plan to say that he gone go get her, so now I have to make those same calls again to go back to the original plan. Why do things have to be so complicated? This is how my whole marriage has been since the beginning. Never smooth for long, always complicated. Anyway, he picked her up, but he was mad about it. O.k., thanks Edward.*

*January 22, 2007- I can't believe this shit. We beefing again. Like we ever stopped. He been sick since Wednesday so I rush home to cater to him. I made sure he got everything he need. Soup, juice, Nyquil... I haven't been able to get anything done at home cause I'm taking care of him. The kids also made sure he was comfortable by helping out.*

*He finally fell asleep about 2:00am... so I go to the job to type my paper and can you believe this nigga mad cause I got up. He so worried about the time I left and not what I was doing with the time, so he called me about 5am at my desk and I answered the phone. He didn't have to look far. Any worries about me should have been over. But not with Edward. Its not like he didn't know about the paper. I tell him everything. The paper was already late. Now if he listens or not, I don't know. I had to find a way to get my paper done so I had to do what I had to do. On the way home I thought I had resolved everything and we were all good. So I stopped by Farmer jack to look at the lot one good time in hopes of doing a carnival there. I was surprised that they were open. I've been up since yesterday. Since I'm there I go grocery shopping so I wouldn't have any reason to come back out. That way hopefully this shit can blow over. After I get home I laid down for a few hours just to be woke up by him telling me that the furnace was off. So I get up, shake off the chill and as I'm putting on my house shoes he asks what happened when I tried to reset it earlier. I say nothing and kept walking. Why did I do that. I go downstairs and next thing I know he comes running downstairs with his jacket on. He mad as hell. So I ask where he's going and he says, oh now you're speaking to me. He goes on and on about how he will not be ignored anymore and how he's tired of talking and nobody in this house listening to him. I'm like damn, where this come from. I was talking to you and you walked away like I wasn't talking about shit. Damn baby, I'm sorry. I'm damn near on bending knee pleading with this nigga that I really didn't hear him. What the fuck! I ain't got no beef with you, Edward. This nigga don't get it. I forsake all others for him. I have nobody else. It would be one thing If I had somebody to run to when we got into it but I don't. When we beef, I'm home miserable, praying that it will all blow over soon.*

*January 24, 2007 Mody Wowo had a bouncing baby boy. I went to see them on my lunch break. 7lbs, 4ozs. He is a handsome little tyke. He wouldn't open his eyes for me but it's cool. Just holding him made me feel like I did when I had my own kids. I want one so bad. That is probably a dream that will never come true at the rate me and Edward going.*

*I finally got the house out of the young lady's name it was in, just to put it in someone else's for a minute. I called her to make sure everything went ok considering when I got there she had already signed and left. She left word not to ever speak to her again. That if I see her in the street don't even speak. I guess my feelings would be hurt if we were friends, it wasn't like I set out to ruin her credit, I was never late for almost 2 years. Well, maybe once, and that was because the bank representative read my account number wrong*

***and when I corrected her she still had it wrong and I mistakenly said ok. So they never took it out but I did call and get it straightened out. I ended up having to pay a late fee. My paying late was not intentional. I really appreciated her. Thanks to her I was able to clean up most of my credit and pay off one of Edward's loans. I wouldn't dare purposely try to ruin her credit or anyone else's.***

10,9,8,7,6,5,4,3,2,1. Every year I made it a habit of watching the Dick Clark New Year's special. This year, in order to feel more like a part of the celebration, I begged my mother for some of her Night Train. She gave me a sip or two, and I'm not gone lie, it was good. But it went down rough... hot. I really couldn't see how people drank that stuff on a regular. The shit was so potent that I got a buzz off just a couple sips. I didn't think anything could replace the feeling I had when I smoked weed though. Now that was my thing.

***January 31, 2007- This month Is already gone. School is alright. Aunt Hattie had her surgery yesterday and they took her other breast. They also found cells that could eventually turn into cancer in a few years. Hell, Aunt Hattie said she 82 years old and they have served their purpose. She is such a trooper. A group of us went with her to her consultation and she told the doctor to go ahead and take it. She wanted to set up the operation as soon as possible. The next day she called me with a date. The day of the***

***operation Aunt Jackie and Aunt Hattie's God daughter stayed with her. I couldn't take that day off since I took off for the consult but I took a break to see her before she went in, and I took another break to see her when she came out. Edward still sick. He's now actually in the hospital. So between him, her, work, school and kids I'm spreaded thin. But my W2 came yesterday and it made everything alright.***

Nana's stomach was now getting big as hell. Her friends Ruby and Rena were still hanging, but Rena, who was a nurse, was really starting to look bad. When she first started coming around she use to look pretty. She had a bad ass body. I hoped she would somehow come to her senses and stop smoking that shit. But I knew that was a long shot.

I'd come to the realization that I was having another brother and I was starting to actually get excited about it. Me and Victor had started talking about what we were gonna do for the baby and what we were gonna buy it when we got some money. I hated the fact that she hadn't stopped any of her habits though. I hoped that the baby would come out healthy, but again that was a long shot. I had seen pictures of babies born addicted and it wasn't a pretty sight. They were generally under weight and they would have shaken fits and all type of medical issues.

My grandmother was ready one way or another. She said that it didn't matter how the baby came out, we were gonna take care of it all the same. She said that God didn't make mistakes.  She was always good about making light out of a would be dark situation.

## Chapter 8

## JACK OF ALL TRADES MASTER OF NONE

When I was coming up, I use to try a lot of different things. One of them was cutting hair. When they were younger, I use to experiment a lot on Travon and Victor. I did the best I could, and actually thought I was pretty good, but let's just say a bowl cut with no blending didn't play too well with them or the cruel ass kids on my block. When the boys started getting older and began to care about their looks, I had to chase them down to cut their hair. I don't think they liked the fact that I had to tighten a belt around their heads to make the lines straight. I have to admit, that I probably jacked up every boy head in the neighborhood at least once.

I also liked to French braid. Aunt Mona taught me that, too. I use to love to braid her kid's hair. They had that good hair and I loved putting their hair in ponytails and braids and then adding the pretty beads.

Aunt Mona use to hate when anybody but her did their hair though. It was always something about it falling out whenever someone else did it, but I don't know. I tried to imagine their chunky asses running around bald, but I just couldn't see it. I think she just didn't want anybody else doing their hair. When I did their hair though, she always changed her tune. She would always say thanks, but she would do it under her breath.

I depended on Aunt Mona a lot during my early years. I remember she use to drive this reddish orange Chevette. She used to drive the hell out of it. It had a stick and I remember how much I use to admire how well she drove that car. I could drive, but driving a stick was another story. She would always tell me that when I turned 16 and got my license that she would teach me how to drive it and then give it to me. Shit, that car had a clutch, different gears, which you had to switch, and at the time I just couldn't see successfully learning how to drive that thing. But for the sake of owning it, I was willing to try.

***February23, 2007- I'm sitting at the airport tired as hell. I have been running around like a chicken with my head cut off trying to get ready. I hate going out of town and then coming back cleaning and washing clothes, so I did that before I left. Me and Edward celebrated our four-year anniversary on valentines day. It was nice. We stayed home and watched Departed and fucked really really good. That was until the kids started knocking on the door, because of course it fell on a week day. We both took off and wouldn't you know it we had a snow storm and all the schools were closed. We were both broke as hell so we didn't trade gifts but that was o.k. We just enjoyed loving each other.***

***It is 8:40am and my flight leaves at 9:40am. I'm nervous. I haven't been on a plane in a nice little minute. I have been***

*driving wherever we had to go. They take you through so much at the airport, and I know it is for our own safety, but damn, you would have a better chance just coming through the terminal in a sheet, your boarding pass and ID. When I pulled up in the long term parking structure I almost had a heart attack when I noticed it was $17.00 a day. In heels, I drag my big old bag, my laptop, another case, and I'm stepping. I get off on six and this little foreign man tells me that the terminal is directly ahead. I get there just for them to send my ass upstairs where it is a long ass loop around line. I'm about to get in the line until this angel in a red jacket came along and escorted me back downstairs where there was less people. But I get there just to stand behind a couple who is being held up as suspicious characters. So I stood complaining to the man behind me and he made me realize that it's better than the line upstairs. After about 10 minutes I reached the front of the line. This time another nice young man, another angel in a red jacket came and walked me through the kiosk machine. I don't remember going through anything like that the last time, however, after going through it, I was then hoarded back downstairs to go threw security check where there was only one line. After standing there almost 15 minutes a short stocky white guy comes and urge us to go back upstairs. He said they had more check points up there. He instructed everybody from me on back to follow him. I gave him the I had on heels* *speech and refuse to go. I turned my head... thinking to myself I aint scared of him so I turned and started talking to the nice gentleman standing behind me. He looked sort of Mexican mixed with something else. He was kind of cute. The last time I flew everything was different. This time people were grabbing tubs to put stuff in, they were taking off their shoes, some were coming out of their coats. So I asked the guy I was talking to what I was suppose to do first when I got up to the front because I didn't want to look like I didn't know what I was doing. He told me to just wait until I got up to the front and everything would be fine. So that's what I did.*

*As soon as I got to the belt, I took off my coat, then the man told me to take off my blue jean jacket. Damn, is your name Edward. I'm practically stripping for this man. I could hear Luke playing in the back ground. I put all the clothes in the tub then take a few steps up cause the line is moving like it's the first of the month and we getting our government cheese. I then take off one boot then I take a step and take off the other. I was glad I got my toes done. I set my bag with my laptop on the belt just for the security to ask me if there was a laptop in it and I replied yes. He said to take it out. He used me as an example as he hollered, "if you got any laptops take them out and put them in a bend." Then he started talking slow like we special Ed, so I turn around to walk back and get a bend but the little foreign guy had already gotten me one. I say thank you and got back in the line. I get through the line just for the big bad security man to say in a deep voice, "Mam, can you hurry up, we need that table," referring to the table I'd just sat my coat, jacket, shoes and laptop on. I say ok. I'm thinking I just did a strip tease for your ass and you mean I can't stand here for a minute and get myself back together. So I move as fast as I can, hook my belt, zip my boot, adjust my bra and I'm out. I find my destination, look around and I see no sign of Renee. So I play on the laptop for a few. After about 30 minutes I called my loving husband just for him to tell me to go to one of the bars in the terminal and get bent, so I did. I get to one of the bars and I was able to get connected to the internet and get bent at the same time. It's almost 9:30 so I pack up everything, drink the rest of my Corona and head back to the boarding area. That's where I ran into my girl, and later her friend. Hey you. We both hug and the adventure begins.*

*February 26, 2007- Well... just getting back from what was an almost perfect trip. My agenda went from eating, drinking, socializing and sleeping to soon as I drop off Renee and her girl it's off home washing that load of clothes by the washing machine that I know ain't nobody bothered to wash. I fold the load that was in the dryer, clean my room and the girls' room, clean the bathroom and make my way to the living room then the dining room. If pops not there when I get there I can straighten up the family room, then the kitchen. You would think that I didn't clean before I left. I'm gone try to get to the basement and in between that I have to call AT&T and pay the phone bill. Back to real life.*

*April 06, 2007- Its 5:00a.m. and we just about to hit the road. Oh, that is after we leave the Laundromat, because Mr. Man just packed and neglected to go to the Laundromat the night before. I wanted to leave at 10p.m. last night. We would have been half way there, now we won't make it there until 1 or 2 in the morning. I have never been to Florida so I'm looking forward to it. My birthday tomorrow. Happy birthday to me. We will be gone for a whole week. This is the longest me and my husband been away from home with out the kids. Sort of like a honeymoon if you ask me, because we never had one. I'm pissed now but I'll be alright once the climate change and I feel the heat from the sun and see the pretty beaches that I hear people bragging about.*

*April 8,2007- We made it safe and sound. Its great... I am loving it. It's not as hot as I imagined it, but its beautiful. The palm trees, the sun, everything that I could imagine. Its Florida... I spent my birthday in Florida with my husband. It don't get no better then this.*

For a while, I began to spend a lot of time during weekends and summers with Aunt Mona. When I started spending time with her, she no longer dated Robert the drunk abuser, she was now dating my cousin's ex boyfriend,

Mark the drunk pervert. Whenever I was over Aunt Mona's and she'd leave, I would always go over my friend Aaron's and chill until she got back. I would stay until the street lights came on and then head back over there. I hated sitting up there with Mark. To me he was creepy. I couldn't help but think back to him messing with my cousin and how he was now living with my aunt.

I remember once, sitting on the kitchen floor playing with my jacks, and I had on a pair of shorts and a tank top and how this fool came in the kitchen and asked if he could play. My Aunt thought it was cute. She was laughing and giggling, not knowing that all along her man was a pervert. I watched him try and play jacks with those big boxing glove hands and knew he was up to something. He couldn't even play. I soon found out. Turns out every time I would throw up the jacks, and lean over to catch the ball, his eyes would become glued between my legs. I just couldn't understand what his grown ass was looking for. He was fucking my cousin, fucking my Aunt, and trying to look at my coochie. I guess he was tryna keep it all in the family. After that day I really tried to keep my distance from him. Every time I saw him I couldn't help but think of Tione Bells.

***May14, 2007- I am trying to stay awake. My boss signed me up for some crisis prevention seminar. It has its good points. I don't have to go to work today or tomorrow and we get free coffee, juice, and donuts. They***

***fed us lunch and at the end you get a certificate stating that you are qualified to assist in the debriefing and defusing in crisis situations. The down fall is I'm bored to death. We have to be here the whole day from 8:30am to 5:00pm. It's not all bad though, one of the instructors managed to crack a few jokes so that was cool. Edward picking up Denise for me. Other than that I would have had to leave at 3:30 which would have jeopardized my certificate. I already have to leave at 4:00 to get Alexis on time. The instructor said they will work with me leaving at 4:00pm. Shit, to be honest I was hoping this seminar would help me to deal with Edward better. Can you say man in crisis?***

While at Aunt Mona's I became hot for this boy that worked at the corner store. Every chance I got I was walking my hot ass down there to buy something. I was too shy to say anything, so I'd just buy something and leave. I didn't care if I just bought a pack of gum, I was at that store.

One day after visiting Aaron, I get back to the house and the dude from the store was sitting at the table talking to Mark. I froze in my tracks. Mark introduced me as his niece but it took me a minute to get myself together. I started blushing and got all tongue tied and for a few seconds didn't know if I'd lost my voice. After I finally got out a hello, he said that his name was Glen. I was so shy. After speaking I went into the living room and sat down on the couch and turned on the T.V. and pretended like he wasn't there.

After about ten minutes, Mark got up and went into the room with Aunt Mona, leaving Glen sitting there. But he wasn't shy. He got up and came into the living room and sat down. I was really sweating now. He was so cute. He was like a funny brown with like a red tint, and he had these pretty brown eyes. They weren't quite hazel but they were a light brown. He was taller than me, maybe about 5,7' and he was slim, had a mini afro and last but not least, he was bowlegged.

He asked if he could watch TV with me; the Incredible Hulk, and I said, sure. That program turned out to be the perfect show. When the Hulk got to his famous line, "don't make me angry, you wouldn't like me when I'm angry "we both said it at the same time and that was all she wrote. We both started laughing and from that point on we were in love.

***June 6, 2007- My teacher funny as hell, he good at making up stories and having us think about shit. He likes to give us things to think about and is good at using us as examples when demonstrating how prosecutors have to prove their cases beyond a reasonable doubt in order to win. Today he gave this scenario. If my classmate seen her boo pull up to a hotel with a lady, and after a while they leave. Then the next day my class***

*mate calls and ask where he was and he says he went to the airport. She say's no you weren't, you were at the hotel and he said yea I was. I was with the wedding coordinator. We went to the hotel to try and plan the wedding because he couldn't do it at any of my classmate's family members house, because they can't keep a secret. His question to the class was, do you believe him. Which brings us back to can you prove beyond a reasonable doubt that he was cheating. The class was in an uproar. Of course my gullible ass said I believe him and the class went crazy. We debated a good 20 minutes. I love being the devils advocate.*

*On the flip side, me and that damn Edward got into it again. I swear we still ain't made up from last week. I'm getting real tired of this shit. Yesterday he tried to choke me again, but I was able to push his fat ass off of me. Chavez heard us and he ran upstairs and grabbed Edward and told him, "You not gone put your hands on my mama." Of course the windows were up so all my neighbors heard us. The shit started that morning because he started working midnights. This change was made so he can have time during the day to do some of the things that he need to do with his truck and the car wash he trying to get without consulting me. Another selfish act that I have to deal with. So the first night he asks if I can take the baby to school and of course I try not to say no to my dear sweet husband that can do no wrong, so I said yea. Before I left that morning I remembered that I only had four people on schedule… meaning I couldn't leave. I calls him on the way to work to tell him that I left the baby at home and she can stay home today. She is in preschool, what the fuck. This nigga went off about how he got to get some sleep and how I did this shit on purpose. That I was too lazy to get up and get her ready. He couldn't understand that I was the only one at the desk and that we only had four people instead of the usual eight. I wouldn't even be able to take a lunch. So he takes her to school, hair not combed and she got on some fucking corduroys. It is May so when I find out you know I'm pissed. She could have missed one damn day.*

*The day before I had to go east and take care of something. I called him to pick up Alexis cause he was already west and of course he had so much to do and couldn't so I had to come all the way west and then back all the way east. His mother went to the hospital that Monday so when I called that morning he ranting and raving. So I said your father there he can watch her or ask your mother. Why did I say that. I really forgot she went to the hospital Monday. He goes to say I don't give a fuck about his mother, blah blah blah. I'm like where do he get this shit from. His daddy lives with us for Christ sake. Me and his mother are not on the best of terms, thanks to him, but we alright. I prayed for her a speedy recovery but I'm not gone be fake and act like we are so close, and on top of that, it is like pulling teeth*

***to get info from Edward. He don't volunteer shit, so he didn't tell me much but he mad that I am not showing a lot of concern.***

***June 20,2007- It has been almost a week since Mr. Little passed. His funeral is this Saturday. The viewing is Friday. I think it is finally sinking in that he is gone. He will be truly missed. He was a man beyond his own time.***

Glen was cool. After that first day he started coming over every day after work. Aunt Mona liked him and would allow him to sit and talk. But she was careful, she never left the house while he was there. But I don't think she had too much to worry about, Glen was a nice guy. We basically did a lot of kissing and he never pressured me to do anything else, which was good, because he may not have been ready, but I was. I was hot and ready.

***July 10, 2007- I feel like my life has turned full circle in some sense of the phrase. The boys are back in my house. Some shit done jumped off on the eastside. Let's just say guns and knives and severe beatings were involved. So of course the end result is Arcyle and Darshawn are back with me in my little humble home. I'm thinking this happened to give us all a second chance to do what should have been done years ago, such as somebody getting a job, a GED or diploma. I'm hoping their near death experience gives them the motivation that I was not able to instill in them when they***

*were growing up. Arcyle was hurt pretty bad so after he heals I will work on him. By him having the baby and baby mama his situation is a little different than Darshawn's. On the other hand they both are able body men and the only baggage they have is mental. That is they don't want nothing out of life baggage. But we gone make it do what it do.*

*I woke up this morning Chavez in the bed next to me, Alexis and Denise on my floor, I go downstairs Arcyle on one couch, Darshawn on the love seat and pops on the couch in the back room. Lord give me strength.*

*July 19, 2007 -So much has been going on since the incident with the boys. They haven't been in any trouble but its tension in the air because they are here. Edward been cutting his eyes... he hasn't said much to me so I'm sure he don't even speak to them. He's so immature and honoree and the sad part is this was their house before his. Edward is not a bad guy it's just he is very, very, very very... moody and it seems that the mood swings are tearing this marriage and family apart. As soon as we get on good terms it don't take much to send us back to beef mode. He just so mean and selfish and self centered at times. How do you wake up mad every morning? I still be thanking God for waking me up. The day before- evidence- it makes me just want to throw in the towel. Like this pass Friday he was suppose to give me 700 dollars. I had to pay my car note, pay the water bill and get the*

***tub snaked. But of course his car been acting up so the repair will cost $200. This would only leave him $130 so I told him to take the extra 70 or 80 dollars out of the $ 700 and get his car fixed. The only thing Edward cares about is his car, his clothes, Denise, his mama and his sister.***

***The kids are gone, Chavez is in California and the girls are over Edward's mother's house. It's rare that all of them are gone at the same time so I wanted to take advantage, so by him getting his car fixed that would be less drama I would have to deal with. Edward acts like such a bitch sometimes when he don't get his way and if he feels like I'm not making something that is important to him important to me, like his car for example, a priority, he wants to argue. I'm like in a nice e-mail. Edward please go ahead and fix your car. Why this nigga wake up with some bullshit about us checking in with one another when one of us gets up and leave. First of all, why you picking shit. That comment was made to him, because he had a habit of doing dumb shit like getting up in the middle of the night to drop off one of Arcyle's friends; male or female. So I asked if he does something like that, wake me up so I can either ride or at least know where you were going, so if anything happened at least I can tell the police something. Edward ain't got no license and what if one of the young lady's people see this grown ass man dropping them off, what will they think. So just play it safe. So he wakes up***

*Saturday morning, looks at me, I'm dressed because I just came back from the grocery store. Mind you this is something I do almost every Saturday. He went with me last Saturday which was nice. I felt like we were a married couple, but any other time I go by myself and just look at the couples and wonder why am I by myself. But anyway he wakes up and says good morning with attitude so I say good morning baby. He goes on to say I thought we were supposed to wake the other person up if we leave. I'm thinking what! It is 10:00am, I just came from the store, you just got off work at 7:00am. Wake you up, are you serious. I leave out the room to wash a load then I go back upstairs and I ask him, "you mean to tell me that I'm broke so you can get your car fixed so you wouldn't have an attitude this weekend and you wake up with one. I'm so tired of this shit."*

*So I goes outside to the back yard. Normally before marriage me and the boys would clear the alley, but since I have been married I felt like I didn't have to do man's work any longer. Why did I feel that. I look into the alley and it looks like Jurassic Park. I was almost scared to go out there. Every noise or movement I heard or saw made me flinch. I didn't know where to start so I borrowed my neighbor's tools from across the street. I got her weed whacker and her tool that looks like a chain saw and I just started cutting a trail. Then I started clearing in sections. I made piles and by this time Darshawn came out to help and before long his friends Ralphy and Carter joined in. I was out there for at least 7 hours. I cleared from the end of the gate to the end of the garage. When I came in do you think bath water was ran or a massage was offered. His fat ass laying up watching TV in the same spot he was in when I went outside.*

*Thank God for Di she had a room, so Sunday, she invited me and the kids to the room. So I took Alexis, Darshawn, Carter, and Ralphy and we had a ball. I was able to sit in the Jacuzzi and I swam and played with Alexis in the water. I got dunked by Ralphy big ass... I had a ball.*

*July 26,2007- Since the ordeal, Darshawn has been enrolled in school and he has a job interview Tuesday. They told him to get his food handlers card so I think that that is a good thing. It is at a hospital full time in the kitchen with benefits. Arcyle ass still ain't did shit, he just laying around eating up all the food. I'm bout to lose my mind. I have been thinking about ways to make myself happy. I want a motorcycle so bad I can taste it. Every since I rode my co-workers Harley I can't shake the bug. When me and Di were younger we rode on the back of bikes and I have ridden a spree before when I was much younger but this new fascination with wanting one has taking over. It got so bad that last week I had my credit ran to see if I qualify. Last time I did that they just laughed and said hell nol... or I had to put at least $2,000 down and the payment was*

***gone be higher than what I could afford. I had them run it last week and they said 0 down 99 a month but I need a co-signer. For 8 months I called everybody I knew. Relatives I haven't spoken to since the last funeral or holiday. I know- that is bad. I asked co-workers and the killing part was 3 of them had their credit ran for me, but they were in the same boat credit wise. So to make a long story short I have to wait until Feb. the black people lotree. If I could have rode the rest of the summer, it would have been sooooo nnniiicccee***

After chilling with Glen for so long, after awhile I just stopped calling any of the other numbers that I had. I still didn't see anything wrong with getting numbers though, after all, I was young and wanted to keep my options open. I wasn't a slut or nothing that's just the way I rolled.

Around about this time Nana was due to have her baby. I'd been praying every day for a healthy brother or sister because she was smoking. Not as much but smoking nonetheless. She was also still strung out on those pickled pig feet. I kinda felt bad for Victor because I knew when I wasn't there that she was running his ass to death.

***August 17, 2007- It is payday and I'm broke as hell. On top of that I almost forgot to pick up the pay roll checks this morning. I'm still a little sad we had to put Gracie to sleep yesterday. She been sick the last few weeks.***

*Not eating, loosing weight. Alexis called me at work and said she looked like she was dying. She tried to make her eat. I talked to Chavez and he said Alexis been holding her all day, so when I got home I couldn't take my uniform off. She and Denise were ready to go to the vet as soon as I walked in. Alexis wrapped Gracie up in a blanket and we went to two vets. They were both closed. I called home for them to look up one close to the house on the internet and Darshawn suggested we go to the humane society. Their clinic was also closed when we got there, but the adoption part was open so I asked one of the clerks to just come and look at her. They see just as many animals as the Veterinarian, Hell I figured they might know more. When he came out he said it looked like feline leukemia and it would have been a fortune to try and get her treated, so I had to break the news to Alexis. As he took Gracie out of her arms, I explained that Gracie was real sick and she was suffering and they were going to put her to sleep forever. Before I knew it she started crying, then I started crying. I then called Edward cause he been waiting on his pussy since 4:30pm, and here it is 6:00pm. I'm telling him what's going on and his response was, why the fuck was I crying. I'm like you don't understand and hung up. I didn't want to cry it just happened and I couldn't stop. I promised Alexis we would get another cat and we held hands all the way home. Denise in the back knocked out. I'm glad she slept through the whole thing. I don't think I could have*

***taken both of them crying. Edward been acting sweet as pie almost as sweet as he was when he proposed to me In the middle of the lobby at my job. He gave me such a passionate kiss yesterday while we were doing the nasty. I thought I was on the soap opera. I even heard the music in the back ground***

On April 21 Nana's water broke and we had to rush her to the hospital. She wasn't due for a few weeks but when we got there her contractions were just a minute apart so they rushed her straight to the back. Before any of us had a chance to do anything, the doctor came walking back up to the front with the news that it was a boy. They'd had to do an emergency c-section. He said that the baby was a preemie then grandma asked if my mom and the baby was o.k. and he said yes. There were some concerns though. He said that she had drugs in her system and there was a chance that the baby might experience some long term problems as a result. That he would have to stay for awhile so that they could monitor him.

I figured this was not the time to turn to my grandmother and tell her that I told you Nana was a crack head so instead I just stood listening to the doctor. I later found out that Nana's blood pressure had dropped so low while having the baby that she almost died. After about an hour we were able to go see the baby and Nana.

***September 4, 2007- Edward packed his stuff and this time I don't know how to feel. There have been times where he would threaten to leave and he would go through the motion of packing and me and the kids would have a crying session as if we were at his funeral. I mean real tears. Believe it or not it hurt equally each time he left. I thought I would have gotten used to it by now. But how can you get used to losing the one you love just for him to reconsider and put his stuff back and make everything better. It was like each time he came back from the grave and we had a new chance at life and rebuilding our marriage. But we go through this shit just about every 3 to 5 months and have since we said I do. Even though him leaving the house causes much grief for us in every since of the word, I vowed to myself that if he threatens to go one mo gen I was gone let him and I was gone make it easy. So no more fucking burials and begging him to stay. This time, I told the girls to prepare for some rough times. That is what I call it when Edward leaves. It means there will be little food in the house. That mommy's money is bill money, gas money, grocery money or just no money. Alexis devastated. She was like ma, not again. I'm like yea baby. She then asked does that mean that we wouldn't be going on any more trips no time soon. I told her no, and that we would not be going shopping, no money for dance class, piano lessons or karate. Things that I promised them when our finances were out the***

*red, but because of Edward's two month vacations every year, it is impossible to sustain any real lifestyle. We living in poverty in this bitch. A two income household now reduced to a one income household over night. Mind you when he takes his two month vacations we still have relations. We living in separate homes, and he in the street and he don't give me any money. I know... crazy. But what is the magic word people, "Marriage," say it with me- Marriage. This is my husband, this person I stood before God and promised to love, honor and cherish. When he gets on my freakin' nerves and when he don't. When he got that flu bug and driving my ass crazy and when he healthy and not. When he got money and even when he can't afford to take me shopping, on trips, can't buy me a Lexus for my birthday and park it in front of my phat ass crib he just put me in last year for my birthday- with a big bow on it- and when he broke, I vowed not to fuck no other nigga. I vowed to put up with his bullshit until one of us keeled over and died. He is my husband no matter what. I chose him. He had already told me earlier that day that if it wasn't for Denise he would have been gone already. That is deep. I agree shit aint right and don't look like it's getting better any time soon but I got faith and I still believe in the sanctity of marriage. Call me crazy but when you join in holy matrimony I think that puts you closer to God in a way. However, we've been arguing all week and now with all my good faith and good intentions, I look up just for my loving husband to tell me he couldn't see us together in the next five years. He didn't take his vows serious I see. I vowed to stay until death but this nigga didn't even give us five years, which also hurt like hell. I still haven't gotten over that shit he said earlier. Ain't this a bitch. After all we have been through in these five years... all the bullshit I have taken from him- just going by this particular week which really wasn't nothing in comparison to the bullshit I have tolerated. I thought I earned my stripes that dreadful night when I decided to stay after that dumb shit he pulled. Make it so bad all the shit I do for him is because of that dreadful night. Not to mention seeing him with the white girl where we shoot pool after the last time he left. And I know he couldn't just met the chic... and he don't see us being together. So I decided all that hurtful shit he say was not going to be taken lightly anymore. No more just letting shit ride and being mature- meaning I know people say things out of anger- but damn after 5 years I'm not worth you thinking before you speak. I do. I'm not worth you not saying hurtful shit. I try not to say hurtful shit. I love him but I love myself more. I refuse to allow him to keep disrupting my life and my kid's life. If he wants to leave... fuck him, bye. I made it real convenient for him to go this time. Me and the girls stayed at the laundromat long enough for him to pack. Not like I had a real choice. I had to wash 11 loads then I get a voice message telling me he still had to get his car out of the garage and he needed to get his machines from up under the steps and his speakers from behind the dresser. I came home and took everything off the dresser so he could move his speakers with no problem. I had Darshawn move the machines from under the stairs and then left him a message that he could come get his things whenever he was ready. As bad as I want to cry, I can't. I thought of all the things I would miss and nothing, well I won't say nothing. We had some good times but damn not good enough to go through this shit. It aint like I'm shopping at Summerset on his pay weeks and in between and living off the water and riding a Range. I'm living pay check to pay check. I'm broke and busted and I'm unhappy. Make it so bad me and my kids were not living like this when he met me. If I have to go through three weeks out a month of hell just to have one week of him being nice to me it's not worth it. I think I jumped the gun with this marriage. He is not who the Lord had for me. Speaking of the Lord he does work in mysterious ways. The adjustment was quite smooth- a few bumps but I can't complain. Edward been working midnights for a few months so I have gotten used to sleeping without him and that was the hardest cause I had gotten used to rolling over and him being there. So before school let out I had started bringing the baby to work with me and we walked down to the school because it was the most logical thing to do. Alexis was the only dilemma because when he announced he was leaving me again he said he would take her to school. He knows I don't have anybody to take her to school. I didn't rely on Chauncey like that, which is Alexis dad and he knew that.*

*Anyway, I'm sorting clothes with my head down and he walks into the basement. I don't look up 'cause I don't want him to see my face because I know my eyes are red from holding back the tears. I gave him nothing so he went back upstairs just to come back not even 10 minutes later and say he ain't taking her nowhere. He was so mean. So I said she got a daddy he will take her then. All I hear as he's leaving is "fuck you bitch, I hate you. That's why I'm leaving your dumb ass, because of your smart ass mouth." Just mean... but he says it be my mouth. But look what I go through. Look what I tolerate before I say anything back. He pushes my buttons until I get out of pocket 'cause if I wouldn't have said anything then he would have come back 10 minutes later and said some more foul shit, cause that's what he do. He already said he was leaving, that was enough. When he said that I barely had the strength to stand. Not again. The house can't take another one of Edward's vacations I see any new uniforms for Chavez or Alexis. No new clothes for Denise who has grown two more sizes since last year and does not wear a uniform. So she has to have a change of clothes every day. He, his mama and his sister buys her things but they don't send it home, so she already wearing*

*Alexis's clothes rolled up. I will be driving on E-killing my engine- very little school supplies, the weight lost from not eating a few nights out the week so the kids can eat. Borrowing money only to owe out most of my check, leaving me with less to work with. My check I just got is spent 'cause I paid the bills that were due. Come Friday is his pay week. How convenient. I wish he would have told me this before I spent my check, I would have prioritized things a little different. I have about a 100 dollars and 30 cents to last me 2 weeks. That's groceries, gas and bus fair. My car note due... this is a fuckin' joke, right. This is my husband. Why do he keep putting us through this. We are a family. We are raising children.*

*Thank God for my kids. Darshawn took her to school on the city bus. Problem solved, temporarily. Her father Chauncey and his wife going through changes too, but we are going to have to come together and do something soon. They do what they can for Alexis, but since I have been with Edward I have not had to depend on them for her daily needs. I had a husband and we worked it out. I cannot afford bus fare for her, Darshawn and Chavez much longer, not to mention he left me with no extra money and no time to prepare. Nothing. That selfish bastard. How could he not give a fuck about us. I have been good to this man for almost 6 years, but I have faith that the Lord will make a way. He always does.*

When I first saw my little brother, I was like, "oh my God." He was so little and red and they had him in this little incubator with all these lines coming out of him. It was hard to watch. On top of that they wouldn't let us touch him. The nurses called him a miracle baby. I can still hear the nurse's telling my grandmother how the drugs that my mother had taken had had an effect on the baby. She told her it would be a while before he would be able to come home. They first had to get him to where he could eat on his own and could maintain his body temperature.

When I went to see Nana, she was just laying in the bed looking helpless. Her body was still numb from the c-section, but she was awake. She looked at me with tears in her eyes and said, "Wep, we made it through. You got a baby brother."

Watching her like that was hard. I couldn't help but feel for her. I told her that she had done good, and that the baby was cute. She hadn't seen him yet so she had to take my word for it. They had been working on him ever since he was delivered so they hadn't brought him to her yet.

For the next five days me and grandma went to visit. After the fifth day my mother was allowed to go home, but the baby had to stay for another week or two. On that fifth day I asked my mother if she had named the baby yet and she said, that his name was Arcyle.

Before leaving the hospital, my mom had to consult with this special nurse who dealt with babies born addicted. She had to sign papers and agree to participate in a program for addicts. During the course of the program they would evaluate the baby and test him during the different stages in his development. If for any reason Nana decided not to participate, then the baby would be taken away and put in foster care, along with the possibility of me and Victor being taken away too. The nurse mentioned something about being unfit so she signed the papers and the nurse gave her a hug and wished her well. It was strange leaving the hospital with no baby.

It was several weeks before Arcyle was able to come home. He was a cute little kid. He was still real little and we had to be real gentle with him. I was good with babies though. I loved holding and playing with them. But when they started that crying it was time to give them back to their mama's.

Arcyle turned out to be no different from the other little babies his age. He was cooing and mimicking like the other babies and he started crawling and walking on time. He was fortunate. Every month Nana took him to the program to get tested, then after awhile she only had to take him every few months or so. I went with her sometimes, but for me, it was just good seeing her being a responsible mother. She never missed a meeting and for my mother, that was saying something. When we were younger grandma took me and Victor to all of our doctor visits, so this was a different person I was seeing. She had definitely slowed down. It was good not seeing her ripping and running the streets like I was used to seeing.

***September15, 2007- It hurts so bad. I've been keeping myself busy trying not to think about this nigga leaving us again. He aint making too many moves to get me back. No flowers, no dates, no I'm sorry. The last conversation I had with him he was still trying to tell me about the issues he got with me and the shit I'm doing. Hell every man wants hot meals, some warm pussy at least 6 -10 times a week and some head from time to time. I work hard. I'm in school... I got some good things going for me. My program and the janitorial service are all in the making so I got plans. I told him even with my issues, I was doing enough, I thought, for him to step his game up. So as we talking, in the middle of the conversation he just up and raised his voice. I had to let him know ain't nobody been hollering at me since he been so called gone and I told him if he couldn't lower it for him to call me later. So he lowered his voice. It took this nigga to move to respect me. Shit when he was here we would holler, hang up, not come home, just very disrespectful. Although it hurts not having no one here, wearing some one's ring in this condition, gave me a lot to think about. Money tight as hell, I'm juggling which bill I'm gone pay, but for some reason I'm good. I haven't had to call him for shit. The***

***last few times he left I had a fit calling him crying on the phone begging him to do shit with me, and for me. This time I prayed about my marriage and I asked the Lord to give me strength to go on if he chose to leave me again and he did. I'm holding on.***

Chapter 9

**MY DADDY**

I had watched my father practice for years with the hopes that he would one day make it big. At last, it seemed that things were finally looking up. He'd gotten a gig with the Dramatics and was set to start rehearsing immediately. I was so proud of him. I even got to meet Ron Banks. Up until that time, that was one of the big highlights of my life. You know, for an old head, the man wasn't bad looking either. They were coming out with the Truly Bad album and I was thrilled that my father's name was going to be on it. All I could think about was that my daddy was gonna be famous. I imagined myself ducking paparazzi, walking the red carpet, traveling, the whole nine.

***October10, 2007- I feel good. I feel at peace. I have come to grips that this marriage is not healthy and he is not going to change. I think most of his problems stem from childhood but he refuses to go to therapy. When you can not admit that there is a problem you can't fix it. I have pleaded for us to both go and he still refuses to make an appointment... and I say him 'cause I did. I made the appointment and we went a few times and then stopped for whatever reason. I am tired of being the only one that wants this marriage. I want for him to want it to and by him making the appointment that would have been enough to prove to me that he wants the***

*marriage as much as me. One of our problems is communication; I feel that communication is a major part of any marriage. I feel* that *maybe a therapist can help us find a way to communicate and also help Edward control his anger and mood swings 'cause after being called bitches, hoes, motherfuckers, and dumb ass every other day- communication is bleak. After a while, I shut down and don't listen to shit. So I had to learn how to tune him out. But the drawback is some of the important things that he might be trying to get across to me I can't hear because of all the other cruel shit that comes out his mouth. He says its things that he can teach me... but he tries to teach me things I already know and my way works for me. He also says that I should do the things that he asked me to do and not the things that I think I should do. I do both. The things that I choose to do... hell, fuck him and feed him and what he wants me to do... let him do him, whatever that means. So I don't trip when he in the streets, he come and go when he please. I try not to nag. When I need something done I just get it done. I'm working twice as hard. I am not perfect but it is not all me. But until he realizes it we're doomed. He also has to realize that he is not always right and I am not always wrong. Through this marriage I have learned to let go and let God and since I have done that I feel much better about myself and I have been concentrating less on us and more on me and the kids. I have been keeping busy... the basketball tournament has been taking up a lot of my time and it will bring in the money I need to pay for my application fee for the non profit status and my insurance for the janitorial service is in the works. School is keeping me busy. I am a survivor and I will get through this. The boys done stepped up their game. Chavez won't let me miss a day of school and Darshawn ass be up every morning helping me with the girls. If I had one wish I would wish for Edward to act right and act like my husband but I know that that wish will never come true. But at the end of the day, I know I have done all I can do and I have no regrets. I hate the kids are going through it, I just wanted the best for them and I thought I was doing that. I wanted to provide them with a more stable environment. Not that I wasn't doing that, I just felt it was time for a balance. A mom and dad. They are fine but it has been an adjustment. Alexis has to stay with her dad and his wife until I get the Intrepid running. That's cool though because they live right across the street from her school. Denise has little fits 'cause she still does not quite understand why her daddy does not live with us. He gets her like clock work every weekend and she knows his cell number. She calls him whenever she feels, which is fine by me. I actually encourage it.*

*October 22,2007- I feel good. I filed for my divorce Friday, served Edward his papers Saturday and I got my Jesus on Sunday. All I can say is thank you Jesus. I am not an advocate of divorce but baby that man had me working 3 jobs at minimum wage and no benefits. Like they say, sometimes we hold on so tight to things that the Lord himself is trying to break apart and that is exactly how I felt damn near the whole marriage. So I threw in the towel and I feel like a load has been lifted. I'm back at peace. I have a peace of mind in my home once again. But Thursday I was a shitty mess. I'm not gone act like it's all bells and whistles. I see why lawyers charge so much... they took me through the ringer. I was told to go to one place just so they could send me to another place, just so they could send me back to the first place, so they could send me somewhere else, then send me back to the first place, then again to the wrong place. Luckily, they helped me anyway then sent me back to the first place just for that precious young lady to tell me they don't take checks. So I would have to wait until Friday. But she was nice enough to tell me that Friday just come and look for her and she would take care of me.*

*I cried at every stop. The notary was nice enough to give me some tissue and some words of encouragement. But even thou I know it was for the best I still love my husband. The saddest part is he didn't love me. At least not the way I needed him to for the sake of marriage. If we were boyfriend and girlfriend yea, but we were husband and wife. Marriage is a commitment and both parties have to be prepared to do whatever it takes with no stipulations. The love has to be*

***unconditional. Maybe the next time around I will have that.***

***December 3, 2007- Alexis birthday was the 28th of Oct., and of course thanks to my loving husband I'm broke as hell so I have to be creative. Alexis is such a girly girl... she loves to be pampered, so I did her nails, I gave her a nice manicure and polished it clear and I gave her a pedicure and massaged her feet. She was so happy. Then I dropped her off to her dad's and he and her stepmother took her to jeepers, as well as to some ice cream place. We all struggling, but we working it out. I'm behind on the house note, the bills, car note, everything. I'm killing old boy credit but what can I do. When I tried to get the house back in my name last month it was right when Edward was threatening to leave. I stressed to the man how important it was he got it done ASAP. I told him I was going through a divorce and if we don't close I couldn't afford to stay here. But he dragging his feet. On top of that, I couldn't show 12 months of paying history because Edward left. If he could have closed before the month ended I probably could have gotten away with it, but again ol boy dragging his feet.***

***Meanwhile, I done hooked up with the good Doctor, it was the least I could do for him helping me out with the divorce, and also to assure me that it wasn't worth going back to Edward. Being with Edward is the last thing on my mind. The good Doctor aint looking for a***

*woman and I 'm not mad at him. He fine and successful. He can have whoever he wants, hell I'm lucky he gave my hoodass the time of day. Edward's daddy still living with me and it's working out, he should be working soon so that will be a big help. I haven't spoken to Victor since I asked him to loan me some money right when Edward left but he called me a few days before thanksgiving and I was happy to hear from him. I couldn't bring myself to call him but I said if he called me then let bygones be bygones. When he called, he invited us down for thanksgiving. I was so excited that I didn't even sleep. I got off work Wednesday, went home and loaded everybody up. By 7:30pm we were on the road. I said a prayer, everybody said amen and we were off. We made it to Tennessee about 3:30am. The weather was really bad and it rained the whole way so I pulled over at a rest stop and slept for an hour. Chavez ass was knocked out most of the way however the girls stayed up the whole time watching movies. It was hell driving through those mountains but we finally got there about 9:30am.*

*During the trip, my brother took good care of us. His house is beautiful. We ate good, slept good, not a care in the world. A few of his buddies also came down and we hit this strip bar. Can you believe the strip bar is in a strip mall. Hell no! The way the rappers talked about it I thought it was gone be the shiz nik. Nonetheless, we had a ball. Me and Victor shot pool and got drunk then I made it rain on some little chick. She climbed to the top of the pole and did a little trick and slid down. As I walked back to my seat I stopped for a minute, watched her do her thing then went back and threw some more money on her. Man, why did I do that. That just opened up the flood gates for all the hoes to holla at me. After that I was letting hoes down easy all damn night. All in all, I had a ball. Victor tight ass paid for the gas coming back. After that we followed each other back to Detroit. I was behind Vic, and his boys were behind me. We did 80 all the way back. We stopped to fill up and eat then jumped right back on the freeway. It started raining when it got dark but we still maintained our speed. We would have gotten back home around 9:00pm but it was a bad accident in Ohio which held us up about 3 hrs. So we got to the city around 12:30 a.m.*

*Well back to the real world. Struggling with these bills, trying to make ends meet and waiting on the black peoples lottree as Mody Wowo would say. We making it. Some days I be wanting to fuck Edward up then after I pray about it I realize he aint worth it. I know I was the best thing he ever had. Shit, let him settle for second best 'cause he will never be able to replace me.*

After Arcyle came home he now had the spotlight. That was o.k. though because as far as I was concerned he needed it. He was constantly growing and so far, so good. No signs of any problems. Thank God. The nurse said he was developing but still had to be watched as he got older and started school.

I was also glad that both of his parents were still in the house. Leon was still around tryna play daddy so that was good. He did a pretty good job. He got him dressed every day and sometimes took the baby with him to the store. Meanwhile, me and Glen was still hanging like wet clothes. I loved him so much that I was convinced when I turned 18 that we would get married. Aunt Mona still allowed him to come over whenever he liked, with the stipulation of course that we behaved ourselves. It was hard to have any privacy when they were there anyway. Mark was always coming out of the room hoping to see something. I don't know if he was spying for Aunt Mona or if he was getting his rocks off by watching us kiss.

Like I said before, Glen never went too far. He would feel on my tidies but that was as far as we went. I wanted him to have the coochie, but I was willing to wait until we got married.

Whenever I spent the night over Aunt Mona's I always had to sleep with one eye open. One night I woke up and that nigga Mark was on his knees on the floor next to the couch trying to put his hands in my shirt. Aint no telling what he would have done if I hadn't woken up when I did. I knew he was a pervert. When I woke up, I hollered out "leave me alone" and he took his drunken ass back in the room with Aunt Mona. After he disappeared back in the room, Aunt Mona hollered out if I was o.k., and I said yea. The next day, before I left for school she asked me if Mark was tryna mess with me and I told her no because I didn't want to upset her. I told her I must have had a bad dream.

***December 7, 2007- I went to Di's church last Sunday. Me, Alexis, Chavez, and Tab; Chavez's little friend. We really enjoyed the service. The Pastor made me feel like he was talking directly to me. He was also entertaining. We will probably go back next Sunday. I can see the light just a little. The black people lottree gone put things half way right for me. I can pay the young lady to do my paperwork for the janitorial service and everything else is gone jump from there. I will also be able to pay the application fee for the program since the tournament did not happen. It's hard to concentrate on things outside of this marriage. I can't wait to start doing some things to help these kids that need it. I hate I had to put everything on the back burner until then but due to Edward leaving I had no choice. I been sitting on this pussy though. Won't be no fucking this time around. Hell, I just wash it and go. I act like it ain't even there. The next man that get this ass is going to be a very lucky man.***

***We're having a gala at my job soon and I'll be modeling fur coats. They gone hate***

***me. I'm walking in with my fur on, then modeling a few, then walking back out with one on. Everybody don't have to know how much grief I'm going through right now. Trust me with a full length mink on my back troubles is the last thing people will see from me tonight. God is good and I feel good. I have too much to be grateful for to be bitter. It still hurts now; I won't lie about that. But I tell you this. It hurts less today than it did yesterday.***

The only drawback that I had regarding my father's success was that I couldn't always see him when I wanted. He would sometimes leave for a week at a time so I would have to chill until he got back.

Everything was going good with Glen, until one of his ex-girlfriends, who lived in Aunt Mona's neighborhood found out I was dating him. Her name was Nicole. Every time she saw me, she would give me these dirty looks. Come to find out her and Glen's sister were the best of friends and she stayed right across the street from them. She and Glen only kicked it for a minute but you could tell she was still jealous. As a result, just in case they were still together, I kept my distance. It was also rumored that Glen had some girl pregnant but he never said anything to me about it. It was more like I knew somebody that knew somebody that knew the girl's sister.

Chapter 10

## LOVE THY NEIGHBORS

As I got older, the people on my block began to change. People moved in and out a lot more than they had in the past and as people got older they would bring other people to the block in the form of relationships and the like.

One new person to move to the block, was Big Willie's girlfriend Toyia. Toyia had a reputation all over the east side for whipping ass. She and her sisters had a reputation. They weren't known for that girly scratching an' shit, they were known for busting' niggas upside the head. I heard that Toyia had once dropped a dude for touching her booty.

Even before I could introduce myself, she and Big Willie were already tearing up the block. Toyia was 14 and Big Willie was 18 and they would both get drunk and fight. I could hear them all the way from my house. I remember them once fighting after she found some other chic's number in his pocket. They were something else.

All sorts of things went on as I began to get older. I had a friend, Tanisha, who was Cory's sister, who use to run away from home a lot, and one of the places she would go was my house. I'd be sleep and she'd wake me by throwing rocks at my window. I would open the window and sneak her in and she would sleep on the floor at the bottom of my bed. When it was time to go to school she would climb back out the window, then disappear for a few months before popping back up again in a few months. For some reason she just couldn't seem to get it together at home. She would show up musty and wear the same clothes for days. I never knew where she went when she wasn't sleeping in my room, but I knew that's not the kind of life I ever wanted to live. I don't think I would have made it. With grandma's cooking calling, I would have had to come home and eat.

My grandma knew about her running away, but she never knew she stayed overnight with me. She said she acted that way because she just wanted to be grown. I concluded that if that's what being grown was, that I didn't want any part of it.

***December 11, 2007- I seen my old school friend Aretha at the library last night. Me and Chavez were both there trying to get our school work done. I have not seen her***

***since middle school. She looks the same- face looks the same. No stress in her face whatsoever. She was there to meet some of her business partners that she's working with to launch this hip hop magazine. She's engaged to be married. They haven't set a date yet. I hope to get invited. Its good to see people that I went to school with doing well for themselves 'cause I have seen some in the street or at the hospital visiting... and baby, they look like they need to be visited. But when I think about it, when I was younger, the crack heads and heroin addicts who looked old as hell, were the age that I am now- go figure?***

My 8th grade school year seemed to fly past. Before I knew it we were getting ready for our annual spring fling. That year we were also invited to march in a parade. We were to march up Warren all the way down past Finney High School, then stop at this new senior community complex as a way of letting people know that the new nursing home was there. Once there, refreshments would be served and we'd mingle with the residents.

I was excited because it was my first parade. On top of that, we were going to wear the cutest outfits. They were red and white with short skirts, white leotards and tights. Like I said, I was also preparing for the spring fling so I was also excited about that. That year I would take part in five dances. Also I was a lot better than the year before. The classes Ms. Jones had sent me to at the church had really helped. I had become more graceful and flexible because of them. To top it off, Ms. Jones also sent me to tryout for the All City dance team. I didn't get picked, but Nana told me that the fact that she even thought to send me was an honor. I still had not made the company but she still had me in damn near all the dances and she let me travel to the other schools to perform. The only thing I was missing was the Jackson Dance Company shirt, my picture hanging up in her office, and the recognition. But I wasn't tripping. It was my last year so from where I started I was just glad to make it that far.

The weekends had become pretty busy for me. At this point I actually had choices about what I wanted to do. I could pick between my father's, hanging with Di, Aunt Mona's, Grandma Sheryl, visiting my cousin Robin or I could just stay home. On this particular weekend I actually decided to stay home. I decided however that if Di called I would hang with her but I really preferred to stay home because I was tired. I had been practicing for the concert a lot and it had taken a lot out of me.

One thing I was grateful for during this time was my health, because the year before, during this same time, I was stuck in the room, smelling like sardines with the door closed with the mumps. My neck and jaw was swollen up so big I looked deformed. Of course grandma had the remedy- sardine oil and a hot towel. I had to stay in my room by myself I believe for a week. I don't wish the mumps on nobody. That total isolation was horrible. So tired or not, I was grateful to not have the mumps.

That night, if I thought I was going to get the rest I desired, I had another thing coming. As soon as I lay down, all I could hear was the loud voices of the new neighbors across the streets. It's was the new bunch that moved in next door to my neighbor Carol. They were a strange bunch, too. One of the ladies even had a girlfriend. Now that was nasty.

They also had kids. Rel was our age and he had a little brother who was about 5. They also had some cousins. One who was also about 5, then another cousin about Tanisha's age, another cousin who was older than us, and also in the house was the lady's boyfriend, her sister Sharon, her girlfriend, and Rel's mama. Phew, they were one big happy family.

Normally we didn't go into people's houses. The only house that we ever went in was Cory's. And that's because his grandmother was the candy lady. But I did go into the new neighbor's house one day and man, let me tell you. When I walked through the door, I had never seen so many roaches in my life. It was like they stayed with the roaches, the roaches didn't stay with them. I mean the roaches were everywhere. As soon as I walked in they met us at the door. They were on the walls, on the ceilings, in the doorway, everywhere.

As we walked through the house, Rel was showing us around like it was a mansion. My only thought as we were walking through the house, was how come the roaches couldn't just be contained in one part of the house, like most of the clan who lived there, which seemed to be in the living room. Every where we went, they were there waiting. The house was also very dirty. Stuff was every where. Clothes on the floor, boxes every where, they had no shame. We couldn't have company if our house was the least bit dirty. Grandma or Nana wasn't having that. That house also stunk...bad. I'd never been to a fuck fest before but I concluded that had I ever gone to one, that's what it would probably smell like. It smelt just like unwashed ass.

When we finished with the tour and went back out on the porch, I took a deep breath and shook off any roaches that may have managed their way onto me. The last thing I wanted was to take those disobedient ass roaches back to my house and mix them in with the domesticated ones we had. Our roaches wouldn't have a chance. They would have been run outta there in no time.

After I got myself together, Rel came out and whispered if we wanted to see something exciting. So of course we said yes. We looked around and made sure no grow ups had heard him then let him lead the way. By this time the sun was going down and it was getting a little dark. So he told us to come on as he led us to this window on the side of the house. As we followed him I started to get nervous because I didn't know what to expect. Plus, what we were doing was spying and I knew that was wrong. It felt kinda like reading somebody's Diary, or ease dropping on somebody's phone conversation. But I still wanted to see. So the closer I got to the window the more nervous I became. I tip toed on up and as I got closer I could hear the heavy breathing. O.k. I thought. This was the same sound I had heard down in the basement when Edward and his girl was down there doing the nasty. So I knew it was some nakedness going on. Anyway, Rel points to the window and I walk up to it and take my turn peeking in. Oh my God, I thought as I focused my eyes on these two big fat people moaning and groaning. As I looked closer however that's when the shock hit me. Hell nol, I whispered. Turns out Sharon was sitting up with her legs wide open while the head of her girlfriend was buried pussy deep between her legs. All I could see was heads bobbing and hips moving. I ducked back down away from the window, but after everybody else finished their turn I had to go back and look again. Sharon had to weigh about 350 and her girlfriend Sherri about 250. They were sweating and flopping around it was crazy. After about my third peek we finally backed on away from the window.

When we got back in front of the house, our attention was immediately diverted toward Rel's girlfriend who was walking up toward the house. So before we could really discuss what we'd saw, she and him disappeared back in the house. After that I went back home. When I got in the house, I go upstairs and Cassandra on the phone. She done discovered something too. A hot line. Turns out when you called the number for the time, you could actually hear other people talking in the back ground. I was immediately hooked. For the next few months I spent all of my extra time on the phone. I actually even met a few people while ease dropping.

When final exam time came around I passed every class. I didn't have the best grades, I got a C- in English, a D+ in Mr. Johnson's class and I did decent in all my other classes. Those were the only two I was really concerned about so I was relived that I passed them. When my father picked me up for the weekend, he was somewhat disappointed about my grades, but like I told him, I did the best I could. Books just didn't come that easy for me. I didn't have a problem with it, I just did the best I could and hoped I never failed anything, and I never did.

So anyway, as soon as we got to my dad's house, I immediately ran down the street to check out my girl Shawnda. It had been a while since I'd seen her and we were both excited to see one another. We hugged, chit chatted a little then hit the streets. The first place we went was over a few blocks to our boy Timothy's. When we got there he and his cousin were outside kicking it. So we hung out with them for awhile. I had a little crush on Timothy so when we saw each other we hugged and he gave me a little peck on the lips. I think Shawnda was kinda surprised because when we kissed she blushed more than me. So just to pick with her Timothy kissed me again.

After we kicked it with the them for a minute, we left for the store but not after promising he and his cousin that we would stop back by on our way home. After we got back from the store, this time Timothy invited us in. When we went in the house, we walked to a back room to where a television was and sat down. But you could tell they'd planned something because as me and Timothy was sitting on the couch all hugged up, his cousin grabbed Shawnda's hand and the two of them went back outside. Anyway he sitting all close, the lights all out... but his mama was upstairs so I didn't think he would try anything. I didn't think he was that stupid. So we're looking at each other like we're both a box of chocolates and the next thing I know, his tongue is all down my throat. We were ready. I could tell he hadn't kissed a lot of girls because after kissing 17-year-old Glen I considered myself experienced, but that didn't matter, I felt good nonetheless.

We stayed wrapped in passion for awhile. It wasn't until we heard his mom walking toward the room that we jumped up and sat back like we were the most innocent teens in the world. This was my first time in their house and the last thing I wanted was to get banned on my first visit.

When she walked in the room, Timothy introduced me. She then asked if I was the girl who had been calling the house. I looked at Timothy, then back at her and said no. She then placed her hand up to her mouth as if to say, oh shit. But I told her that it was me, that I was just kidding. In fact, I was calling the house every other day.

After meeting his mom, he walked me back outside and me and Shawnda said our goodbyes and we were on our way. As I mentioned before, Shawnda's neighborhood was nothing like my street, Cope. It was real quiet. They didn't have bullets flying over their heads, or project chicks tryna whip ass every other day. The only incident I ever heard about was this dude down the street from them getting killed after crossing some people the wrong way. So chilling with her was peaceful. We would just sit on the porch and chill.

The following week, when I got back to school, it was time for the big parade. It was one of the biggest moments of my life. All the teachers came out to support us. It was very exciting. The police had the entire marching route blocked off. Our school as well as a few others took part. As we marched, every few blocks or so we would stop and do our little routines. We looked so cute out there. We had on our makeup, some of us had pom poms, and some carried flags. I was one of the ones with pom poms. We were really doing good when out of no where, a damn bee came up and stung my ass on the back. I saw the bees coming and tried to swap them away but to no avail. I guess the perfume I had on was too much for it because that bee got me good. I tried to keep my pace and maintain my smile but I have to tell you, I was in pain. When Ms. Jones saw me marching in place like I'd suddenly lost all understanding as to why I was there, she motioned me over to her. When I got over there she asked what was wrong and I told her I'd gotten stung by a bee. She then pulled the stinger out and then removed a piece of ice from her cup and placed it on the wound. After a minute or so, I was able to catch up with the rest of the girls and continue the parade. I'm just glad I wasn't allergic to bees because that would have really ruined my day.

The parade was nice though. And when we reached our destination everybody had a nice time. There were clowns, plenty of food and refreshments and the elders really enjoyed and appreciated our efforts. And if that wasn't enough, the spring fling was the following day and being that I was a senior, I, along with Di and Melanie, would be the stars of the show.

***December 14, 2007- I have a Christmas tree, thank God. A good friend made sure we had one. It won't be any presents from me under it but at least we can have the spirit***

*floating through the house. I think I'll have Christmas in July for them at the resort in Florida. When me and Edward were there we went to a time share and I signed an agreement for them to take money out my account every month to pay for our next trip. I just have to get us there, which will not be a problem. If we have to hit the highway, then so be it. I will get some gifts and let them open their gifts there. I'll also decorate the room like its Christmas. It's sad this year. Our Christmas present is that the house note will be paid one more month and we got a roof over our head. But God is good 'cause in spite of all that we're going through and all that we have been through it is still laughter and happiness in my home. Pops seems to be comfortable and the boys have been staying out of trouble. Denise is fine and Alexis is adjusting. Me, its still hard financially and emotionally, I still feel like somebody is suppose to be in my life right now. I wish I was in a wonderful marriage right now especially during the holidays. Now physically, I'm straight. I have been doing my sit ups and my goal is to have a six pack by my birthday so I can get my naval pierced and a tattoo on my stomach. 35 is going to be the new 20.*

The concert went real smooth. We finished the African number but when it came time for the finale, I felt my self getting really nervous. The crowd was going crazy, but I was ready. We would do it to Aretha Franklin's song, Pink Cadillac. When we ran back stage everybody was excited and ready for the next number. We hurried and changed and when we went back out on stage, we killed them dead. It was the best performances of our lives. As the crowd jumped to their feet, for that one moment, I can honestly say that I knew what it was like to be a star.

***December 16, 2007 I am so stressed. I am going through my mail because I have turned into one of those people that let mail stack for a few weeks because the bulk of it is bills I can't afford to pay right now, so if I'm not expecting a check, what the fuck. I owe so many people, a couple of them are people I paid off and now I owe them again. Now how does that happen. I'm so close to putting this ass on e-bay to the highest bidder it ain't funny. I even thought of selling a vital organ like a kidney or a lung... maybe one eye. I wonder how I would look with a patch. Knowing me my ass will have Mody Wowo stone it so it can look sweet. Edward came by; he hugged me and although I didn't have the strength to hug him back it felt good to be hugged by him. I still love him. Through all the shit we been through over here these past three months I still wish we could be a family. I hate so much to have to start over, get to know somebody else's habits, wants, desires, likes and dislikes... I just hate it. At least I know Edward's issues. In my heart I know if I took Edward back I'll give it a week and he would be back to the same shit. The attitudes, the***

***mood swings, the bull shit, the arguing... the same shit***

School was finally out and Nana was allowing me to go to Flint with my friends Aaron and Erica. Erica hung with us at school but I only had one class with her. We would also walk home together sometimes. A friend of her mother's, a real nice white woman, had invited us to visit and hang out at her family home in Flint. She had a big house out in the country and also had about four or five four wheelers which she said that we could ride. I was ecstatic. I actually packed before asking to go. I don't know what I would have done had Nana said no.

When it was time to go, Grandma dropped me off at Erica's. When I arrived, Aaron pulled up right behind us. Me and Aaron hugged, then knocked on Erica's door like we had never been any place in our lives. When she opened the door, we all let out a big scream. We were so excited.

The lady, Ms. Williams, picked us up and we made the hour long trip to the house. When we arrived, it was dark, and time for bed, but we were too excited to sleep. We ended up staying up till about 2 a.m. just talking. The next morning was even more exciting. As the smell of pancakes and bacon swept through the old country house, we hurried, threw on some jeans and long sleeve shirts and hurried to the kitchen.

Once outside I was surprised at how far in the woods we were. But I was ready. As they arrived, we also met some of the other family members. They were pretty cool. They acted like it wasn't the first time they'd ever seen black people so I was relieved about that. After greeting her family, Ms. Williams then took us out back where we had our pick of four wheelers. When she showed us the path, it seemed to stretch for miles. We each jumped on a bike, she showed us how to work it and that was it. I started off kinda slow, but after I got the hang of it, there was nothing but sloshing. We had a ball. At first we just rode around the house for awhile, and that by itself was fun. They had this real deep ditch back around front and when you'd ride down into it and come up, it would toss you in the air like a rag doll. We ended up riding those bikes all day. The only time we stopped was for lunch. They fixed fried chicken so you know we weren't too excited to stop to eat that. That right there showed us they knew something about black people.

I concluded that day that white folks knew how to have fun. Four wheeling was not something that you saw in the hood, and until this day the only time I've seen anything close is people shoveling snow with them.

When we got back to Detroit and grandma picked me up from Erica's, I drove her crazy with details of the trip. I talked from the time she picked me up until we got home. Then once I got in the house I did the same thing to Nana. "Nana, you should have been there...we rode these big four wheelers, and when we went up the ditch, it threw you in the air, and we was way back in the woods, and we ate fried chicken, and at first I didn't know what to think of them white folk, but then after we was there for awhile and got use to them and realized that they weren't that bad and can I go back again if we get invited..."and I just went on and on until she finally told me if I kept talking I wasn't going back no where and why don't I go outside and play before I drive her crazy. So, that's what I did.

When I got outside, it didn't take long for me to snap back to reality. Come to find out, somebody done told everybody that Rel said he liked me and the news had traveled quickly back to his hoodlum girlfriend who was now looking for me to resolve the problem. So I get outside and everybody's in a circle waiting on me to arrive. So I walk to the circle and here comes her amazon ass walking down the street looking mad as hell. When she gets to the house though the first person she walks up to is Rel. She jumped in his face and demanded to know if he had a crush on my little yellow ass. When she mentioned my name I was dumbfounded. I mean damn, I had gone out of town, had the best time of my life and as soon as I got back I'm in the middle of what could turn out to be the biggest bull shit of the summer.

I prided myself on staying out of trouble, so I zoomed in to ear hustle and see what she was talking about. When she asked him again if he liked me, I answered for him. "Ugggg, I groaned. No you don't. He don't like me. I don't know where that came from," I said, hoping that would save me from a lot of unnecessary grief.

I started thinking to myself, that yea, he had some nice teeth, that is when he brushed them, and maybe if I could get past the body order, but, NOT. He was not my type. So after a few minutes of going back and forth, he kinda manhandled her and walked her on into the house. After about thirty minutes she came back out, hair all sweated out, looking like she's just been fucked and then walked on down the street without saying another word.

Well, if I thought that was the end of drama for the day, I had another thing coming. Big Willie, who called me Banana, yelled from the corner for me to come down and walk with him to the store. He'd been in an accident a few weeks prior and hurt his hands, so he couldn't carry anything so he would ask me to walk with him so I could help him out. So we're walking to the gas station and here comes this Rel's girlfriend Shay, along with one of his cousin's who's riding barefoot on a bike. When they see me they block my path and Shay says something like, "now what's up with you liking my boyfriend." I'm thinking, damn, I thought this shit was over with. I look at them and I know they both gone try to jump me, but I really didn't want to fight. It wasn't that I was scared, I just didn't want to fight. Plus, once again, the information was wrong. I didn't like her boyfriend and I told her that. Then I started laughing and started walking away. When I got to the corner this big 5ft9inch a hundred a seventy-pound bitch jumps in my face and pushes me. So I pushed her back and the fight was on. We were like two bulls locking horns. She had my hair and I had hers and with our free hand we were both swinging for the knockout. Before I knew it we were in front of this girl Tammy's house and when we got to the grass she tripped and I landed on top. At that point she was in trouble because with the advantage I started wailing away on her ass. I swung so many times that about twenty percent of my punches actually hit the grass. Next thing I know, I could fell what felt like punches hitting up against my back. But I didn't stop. I just kept swinging. I couldn't stop hitting her long enough to see who was hitting me so as she continued trying to flip me over I eventually looked up to see, Landrel, the barefoot bike rider kicking and punching me in my back. The fight went on for a while. Finally, after about what seemed like 15 minutes, somebody mama came out and broke us up. By this time everybody on my block done came around the corner so Rel he mad at the lady who broke it up, cussing her out talking about she helped me by holding down the chick I was on top of, and blah, blah, blah. All I knew was the bitch had torn my shirt, my tittie was hanging out, and it had a big bite mark on it.

When I got back to the house, I immediately called Di and told her that I had just got jumped by the dirty people from across the street. And true to her character, she didn't even want to hear the story. Within 45 minutes Di pulled up in a cab with Tae, Lashawn, and two other girls. I hadn't seen these girls before but they came ready to fight. As soon as Di and her crew jumped out the cab, I heard one of the girls from across the street, ask in a threatening voice, if they were now supposed to be scared. Of course, my answer to that was yes, because Di was dangerous. At all times she either kept a gun or one of her grandmother's butcher knives in her purse. By this time the block was filled with people ready to see a fight. There was a barbeque going, people were milling around, the people across the street were ready and we were ready. Everybody on the block hated the fact that the new people had jumped on me so although they didn't know it, they were outnumbered a hundred to one.

Roni who was manning the grill had called over a bunch of people because he had already gotten into it with Tammy's man a few weeks back. Something happened where Roni, who was gay started getting harassed and called all kinds of faggots and after he couldn't take it any more, he'd snatched off his wig and told Tammy's man that Tammy's man had been fucking with Roni, which was his pet name, and now he was fucking with Tony and that he wasn't gone be too many more faggots. So as a result of that run in, he and his crew were ready.

After about an hour of us standing around staring each other down, both sides kinda reached the conclusion, that whatever drama had unfolded, that the end result wasn't worth the hassle. So the people across the street finally went on in the house. Meanwhile, Roni and his friends, a group of about 10 gay dudes from every spectrum of the gay community were too fired up to call it quits. They'd been out there drinking beer and talking shit for hours so they were ready to burn some shit down. About 10 minutes after the girls went in they started calling for Tammy's man to come out. They were so mad they even started throwing bricks at the house. Finally, he came out. When he came out, I ran in the house to use the bathroom because I wanted to see this man fight Roni, and I didn't want any interruptions. The crowd had decided that they would go one on one and I didn't want to miss it. Rel's cousin had even pulled his van on the grass so that everybody could see and the two of them would have light. They were both ready so I had to hurry. I think I was in the bathroom for about a minute, and by the time I get back on the porch, all I heard was, oooooh, did you see that.

I was like, what, what. See what! Come to find out, Ronie done knocked the nigga out with three quick blows to the head. It was like a real live prize fight. All of Ronie's friends were out there cheering and I'll tell you, the block was on fire. People were talking shit like Ronie was the greatest fighter since Muhammad Ali. They say her man didn't even get in a punch. I couldn't believe I had missed the whole thing. I had betted on Roni walking over to the the guy, and taking off his earrings, then his wig, then talking a little shit, then getting it on. But he'd let me down. His ass went right over there and knocked my man right the fuck out.

After that night, it took a few weeks for everything to die down. Eventually, we started back speaking, but it was never the same. I could never trust those hoes after that.

Chapter 11

## HOUSE PARTY

*December 24, 2007- Its Christmas Eve. I'm still having my annual Christmas brunch, but its tight so whatever I cook is gone be real simple. Hell my family don't care, they love me and they gone come just because. Last year we did it big. This year they might have to settle for eggs, bacon, grits and biscuits. I can afford that. The kids gone be shocked 'cause I can't afford to buy them anything. I mean, I can't buy them nothing. But they knew it. I don't know how I paid the mortgage. I barely have enough for my car note. They had a sale at one of the hospitals, so I was able to get the boys an outfit apiece and Alexis some boots. I didn't get Denise anything. I know her dad and his people gone set her out. I got pops and Arcyle some socks, a hat and a glove set.*

*I went to my friend Shawnda's church yesterday. She does a play at her church every year and I promised her that I would come see*

***it. She's very talented. She actually writes and produces the whole thing. Every year for some reason when it came time for us to go, me and Edward would be beefing about something and I would decide not to go. It was hard for me to do anything like that if my personal life wasn't right. When I'm beefing its like everything around me isn't right, so when that happens I don't like to be around people. When my aura isn't right, I'm afraid the evil spirits may rub off on people so I stay away. Anyway, I went yesterday and it was beautiful. I got there just in time. I am always late... at least 15 minutes for everything. Everybody say I got that from my dad. I'm so glad I made it this year. I told her I can't wait to see one of her plays on Broadway. Her husband is also a producer. He's into music. They looked so good together. After the play the pastor called her up to the stage so she could introduce her cast then after the service she introduced me to a few of the up and coming artists her husband has on his label. I was honored. After that I went to visit Auntie Hattie in the hospital. She's in good spirits but she's not looking so good; at least not to me. After that, I came home, cooked dinner, braided Alexis hair and went to sleep***

Every summer for as long as I could remember had brought something different. There were trips to my dad's, hanging out with my cousins, or just hanging out on the block. This year the new thing would be house parties. Tammy's boyfriend's baby mama who stayed a few blocks over was going to be throwing two dollar parties, and me, Di, Tae, and a few more of Di's girls had already planned our whole summer around those parties.

The first Friday of the parties, the girls pulled up in a cab, piled out and came into the house to freshen up. We were all real excited and looking forward to the action. People in the hood had been talking about this party all week and I was hype. I put on my tight red levis and one of Di's silk shirts, my friend Toyia did my hair, and I was ready. Toyia did my hair in popcorn waves, which is a style where you gel down your hair, then pull the hair threw a net to make it stay. She had everybody in the hood rocking that style. You couldn't tell me nothing, I knew I was fresh.

After everybody made sure they were ready, we walked around the corner and headed to the gig. As soon as we hit the street you could hear the music blaring from the house. When we got to the side door, we paid the girl taking the money and we were ready to party. This was my first real house party without adult supervision so this was it. When we got downstairs I walked in like I was walking into some strange excited place from another world. That first experience is amazing. You get downstairs and the first thing you see is everybody grinding. And I mean they grinding tryna get a nut. You couldn't have pried some of those people apart had the house been on fire. It was hot, dark, and the drinks were plentiful.

Nothing heavy at the time, just coolers, but that was enough for us.

When we got settled real good, and smelled that somebody else had lit a joint, Di took one out of her purse and lit one up too. We didn't want to be disrespectful, normally we would go outside because everybody doesn't smoke weed, but shit, when we smelt the weed penetrating the basement, it was a wrap.

Everybody in the hood was there. I even seen some project people up in there. I hadn't really had no problems with them, but that didn't really matter. I knew how they got down. The girls were worse than the boys. All they did was fight. Don't get me wrong, they came in bumping people, and tryna start shit, but everybody was too caught up in trying to have a good time to let them come in and destroy the party. So after they saw that nobody was paying any attention to them, they went on and settled down and joined the party.

***December 27, 2007- Aunt Hattie still in the hospital. I went to see her Christmas Eve. I hated that she couldn't be home for Christmas. I stayed in the hospital watching Jeopardy with her then I headed home. I hate seeing her this way. She's been taking radiation treatments the last few days; they hope it will stop the growth of the rare cancer that she's fighting. I just pray for a speedy recovery.***

*I made Christmas brunch and nobody came. Everybody called and was trying but just couldn't. It is tight out here for everybody. Poor Christine who has come almost every year was trying to come up on gas money so she could come but Bush got the economy so fucked up it ain't even funny. But I'm glad they called. Me, pops and the kids ate good. The boys' friend Devon ate with us. I was able to pull off French toast, eggs and some bacon. I said a prayer, we ate and then I slept for the rest of the day. The kids... meaning Chavez was upset because we usually visit the family and exchange gifts and take pictures. But I wasn't feeling it. I guess depression had set in because I was really too broke to be motivated to do anything. I didn't have gas in the car, I didn't have presents to give so I just didn't feel like leaving the house. I hate my family is broken... I hate that am still in love with my husband... I hate that I have become another statistic and the fucked up part is I still don't have a concrete reason for why he left. We talked yesterday and I swear he brought so many ill feelings back that it wasn't funny. We started off good- talking about work, bullshit, funny bullshi... but bullshit nonetheless. Next thing I know we back in left field and I think it started after he asked if there was anything we could do to make the relationship right. When he asked the question I got upset because I felt like that was some more fiend talk. He should have asked that question before he abandoned us. He always wants me*

***to fix shit and when I fix it, it aint right, he has a better solution. Then I'm stuck wondering if he had a better solution why he just didn't fix it in the beginning and the sad part is, when I fix it, it is fixed but because he didn't fix it, it ain't right. If he can't take credit for it, it ain't right. So before I knew it, I'm hollering, my head is hurting, my stomach is back in knots, and I'm crying. So many questions unanswered, so many problems unsolved, but I realized through that conversation that he still has not forgiven me for anything I have said bad to him throughout our entire marriage, because he brought up shit that I know I apologized for a million times. This nigga crazy and need some serious help. Boy, bye.***

Another thing that we use to do during this summer was go skating. Everybody and they momma use to be up at the rink. Especially Di, she practically lived at the skating rink. Every week she was at the rink. She was good too, she could skate backwards, dance to the music, the whole nine. When we would hook up on the floor, I could hold my own, I just wasn't as good as her. I could do almost every routine, except those that involved skating backwards. For some reason I just couldn't skate backwards. At least not then.

There would always be a lot of cute boys at the rink too. That's what I liked about it. I knew that whenever I went I would pull about a dozen numbers.

***January 1, 2008 - I am snug in my bed with Alexis- Happy New Year I say to myself 'cause she knocked out. My dad called, we talked for a minute then Edward called and wished me a Happy New Year. He say he was thinking about me... and I was thinking about him too, but I wasn't gone call him, I'm trying to move on, but its hard 'cause I feel like I'm leaving a part of myself behind. Well, on a lighter note I hope to be half way caught up on the mortgage this month and next month when I get my taxes, I can pay the application fee for the non-profit status for the program and I can start helping some of these kids get it together. I can also pay the young lady so she can get started on my paper work for the janitorial service so I will be able to start getting contracts. Then I can start working on bringing this house up to code so I can turn it into a AFC home or a place for borders. Either way I have to start working on my wealth... since I'm already rich.***

Me and Terry, one of the guys who I ran into at the skating rink have been talking every day and night since we exchanged numbers. Terry was someone who I had went to school with, but when I knew him we never paid much attention to one another. Now, it seemed when I saw him at the rink, those pretty eyes, bow legs, and nice smile was about all it took for me to become hooked.

After a few weeks of heavy talking, I agreed to visit him at his house. He'd agreed to pay my cab fare there and back so I was excited about that. This would also give me the opportunity to meet his mother and brother who I'd talked to on the phone whenever I'd call.

When I got to his house he led me to the T.V. room where his mom was then his little brother came running down the stairs and I met him. After the introductions his mom asked me to have a seat then asked if I wanted something to drink. I told her a pop would be good, so she sent Terry to the kitchen to get a pop. After he came back with it she then went into the kitchen to get dinner started. His brother decided to stay and play eye spy, however after watching us watch TV for about ½ hour he got bored and went back upstairs. We started off just holding hands then he moved in and put his head on my shoulder. At that point, I scooted over closer to him to make it easier for him to get to my neck. He gave me a little peck on the neck then started nibbling on my ear. As we were starting to get into it, his mom yelled from the kitchen and asked if we wanted anything, and we both yelled back... noooo, at the same time. When I turned back toward him, his lips met mine and we were off and running. As we were kissing, he put his hands on my knee and started rubbing it around. Something told me to wear pants, but it was too late for that now. As his hand's climbed up my leg, I returned the favor. I put my hand on his knee and then slowly slid it up until I had inched up to this big bulge between his legs. At the time, it just felt like the right thing to do, but soon as I felt the budge, I got scared and moved my hand back down a little, but he grabbed it and put it back. So I left it there. Meanwhile, he had moved his hands so far up my dress, that it was no place left to go except my panties. So he slid them aside then slid his warm fingers onto my hot tingling coochie. He didn't put his fingers inside, he just rubbed softly around the outside. While he was doing that, with his other hand he grabbed my hand in such a way that let me know that he wanted me to squeeze his bulge, so I did. The more I squeezed the more he rubbed. This went on until we heard his mama holler...dinner was ready. He then got up and went to the bathroom while I sat up and adjusted myself and acted like nothing had just happened.

After a minute or so his mother came back in the room and asked if I was hungry. Being that I was and she'd fixed one of my favorites; spaghetti, I said yes. So she made me a plate and brought it back to me. By then Terry had gotten rid of his budge, fixed him a plate and joined me back in the T.V. room. After we finished eating, I told him to call me a cab 'cause it was getting late. I then called Nana and let her know that as soon as my cab came I would be on my way.

The minute I arrived home, I went straight to the phone and called Terry. Now that's what you call puppy lo

## Chapter 12

### LOYALTY

All leading up to that Friday, I was geeked because me, Di and the girls were going to another house party. This time, when we got there the project girls and some of the boys from the projects were already there. They didn't start off doing the bumping thing like last time, but they were staring Di and her girls down like there was gonna be a problem. For some reason, they weren't griming me, but that didn't really matter, I knew that if something went down I would have to fight regardless. That was Di's code. We come together, we fight together. I didn't really have a problem with it, I only wished we had picked girls that were not from my hood to beef with. That couldn't be too good for me.

The griming had come as a result of Di walking over and giving one of her boys, who was from the projects, a hug. Nothing serious, they were cool, so they gave each other a brotherly sister type hug but that was all it took. The kind of hug didn't mean shit to the project girls and in particular this chick name Rhonda because the boy turned out to be her baby daddy. So even though he told her it wasn't about shit, that Di was just his girl, Rhonda and her crew didn't care. So before the night was over, Rhonda finally got around to bumping Di. Di bumped her back, and then the rest of us bawled up our fisted and readied ourselves for action. Before anything could get started though, the dude got in between the two of them and whispered something into Di's ear. I don't know what he said, but whatever it was Di backed away. After that he grabbed his girl and the two of them started dancing. When the party was almost over, the dude made sure he led Rhonda and her crew out first. We left shortly thereafter. On this particular night we were lucky, we had avoided hand to hand combat, but I knew, the next time Di and Rhonda crossed paths, and that dude was not around, it was gone be some shit.

In fact, it wouldn't take long for that to happen. That following Wednesday me, Di and Tae were hanging out at Chandler Park. We'd been there for most of the day so when it started getting late they dropped me off, and the two of them went back to the park; probably looking for trouble. Their thing was starting shit. That's what they did for a living. Shonuff, this bitch come calling me around 9:00pm to tell me that her and Tae seen Rhonda at the park. She said that while they were parked on the strip, Rhonda and her crew rode pass catching each other's eye in the process. A few bitches were called between them, but before either of them could do anything, the poe poes popped up and they had to leave. Any other time the cars would have had enough time to stop, get out, fuck somebody up, or get fucked up and that would have been it. It would've been a slam down boxing match.

So of course as soon as Di got home she couldn't wait to call and tell me what happened. The only thing I could think was how Friday there was gonna be some shit and sho nuff, for the next few days all I heard was how the project girls were gonna get fucked up, and how we were the ones that was gonna do it.

I couldn't believe I had gotten myself into something that I had nothing to do with. I even got a knock on my door during this time, and guess who it was? Rhonda. She'd come to my house to recruit me to fight Di and her girls. What the fuck, I was one of her girls. Her theory was that I stayed in the hood and Di and her crew were outsiders. The killing part was they knew Di was my girl but they still tried to play me. I knew I had to come up with something fast so I told her I was on punishment, which I was, so I tried to explain. I told her because I had gotten back late from the party the previous Friday that my grandmother had nailed up some chicken wire on the window so I wouldn't be able to sneak in. That as a result I had to knock on the door and that was it. I was now on punishment. I had actually served my time but I did what any real person caught between a rock and a hard place would do. I told Rhonda I was still on punishment and I wasn't going.

After she left Di called, I told her the same thing. Of course she knew it was a lie or I was at least stretching the truth 'cause she knew Nana was not gonna keep me from going to our Friday night parties... especially in view of the fact that I could always bribe her and give her a few dollars to let me go. But I held on to my lie. I told her that Nana had extended the punishment. She said Tae had already told her that I was gonna come up with an excuse and that she had even listed the top five excuses I would come up with. Number one being I had gotten shot and was on my way to the hospital.

Well, I got called scary and all type of other derogatory names. They had a field day but I didn't give a shit. Given a choice, I would rather take the abuse from Di then deal with the repercussions from fighting the project girls. I still had to live in the hood, and after they did what they were gonna do at the party, I would have to walk the streets looking over my shoulder, worried about them breaking out my grandma windows- not my windows mind you- I had no windows, or burning down our porch or some other dumb act that I could pretty much depend on happening. To me, it just wasn't worth it. After all, that's just the way that them hoes got down. It was nothing for Di and them to fight. Plus, Di and her crew didn't scare me. But them project girls, now them hoes gave me nightmares. They didn't give a fuck...you hear me, they didn't give a fuuuuuck, I had seen their work.

When Friday came, I stayed home and talked on the phone with Terry all night. He was in my corner all the way. He didn't want me to go any more than I didn't want to go. So anyway, about 3:00am Rhonda knocks on my door and says that she and Di had indeed gotten into a fight and did I know where Di lived. Her boy had told her she stayed by our old school Jackson, but I told her she had moved, but that I couldn't remember the street. I told her we had been beefing ever since they got into it, and that she didn't trust me any longer because I stayed over in the hood with them. Then Di called the next day to tell me how I missed it and how they had fucked them hoes up. She said that they couldn't fight, who had talked the most shit, who had gotten hit first, the whole nine. Although I wasn't impressed I gave the impression that I was. I was just glad nobody got seriously hurt.

Nevertheless, from that day on whenever I was with Di and Tae, my loyalty was questioned. They would not let me forget how I had not shown up for the fight, and would constantly have something smart to say whenever we were together.

## Chapter 13

## High School

By the end of that summer, high school couldn't come soon enough. As an incoming freshman though, all I heard was the horror stories about the fights, the name calling and the ostracizing. Everybody had said the same shit about middle school, but I didn't have any problems. But this was not middle school, this was high school. I had enough sense to know that high school was different. That much I knew. I was now about to go from childhood, to one step from being grown. Now that was scary. The only thing scarier than that was, you guess it...them Project Hoes.

***January 7, 2008- First day back to work after a week's vacation. I feel good, I'm all rested and excited about the business ventures I'm trying to pursue. I am debating if I should do the AFC home versus the room and board housing. I have to talk to a few people to way out the odds for both, but both is steady income for me and my kids and also employment for me and my family and whoever else I can help. I also have been getting weak. I have been calling Edward lately, I don't know exactly why? I don't know if it is cause I'm lonely, horny, miss him, miss having somebody or is it that I don't like to fail at things I work hard at. So for me to invest so much time and effort into this marriage and not to mention money and for it to just end the***

***way it did is egging me. Although we didn't argue, just the way he still talk still let's me know that he hasn't changed. He still blaming me and me pursuing him in some way is still giving him the advantage. I just wish we can get it right but for some reason I know that will not happen. I feel like a charity case. My aunts been taking care of us, giving us food and a few dollars here and there. My girl Sammy even took me out to eat. That was the first date I had in a long time. Hell Edward wasn't taking me out when we were together, let alone apart. I can't wait until I'm in a position to show everybody that has been in my corner through out this whole thing how much I love and appreciate them. I always tell them- I just want to be able to show them soon.***

In getting ready for high school, Pamela and my dad bought me a few outfits and closer to home my grandma bought me a few. This allowed me to change up for a couple weeks before I had to wear the same thing twice. But that was cool, it was actually a step up for me. I was also able to keep my hair up every two weeks with the help of grandma and my daddy. Mr. Little kept my hair looking good. By this time, he was doing hair out of his apartment. He was the man, too. He kept women coming and going. If you didn't know he was doing hair, a person would swear that he was pimping women out of that place.

My grandmother took me to get supplies that year, as if buying supplies was gonna give me the automatic A's I wished for. I had attended school for eight years and I was still just a C student.

When I got to high school, I didn't see anybody I hung out with from Jackson. The genius, Ms. Di had gotten accepted to Cass Tech, my friend Aretha had gone to Murray Wright, Aaron had gotten accepted to King, so I was the only one out of my crew to attend Finney. The first day was wild. The line to get our schedules was wrapped around the building. When I got my schedule it looked like a grocery list. I was like damn! I had classes from 1st to 7th hour. I wondered if I would ever see first hour, though, because I just didn't get up that early. I had English first hour, Algebra, second, third hour introduction to physical science. Damn, I wondered if they knew who I was. I already needed to see a counselor to help resolve this schedule. To start off, I was told that physical science was for the smart kids, so that sure in hell didn't include me. I also had French, Social Studies, and Dance. Then they had a list for people that wanted to join any of the sports teams on the gym door so I signed up for track. Now that I could do. I could beat everybody in the neighborhood running, so why not.

Everyone going out for track was to meet after school in the weight room; where ever the hell that was. Meanwhile, I needed to find my English class. I asked the security guard for directions and he directed me upstairs.

When I got to the top of the stairs another security guard directed me to the other side of the school. It wasn't hard finding my other classes and before I knew it 5th hour had come and it was time to go to lunch. Compared to Jackson, the cafeteria looked like a real restaurant. When I got there, everybody looked lost. It looked like the blind leading the blind.

My grandma had given me a few dollars so I could catch the bus so I had a little money. That's another thing I would have to get use to. There would be no more rides to school. So now I really couldn't wait to get my license. Aunt Mona's car was still there ready for the taking, but she still hadn't taught me how to drive it. She kept saying that she would, so I couldn't wait to learn.

Anyway, as I looked over the prices for lunch, I had to swallow twice just to get the lump out of my throat. Hell I had gotten use to free lunch. Now pizza was two dollars...pop a dollar. I couldn't see how I was gonna survive buying lunch everyday. It looked like I would have to get a job if I wanted to eat. At least eat something other than peanut butter and drink something other than powdered milk, because that's what my grandmother would have ready for me each morning if I told her of my dilemma.

After lunch, I made it back out through the maze of halls and finally located my locker. I put all the books that I'd accumulated in the locker and hurried my ass to French class. I was lucky because it was right around the corner from my locker and I had pretty much spent most of my time just looking for my locker. When I walked in everything around the classroom and on the board was written in French. Talk about culture shock. When I walked in my teacher said bonjour, so I said bonjour back. Then she said Ja ma pel Mrs. Salimer and I said Ja ma pel Shakenya. When I said that, the whole class laughed. But she shhhhsshhhed them because she said I was right.

That little episode gave me confidence that I would do well in French. To tell you the truth though, I was actually just tryna be funny and break the ice, but her body language made it easy. When I came in the class she smiled and made me feel like she was greeting me, so I assumed she was saying hello. Then with the Ja ma pal I wasn't quite sure but she said her name so I thought she was introducing herself so I did the same.

When I got to social studies, it was back to blah, blah, blah. That's how my teacher sounded to me. I wasn't looking forward to that class at all. After that I found my way to the auditorium to meet my dance instructor. When I got there she was a big woman... quite a change from little fit and trim Ms. Jones. She did look the part though. She had braids which she wore tied with an African print rag and she wore a solid colored leotard with a big wrap around skirt, which made her look like a dancer. In addition, although she was big, she walked with a style of grace. There was about 15 of us in the class, and out of that number 5 of us were fresh meat, so she spent the class talking about what she expected out of us and what we needed as far as leotards and tights.

After that I went to the weight room where I was approached by this big burly man with a raspy voice. He spoke, then I spoke back. When I took a good look at him I realized that he looked sort of like Mr. T except without all the muscles and gold chains. He looked like he was probably fit at one time but now he was just a shadow of what he used to be before the cheese burgers and beer got a hold of him. Anyway, he gave me a tour of the weight room then took me outside so I could see the track. After showing me the track he told me to bring my sweats and be ready to work out the following day.

***January11, 2008-All is well. I feel good today... Edward and I went to therapy. We had a conversation Monday, I don't know what was said to make him make an appointment but he told me to hold on and he clicked over and the receptionist was on the line confirming an appointment for Tuesday, so I agreed to go. I don't know how successful it was, the therapist said a lot of things that made sense, but they were some of the same things that I had been telling Edward all along. So a part of me feels like if he ain't listened***

*thus far why the fuck even bother. So I am trying to stay positive since we both agreed to go, but still, he said some things that I can't shake. He said he think I still just want him for his money... what a joke. As if I am not making personal moves of my own to ensure financial stability. On top of that, none of my business ventures requires his help. It would be nice if I had his support, but with or without his support I am still going to do what I got to do. Then he made a comment that I make him feel like anybody can be here. In a way I can understand that statement, but it is confusing for one because it is not my fault Edward picks and chooses when he wants to step up and contribute to the house as far as repairs and yard work goes. So if you not doing much then yea I can see how he can feel that way. Anybody can come in and do yard work and home repairs, but again that is not my fault. I would tell Edward that I want to do a project with the house and let him know when we would be financially able to do it, then when the time come he either in the street, playing golf or just laying around. So of course if you not doing much it won't take much to replace you. The truth is though that just anybody can't be around my kids. I'm doing things for him that I have never done for another man and I have taken shit off of Edward that I would not have taken off another man... and the sad part is I know he knows that. So I was heated. There he was sitting there like he was the victim. I really got mad then. I was so mad*

*I started crying. I got up and started pointing in his face because I was so mad I couldn't talk. All I could do was point.*

*By the end of the meeting I had calmed down a bit. He took me by the hand, walked me out and then to the car where he gave me the most passionate hug and kiss ever. But I didn't trust it. I felt like he was using me and had something up his sleeve. It's going to take a few more sessions to convince me otherwise. In the meantime, I was committed to doing what I have been doing. Staying positive and praying for strength to get through another day. Every day I try to make something happen... the only problem is if we do decide to stay together and make it work it is going to be hard to make him a part of my life since I have learned how to live without him. It has been almost 6 months. That is a long time to be without somebody. I now have the mentality of a single woman... an independent woman... the kind of woman I was before I was his wife. At this point I have been holding things down without him. I have been making decisions without him and doing things in the best interest of my family without him and finally, the fact that I haven't asked him for a dime since he's been gone should speak to the fact that I am not interested in his money. As a man and the head of the family, that comes with the territory. But in terms of me just wanting him for his money, that's bull. He doesn't make that much more than me.*

I made it through my first week of high school without a glitch. With all the homework though, by the end of the week, I was tired as hell. That first weekend consisted of nothing but homework. If I was gonna maintain decent grades I would have to maintain my homework on a consistent basis. No one had to tell me that. I knew me and I knew my capabilities. Therefore, I had every intention in the world to work hard, do my best and get the best grades possible.

Well, that first week my intentions were great. However, Di called that Saturday and asked if I was ready to hang. So, just like that, I was now short on time. I asked what time she was coming and she said she would be at my house around 1:00. It was already 11:00 so I hurried, did my math, read over my English, then hurried and got dressed.

Like clockwork she was there like Johnny on the spot. She was ready too. She'd met this dude and of course, he had a friend so we were ready to roll. Before I left, Nana gave me her usual speech. No sex, no drugs, be careful and be back no later than 10:30.

***January 15,2008 -Life is good. I am getting closer to taxes... I'm sorry black people lottree and getting my new start at life. I'm putting together a skating party for Feb. 11, hopefully I will bring in enough money for my insurance or my application fee or both. I'm very hopeful that I'm going to have a good***

*turn out. I'm going to have a radio personality come and Chavez and his group will perform. Personal note- me and Edward have a another appointment tonight- we'll see how it goes. For the most part he been spending the night and I feel funny 'cause he back to getting the perks but he not doing nothing major. His stuff still at his mama's, I'm still behind on the house note, but hopefully I will be caught up this month. He has not said anything about what he gone do to help.*

*January16, 2008 We agreed to sit down together and do the bills as opposed to me solely managing the money and I think I know how this is going to go. Edward is not responsible when it comes to paying bills and taking care of shit. Let's just say when it comes to prioritizing, Edward will buy a game for the play station before he will buy groceries. This is just another test for me to prove myself to him and prove how much I love him 'cause this was a suggestion that he made that I agreed to in therapy. He really don't want to do them it's just because I want to do it that is the only thing. I requested in this marriage that since I came in with a house, two cars and contribute the most money to the house to let me manage the money. So since I agreed this month to let him do it, hopefully next month when it is time to do them he would have something else to do. I really didn't want him to help with the bills because it was tedious and as far as I was concerned he just wanted to see how much money was left after the bills*

***were paid so he could find something to buy with the money.***

## *Chapter 14*

## *SHARPEST TOOL IN THE SHED*

By the end of the first semester, I was feeling pretty good about high school and also proud of my direction. My first report card marking was pretty good. I got an A in dance, a C in English, a C in math, a B- in science and a B in French. I would have gotten an A but I missed a few assignments. Not so bad for a 1st report card. My intentions were to do better on the next card marking.

Meanwhile, after practicing for a semester, it was also time to start track and field. Our first race was due to take place the following week against Pershing. There would be other schools there, but Pershing was the school to beat. I was set to run three races. The 2/20, the 4/40 and the 400 relay, whatever that meant. All I knew was I would have to run long, hard and fast if I were to win and I was ready. As a matter of fact, our coach, Coach Hill said that I was one of the fastest on the team. I didn't just get on the team and intend to win off sheer talent though, at this point I was actually lifting 200lbs with my legs alone. I prepared for my meets.

While preparing for the meets, I noticed that a lot of the kids into sports were also into clicks. For example, the cheerleaders hung with the cheerleaders, the smart kids with the other smart kids, and the basketball players with the other basketball players.

My friend Melanie hung out with the cheerleaders. Me and her never really hung that much during school, Di said because she was fake, however I just saw it as she just had another group of friends other than me. I had no problem with that. She was entitled to do her own thing outside of me. Plus, Melanie had always hung with the more popular kids. Even during Middle School so I had no reason to expect anything different now.

I didn't have too many complexes at the time so I was straight. I had survived acne, survived being shaped like a boy, as well as survived problems with my mother, so I now felt like I could survive anything. I was also one of those kids that tried to avoid trouble, so I was cool with everybody.

In terms of my popularity, being on the track team helped a lot. By working out with the jocks, I found myself being adopted as everybody's little sister. Of course, I wish they would have seen a little more than just a little sister, but at least I was noticed. I also got a chance to hang with the smart kids because I spent a lot of time in the library. The difference with them was, I was always in the library trying to catch up, and they were their simply to do research, homework, and be with friends.

Despite me and Di going to different schools we still made time for one another. I'd made some friends since getting to high school, but not many. One of my best friends was a guy named Ashley. He was the photographer of the school. He would set up right outside the school store and take pictures. It wasn't an actual store, but an area where things were sold and that's where he would set up. Ashley was what I considered a sheer nerd. He had the glasses, the look, the only thing missing was the pen pouch in the pocket. I was late every day for IPS because I would spend all my time in between classes with him getting my pictures taken.

***January 20, 2008- Besides the furnace being out and it being cold than a bitch, everything is mild and peaceful around the ranch. I can't wait to get caught up on everything. I'm being patient but it's hard to contain myself considering most of my ducks are in a row. Edward made some calls trying to get the furnace working. Thanks Edward.***

After much training and anticipation, I was finally ready to participate in my first track meet. The team left immediately after 3rd hour. Of course that was one of the perks of participating in sports. Not to mention the fact that the teachers were really into sports and supported all the kids who took part. When we'd leave they would give us their blessing, wish us good luck and give us homework that we didn't have to turn in until the following week.

When I arrived at the track, I was surprised at how cold it was. As I warmed up I wasn't sure if I could actually warm up enough to run. But I was ready. My adrenaline was flowing and there appeared to be hundreds of excited spectators in the crowd ready to cheer us on. I hoped like hell that I wouldn't throw up in front of all of those people. I had never run in a track meet before, much less attended one, so to say the least I had a lot of different emotions flowing. I felt like I was at the Olympics and the pressure was on me to bring home the gold.

Finally, after what seemed like forever, Coach Hill called me over to get ready for my first race. My first race was the mile; which meant running around the track four complete times. All types of thoughts were running through my head as I walked toward the start line. I was constantly telling myself not to start off too fast...not to spend all of my energy trying to get off to the fastest start. To pace myself and then give it my all at the end. And most importantly to stay in the heap.

I walked to the start line, shook one leg then the other, then did the same with my arms. I then looked over at my competition then stretched my neck turning it from side to side. I then leaned down, got in the start position, and before I knew it, the gun sounded and we were off. I took off running at a nice little stride. After a couple minutes I made it around once and was headed around for my second go around. By my third lap the crowd had really started to cheer. At that point I started to pick up a little more speed. I was now running at a nice little stride. At this point Cass was in the lead, King was second and I was dead on their heels running third while the girl from Pershing was on my heels running forth. When I reached the last lap, I picked up more speed and went for the gold. I was now running neck and neck with King, who was still in second. I was running so fast; I couldn't believe I was not in first. But those girls were fast. I reached the finished line right behind King in third place.

All I could think as I crossed the line was that I'd made it. King had barely beat me, so for my first meet I considered myself to have done a pretty good job. As I walked back toward my group my team mates were all happy as they patted my back as a sign of support. I had to admit that I liked the treatment. I could get used to that. After a few minutes though, the adrenaline started to wear off. When I turn to walk toward the coach, I started to feel weak. By the time I reached him I fell into him and held on for dear life. My legs felt like rubber. Rubber in pain. After a few minutes of holding on to the coach, my legs gave all the way out and I fell to the grass. At that point my body had literally shut down and I could no longer breathe. I couldn't even move. I could see the coach signaling for me to get up but I couldn't. I felt like I was in a dream. His voice sounded like a vague call in the night. I couldn't hear shit. The only thing I could think at the time was how this would be a really good time to stop smoking weed. Well, with the help of Coach Hill and my fine ass team mate Joshua who also played football, tennis and had a body like Mr. America they managed to get me up. I jogged in place to get my muscles and other facilities back right and tried to prepare my mind for the next relay.

The next race was the relay. We had practiced the handing off of the baton all week, so I prayed to the lord, not to let me drop the baton. I was positioned to run the last leg. Again, the gun sounded and my teammate, Alicia was off and running. I held my breath as she ended her lap and passed it off to Shauwn. At that point I took my position and waited for Shauwn to finish her lap and pass the baton to me. As my heart pounded with the excitement of ten horses, I took off without a hitch. She slapped the baton into my palms just like we had practiced. I took off in first, but the girl from Pershing was really fast and quickly caught up. We raced around the track neck and neck. I was right there with her... but right before the finished line she leaned down and beat me by a nose.

After the relay, if I thought I was out of breath after the first race, this time I felt like I was gonna die. Not only was I totally out of breath, I also could no longer feel my legs. They were so sore they had become numb. I had come in second but I was in no shape for another race.

*January 22, 2008- Fuck you Edward and I mean it this time. He had the nerve to ask me if I spoke to the Good Doctor and I said I did not feel comfortable answering that question. This nigga done went through my phone looking for new numbers. Talk about trust. He got mad and took that for yes then he hung up, so I called back and tells him that if I haven't asked about who and what you been doing these past 6 months we been separated so I don't feel you should ask me. The therapist said for us to move on and get out the past. He went on to say you fucking him, you sucking his dick, that's why you can't give me no head. Head... I'm thinking to myself, that's not the reason why you not getting no head. We only went to one therapy session and you still ain't giving me no real money. Baby steps homeboy, baby steps. Things done changed since he been gone. No more pussy and head on a platter on demand. I'm thinking what the fuck do it matter who I spoke to if I am willing to try again, go to therapy and start over after almost loosing everything I worked so hard for because you chose to up and leave one day. Not caring about how we gone eat, where we gone go if I lose the house... Don't worry about who the fuck I been talking to. Now I choose to forgive and try to forget and you worried about who the fuck I talked to... Fuck you Edward, I think I'll move on now...*

*Feb 16, 2008 We buried Aunt Hattie today. She is no longer suffering. Her bout with cancer this last time took a toll on her. She was having trouble breathing, she was back and forth to the hospital and this is a woman who out of 83 years was hardly ever sick. I'm sure gone miss her good cooking on the holidays. She would make her home made rolls and she made sure I was always the first to get a couple. She would also make me my very own cheesecakes. On many occasions, because she lived only minutes from my job I would eat lunch with her. I looked forward to her call to say," what you doing for lunch," and If I did have plans chances are they got canceled so I could eat some of Auntie's good cooking. I'd leave her house and go back to work damn near sleep. You know how you get after a good meal. The only downfall was when I'd get home I'm still full so I might not cook. So they get mad. Especially Chavez ' cause that means he would have to cook.*

*Edward was one of the pallbearers. We got into our first argument today of all days. We got through it though. I just got to realize he is who he is. If that dreadful night that forever changed my life didn't change him or being without me for six months has not changed his ways then nothing will. I know I keep saying bye, but I just have to decide if I'm going to deal with it this time around. I don't know if we'll make it, but I'm happy that we both have decided to try again... there is nothing more important to me than keeping a family together*

Thus far, high school had been quite exciting. After almost five months into it, I was about to celebrate my biggest day ever; my sweet sixteen! It seemed though, that my sweet sixteen was not the only big event about to take place. Nana's belly had gotten big again, and like the last time, she denied being pregnant. Again, she said she'd been eating a lot, and like the last time, I didn't see any need to argue. Once again, time would tell.

When it got close to my birthday, Aunt Mona decided to give me my present early. She started teaching me to drive the Chevette. I had never driven a stick shift before so before we started she tried to explain how to drive it the best she could. No matter what she told me though, none of it seemed to make sense. The first thing I did was get familiar with the clutch, then the gas, then brake. After awhile, things seemed simple enough. But then we hadn't moved yet. As soon as we started the car and it was time to move I got confused again. There was just too much stuff going on. Foot on the clutch, then one up, two down, three up and to the right, then reverse. The first time I placed my foot on the gas the car didn't move. She then told me to push the clutch down, put my foot over the gas then to put it in one. The hard part was easing up off the clutch at the same time as pushing down on the gas. Each time I tried it, the car cut off so I had to start the whole process over. Each time that I started the process over, I wondered who, other than a sixteen-year-old getting a free car would go through all of that.

Well, after getting started and driving around for awhile, I finally got the hang of it. At least I thought so. I figured out that driving a stick was all about timing. So after a few hours I was good to go.

When we got back to the house, I asked Aunt Mona if we were going back out the following day, and she just looked at me without answering. I took that as a yes.

***March 19,2008- God is good. Me and my husband are doing well. I think we might be closer now than we were before. I still don't know what he got out of being away from me and I am still trying to figure out what the lord was trying to show me. I don't question 'cause I know everything happens for a reason. We don't talk about the six months and I think it is for the best. The girls are good and Darshawn is on the honor roll. I was so shocked... I had to ask him if the name on the report card was his. He had two A's, two B's and one C. Not bad... not bad at all. Arcyle still doing what he has to in order to get into Job Corp. or the army which ever come first. He's supposed to leave in April, right after my birthday, so we'll see. Chavez bringing his grades up but he also smelling himself so I have to refrain from going street on his ass. I keep having to remind him that I'm from the eastside and he won't be satisfied until I snatch***

***his ass up. I noticed that I have to say it with authority then he eases back in his place. Pops still here, he back cooking meaning he ain't been working but its cool. I enjoy having a hot meal when I come home from work, it gives me a little more time for myself to do some of the things I have to do. I am still developing the program. I'm realizing that I have such a long way to go to be up and running, but I'm getting there.***

Well, after begging Aunt Mona to take me back out...and a nice little foot rub, she agreed to do it. This time however, we drove all over the city. The car shut off a few times but other than that, I did pretty good and was ready to take over the car. After realizing that I was actually going to be driving, I quickly realized that I needed to find a job. Aunt Mona confirmed that by telling me that the car would stay parked until I found one. Hey, that was cool. I mean, I knew I had to put gas in the car and I couldn't very well do that without any money.

To help me along my way, Aunt Juanita helped prepare my resume. I had never really had a real job, so she got creative and made the resume look real professional. After it was ready, Aunt Mona referred me to this Nursing Home over on Warren. She also told me that when I went to fill out the application, that I should wear dress slacks, a nice blouse and some dress shoes. So that's what I did. I wore a black pair of pants, a white blouse and toned down my usual red nail polish replacing it with clear polish. I also placed my hair in a nice pony tail, then wrapped it in a bun, put on a little lipstick, replaced my usual big earrings, with small studs and I was ready. Aunt Juanita even let me wear her nice Whitnauer watch.

When I was ready to go, Aunt Mona drove me to the place then waited outside while I went in. I was so nervous. You would have thought that I was doing more than just dropping off a resume and filing out an application. In fact, after I finished filing out the application, the lady had me to take a seat, while she went into another office. A few minutes later a heavy set white lady came from the back and introduced herself. Her name was Mrs. Muler. She then asked me to follow her and as I did she proceeded to look over my application. She then started giving me a tour and after awhile it dawned on me that I was being hired for the job. As she started questioning me about my application, which was made up, she started telling me how nice the place was and how much I would like working there. In the meantime, I answered all of her questions the best I could. I didn't completely lie, although I hadn't done childcare specifically; I had done some respectable amount of babysitting. And although I had not actually worked at a janitorial service, I had done quite a bit of cleaning. Then in turns of the customer service position, you guessed it...I had done quite a bit of talking on the phone so I definitely had good communication skills.

When she finished questioning me about my previous jobs, she told me that since I was not yet sixteen all I needed to do was get my worker's permit and that I had the job. She mentioned something about child labor laws, but hell, I would have been ready to start right then. Anyway, she told me to be back the following Monday and that I would been given 2 weeks training, which was cool, considering we had just gotten out of school for summer break.

The first thing I needed to do after getting my permit was go shopping for scrubs. My grandmother gave me a few dollars and Aunt Mona took me. I was to be at work by 8:00 Monday morning so when Monday came, I gave myself a little more time and got there at 7:50.

When I arrived I was led to the 3rd floor where I was introduced to the remaining staff. Then I was taken to a residence room, where five other women, all drinking coffee, were already waiting. All of the other females starting that day were older women. Mainly in their 30's and 40's.

Our first lesson of the day was making beds. My first instinct was who doesn't know how to make a bed. Well, contrary to my original belief, there is a right way and a wrong way to make a hospital bed. In showing us how to properly make a bed, the nursing assistant doing the training messed up a bed then had us take turns making it back up. The first step in making a hospital bed is laying down the pad. After that you put on the fitted sheet, then the flat sheet, then the blanket, and then the spread. That was easy enough. The next lesson, diaper changing, was a little more challenging. This time we were led into a private room for a live demonstration. The specimen was an elderly man by the name of Mr. Angling. Before getting started though, we had to learn how to give a proper bed bath. Just seeing the little white man laying there buck ass naked gave me the creeps. I prayed then, that when I got older that I could take care of myself. I couldn't imagine how he must have felt lying there with seven women watching him get bathed with all his little secrets exposed... and I do mean little. But then again after I thought about, what old man wouldn't want seven women watching him get bathed. I concluded that it was probably the highlight of his day.

After the bed bath, the assistant rolled Mr. Angling onto his side, rolled the diaper halfway and pushed it under him as far as she could, then rolled him to the other side and pulled the diaper out, concluding by tapping it at the ends. Again, a little challenging, but easy enough.

The next thing we were taught was how to change a bed with the patient still in it. Some patients were bed ridden and couldn't get out of bed. These patients have to be turned every hour so as to prevent bed sores. So the changing of the bed has the same concept as the changing of the diaper. Roll the patient over and then remove the dirty linen, put the new linen down and roll it, then roll the patient to the other side and when you pull the dirty linen the clean linen comes out.

By the time we finished learning the basic lessons, it was lunch time. As I walked to the store, I felt pretty good. For one, I had a job. And not only that, I was the youngest person there, so for me, that told me I was on the right track. Another odd thing about my co-workers was that they were all white. But that didn't really bother me. You could tell that most of them were used to being around black people. That they either had black kids, had dated somebody black or something because they just had that thing about them where you knew they were comfortable around black people. There were also a lot of Philippines working at the place.

After the break we went around and helped pick up trays from each of the patient's rooms. After that, we were taken on a tour to see the rest of the units. I think it goes without saying that the place was pretty big.

Each of the floors was made up of something different. One floor was made up of the patients that needed the most assistance. Another floor for patients that could somewhat do for themselves and another floor for Alzheimer patients; those with memory loss.

For those patients because of the possibility of getting out and getting lost the door leading out had to be locked at all times.

They also had one other area. I called this area the suburbs. It was located near the gift shop and beauty salon and came equipped with a full living room area for each patient. The people in this area needed little assistance and could come and go as they pleased.

On the way back to the area from which we started, we stopped at the little store. The man running it looked to be about 200 years old. There was a juke box in the store and all the songs were from way back to like World War 1. The man was real nice, though. He treated us to ice cream and as I got to talking to him, realized he was actually kinda cool. You just had to make sure that when you were talking, that you talked on his left side, because if you didn't, then he couldn't hear nothing you were saying. I really liked him a lot. He suggested ice cream for us and the ice cream he referred to me, spumoni, turned out to be pretty good. I had never heard of it before that day, but once I tasted it, I was sprung.

***April 22, 2008-Me and Edward back to normal, arguing, not talking and not fucking...oh, I'm sorry, I mean making love. The latest is his tickets. Edward told me he paid most of his tickets but turns out he ain't paid shit on his tickets and to make it so bad, he had the money. Again, not taking care of***

*business. One of the biggest issues I had was him driving while his license was suspended and he gets pulled over and get arrested* then *that will fall on me to get him out. He doesn't see it that way. I don't have that kind of money especially coming from being left to fin for myself these last 6 months during the worst economic times I have seen in my lifetime. I feel like I am living in a depression during a recession if that's possible. I don't want to wish that on him but it is getting hot. Poe Poe's be out. He been lucky so far. That's why he has gotten so laxed. Come to find out, he still owes close to the same amount that he owed when he left. What the fuck did he do with his money? He had close to six thousand dollars those six months he was gone, so I'm pissed 'cause he lied for one, then I find out that all these years after he gives me what he wants to give me he still has at least two to three hundred dollars and some change in his pockets. Do you know what type of nest egg we could have built in these years if he had just put a little something away. I mean I just went 6 months without being taking out, no house repairs, very little groceries, no gifts and this fool hording money. Now why the fuck come Tuesday he need gas money. Mind you, this has been going on for the last few years. Us arguing over this shit. But keep in mind I just found out that he had this extra money. I only found that out after putting in for a loan and seeing his check stub. Then he's gone try and switch things around and say its my fault that he's riding on E because I'm only giving him two's and fews. Hell I'm giving him money out of my gas money I set aside for me after I pay the bills. So anyway I tried something different. I set him up with my lady that helps with credit repair and loans. Since his car is paid for now he has collateral... now he can step up to the plate and get a loan and help us out. Well guess what, he got denied cause he has no license and the criteria is different when you only have a state ID so she said she would do it for me ' cause my score was just a little higher and I had made good on a previous loan. The flipside is he would have to put his car in my name. His response to that was no. All this time I'm thinking we're doing at least good enough for me to ask for something as simple as putting his car in his wife's name so that we could get a loan and this guy says no. I had also suggested that he put his check in my checking account for a few months and live off of a hundred dollars a week until we got out of this debt that we had built up while we were apart and he also said no to that. He said that that was too much for me to ask of him. So from that day on, it was all downhill. Before then all I know is everything was baby this, and baby that...rubbing my feet, kissing...you get my drift. But come to find out, although I had his back, he still didn't have mine. We could lose this damn house and he couldn't give a damn. Hell he always got his mammas house to run back to. Meanwhile, me and the kids would be displaced with no place else to go. This last separation had drained me dry. I no longer had a bank account, no collateral, and on top of that spent night after night trying to come up with a master plan to get out of this mess. Meanwhile while I'm up thinking- this nigga snoring. Not a fucking care in the world. We supposedly had the same issues...the same goals and wanted the same things but come to find out I was once again living a lie.*

*If everything I'm going through wasn't enough, Chavez got expelled. But because his attitude has been good all year, they are allowing him to still get his work and turn it in to receive credit. But he cannot go back for the rest of the school year. The counselor said he is going to see what he can do because he knows Chavez is a good kid but because of all the recent violence in the schools, his school, like most, is a no tolerance school. Everything is taken serious. This time... Chavez and a boy exchanged words... Chavez got on the phone with Darshawn to come down with the crew and blah blah blah. Darshawn called me at work so I leave on my lunch break to get him, but even though I came instead of the crew, he still had to go.*

*Arcyle bull shittin'; he was suppose to leave today. I was all geeked telling everybody and they mama that he was leaving just for this nigga to say he postponed it for May 5th. Ain't shit here why is he waiting?*

*Other than that, I'm good. Minor dilemmas at work. A co-worker reminded me that my job does not define me and that was enough said.*

*April28, 2008- I got my bike; it's a 1981 Yamaha 650. I bought it Sunday. I haven't ridden it yet, but I went out and bought a new battery and some spark plugs. I'll probably put them in tomorrow. I also redid the bathroom upstairs. I still have a few little things to do, cosmetic shit, but for the most part it's a beautiful brown with hints of green and burgundy. I bought a pretty beige color toilet and sink with gold fixtures on the sink and I bought a gold handle for the toilet. The brown flows with the green in the hallway. With the dark wood floors, the house is really coming together. I have been trying to do a project whenever I get some extra money. I have been trying to keep the projects under three hundred. It's a challenge, but I have been making due. When it runs over I just wait until I get more money to finish, so as a result, I have a lot of half done... well I won't say half done... just unfinished projects. I really feel like I am accomplishing my personal goals in slow motion, but I can feel the transition just the same.*

*May 1, 2008- Today marks fifteen years Nana been gone. I have to send my dad a card and visit Grandma Sheryl or she gone kill me. I haven't seen her since Aunt Hattie's funeral or was it Easter. Either way I have to go over there. It use to be bad for me emotionally on this day. I normally take off work and stay home and reflect. This year it rode up on me so fast I forgot to take it off. It might actually do me some good to be around people today. It just gets crazy thinking about Nana. I have a few regrets. I think about how I use to talk to her. Towards the end I had lost a lot of respect. It had gotten to the point that everybody knew she was smoking and she didn't care. She had even started looking like a typical crack head that be at the gas station asking to pump your gas. So it was hard. But the bible say honor thy mother and father, so I feel it... especially since she is no longer here for me to say I'm sorry. I miss my dad more on this day also because it's he and Grandma Sheryl's birthday, so to say the least I'm usually an emotional wreak. Happy one moment, sad the next. I usually stay to myself so people won't think I'm bi polar and shit. I'm just trying to stay strong. Me and Edward still ain't on good terms and that's all I'm going to say about that. Sometimes I wish I did not love him so much. It's going on three weeks and its already back to the same shit. My job is also getting a little shady. I'm trying to hold on until January but I don't know. We have a new boss and with a new boss there are going to be changes. Some good, some bad. I feel no security, period. My former boss made me feel like I was a valued asset to the department. She respected me... she gave us credit for the good jobs we did and made us feel important.*

*This new lady, well let's put it this way. She told me in so many words that if I am not satisfied with the changes then I should find another job. I'm thinking that since I'm the only one that knows how to do payroll and the scheduling in the department you would think, if no one else, should would be trying to keep me happy. Yesterday they suspended my boy for doing his job. He wasn't even able to tell his side of the story. What happened was a state agent of some sort came up to the desk asking to go to administration and she didn't have an appointment so he said he had to call up. We have to call for anybody who wants to go to administration. You can't just walk up to the white house asking to see George so he called and they said to ask her to have a seat. So she refused and said she'd rather stand. So she stood for about 3 minutes before someone came down and escorted her up. Well, she felt that my boy had gotten smart and because of that, they had him sent home. The sad part is that could have been either one of us. All he did was follow proper protocol. I wonder what would have happened if he would have just let her up. They would have had his head on a platter with an apple in his mouth. I have to get my shit together. I thought I would have been leaving before my old boss left but I got laxed... a little comfortable 'cause she was a cool boss and I respected her. I had the feeling that she was going to stay a little longer but turns out I was wrong. I have to get my shit together.*

*June 3, 2008 - I spoke to Dee brother yesterday. I just so happen to run into him at one of the restaurants he manages by my job. He's the supervisor over a few restaurants, which I wasn't surprised. Hell when we were 16 he worked at Mickey Dees with Kevin. Of course he didn't remember me, I was not the cutest back in the day and far from popular. When I saw him I was so ghetto. I yelled through the glass hollering how he looked like my son. I went on to say I know your mama, and my mama dated your uncle and needless to say I knew your brother very well. We laughed and he felt like we should exchange numbers because we had a lot to talk about. So a month went past and now he and his mom wants to see my little man. Long story short, it is a strong possibility ...like 99.999% that Chavez is related to them, so they want to meet him this week. We'll see how it goes. So much time has been lost but if they are related that will be one less thing I have on my list of unfinished business. Me and Dee made contact a few years back and he seen Chavez for the first time since he was about 2 or 3. Chavez looks more like Dee's family than mine so we both apologized to him for them being young and immature. I wanted them to move on and try to build some type of relationship, or even just a friendship but nothing came of it. Last I heard Dee was away, so it was nice seeing his brother and still being able to set up a meeting with them just to explore the possibility that Chavez might be related.*

## Chapter 15

## GIRL STUFF

While hanging out downtown with Di, I met this dude named Phillip. Whenever we went downtown we would always compete to see how many numbers we could get. But this one I had to put a star next to 'cause this nigga was fine. He was built up, with this pretty Californian red complexion, with that good hair, which he wore slicked down in a ponytail. I didn't waste time calling him. He turned out to be a 12th grade student at some suburban school where he was also on the wrestling team. He also had his own car.

Compared to other guys I'd met, having his own car made it a lot easier for him to travel. As a result, he didn't waste any time responding to my calls. He came over the following weekend after we met. Of course, like clockwork I had to have my girl there because he'd also brought a friend. Plus, it was almost like me and Di couldn't function without the other. Whenever she had a date I had to come and vice versa.

When they got to my house, before I could even half pretend to be living a half way normal life, Nana met them at the door with her hands out begging for money for cigarettes. I usually had to give my friends the heads up about my mama before they got there, but this time it had some how slipped my mind. It was always weird trying to start a conversation with somebody by having to tell them first that my mom was a crack head. You know I had to get that out of the way because it was obvious. So I would tell them and then move on with the conversation because I never wanted her to become the primary focus.

Anyway, like I said, Nana was all up in my man's face before I could get outside. Then when I did get out there, I asked her to leave them alone but her response was, if they couldn't give her a few dollars then what good were they. That I didn't need no little niggas coming to the house that didn't have money, so if they couldn't help her then they couldn't see me.

Meanwhile, Phillip and his boy rollin'. They laughing like they at a comedy show or something. The bad part was, the comedy was my life and Nana was good at embarrassing my ass. I don't think she did it on purpose. She really felt like any dude that chose to mess with me owed her something; she felt like without her I wouldn't be. So anyway, after giving her a few dollars, we sat on the porch and waited for Di to arrive. When Di got there, she and his friend sat on his car, while we sat on the steps and looked at the moon and the stars. I know it sounds mushy but our steps are on the side of the house which sits facing against all the lights, so when it gets dark, and you look up, all you see is stars. It was so romantic.

After that first night, me and Phillip got together every chance we could. I liked him a lot, but in spite of everything good about him, he was a little too perfect for my blood. He was an All American football player, had a 4.0 grade point average and he was a virgin. Hell, I was also a virgin and somehow in my mind I just couldn't see where we were going with the relationship. I just couldn't figure out what he wanted with me. So after a while, I just stopped taking his calls. Yea, maybe he was too much of a good thing, but hell, I was from the ghetto, I needed some controversy in my life.

***June 10, 2008- Me and Edward been house hunting. The situation with this old house ain't working. Someone rode past Saturday while me and the boys were working in the yard and took a picture of the house. An appraisal sign was on the side of the truck and the man took the picture like he was sneaking. He took the picture while the car was still moving so I don't know what to think. I have a feeling the man might be trying to sell it so before we get caught up and be homeless I'm***

***thinking about walking away. I don't want to though, we been here 14 1/2 years. This is a buyer's market right now so hopefully we can find something that has what we both want and what everybody needs.***

I guess as a teenager, there was never a shortage of fine looking boys. For me and Di, they came and they went. One of the boys who seemed to stick though was Booky. Every time I looked up there he was. I either saw him at school, walking home from school or hanging out in the hood. All during this summer, I would see him riding through the hood on his new Spree scooter. Of course I would always check him out because he was fine as hell. So you know how that goes. Anyway, he would be on my street a lot because his mother bought the house where Ms. Flower's use to live and he'd moved in temporarily until his mom could find a renter. He didn't actually live in the whole house though, he lived in the basement.

Before moving down, the street, I hadn't seen him in awhile. I hadn't had any real contact with him since my days of walking home from middle school. So when he walked up to me and started his usual antics, I welcomed the attention. Unlike the past however, this time I showed very little resistance. With everybody and they mama outside there we were on the side of my house with him grabbing and groping my ass, tidies and anything else he could get his hands on. Still, I should have known something was up when he asked if I wanted to see the inside of his house. I hadn't seen it since they'd taken over so I was somewhat curious as to how they'd fixed it up. When I got down there, I was impressed. They had done a good job. They'd put in new carpet, painted every room, and upgraded the bathroom and kitchen. From the inside it looked like one of those houses out of a magazine. It actually looked out of place on our block.

It looked nothing like it did when Ms. Flower's lived there. Her house smelled, stayed dirty and was always cluttered. Of course that hadn't stopped us from visiting and watching HBO.

As I followed him downstairs, my inner voice told me not to continue, to leave, to go back upstairs, but I continued anyway. When we reached the basement, again, I was somewhat surprised. It was really nice. It looked like a little bachelor pad. I think I was so impressed that I didn't even think about what I was doing down there. But when I realized I was now standing in his bedroom, that kind of woke me up. At that point, something in the back of my mind told me to turn and leave, but it was too, late. Before I could make my move, he wasted no time getting started. He walked around to where he was now facing me, pulled me toward him, and grabbed my ass. Before I knew what was happening, he was squeezing my ass, kissing my neck and rubbing my back. He then lifted up my shirt and started sucking on my tidies. While my tidies were in his mouth he started unbuttoning my pants. At this point I was hot, I'll admit that, but I was still not ready. I grabbed my pants in an attempt to keep him from pulling them down, but as he was trying to pull them down he was walking me backwards toward the bed. Before I knew it, he had forced me back onto the bed and was lying on top of me. At that point I was holding on to my pants for dear life. But he was too strong. He managed to pull them down just enough to then get his knee in between my legs. When he did that, I was trapped. I couldn't pull them up. He then laid his body on top of mine, prided my legs open and before I knew it, had his dick right at my pussy. I tried not to open my legs any wider than they already were, but again, he was too strong. I started getting a strange feeling that he had done this sort of thing before, because he really seemed experienced at what he was doing. So I began to panic. To get loose I started twitching, trying to squirm loose, but he was just too big. To make matters worse, my pussy was wet as hell. Talk about lack of experience on my part. I couldn't even maintain my composure.

When the tip of his dick finally touched my coochie, it felt like a fist trying to get in. I was so tired by this point but I continued trying to get loose. I was determined to get him off of me and get away with my coochie still intact...but that was not to happen. With his hands he rubbed the tip of his dick on my coochie then he pushed it in a little then he just kind of stopped. After a few seconds, he pushed it in a little more then stopped again. He repeated this a few more times, and this was him just trying to get the head in. Finally, after one last push, my cherry popped.

My coochie was so wet it felt like I had pied on myself. In spite of that though, the pressure was unbearable. It felt like I was on fire. Like I was being ripped apart. As I endured the pain, all I could think was how this couldn't be what everybody had been bragging about?

After a few moments, the realization that I was about to lose my virginity hit me. That's when I began to really panic. I started crying and yelling for him to get up, but he wouldn't. Meanwhile there he was, cool as a cucumber. Telling me to relax and that everything would be alright. But he didn't understand. How could I be alright with a big muscular arm rammed up my pussy. No, I wasn't going to be alright.

After what seemed like forever, he finally groaned, grunted, then fell flat on top of me. This time, when I pushed him to get up, he rolled over with the weight of a feather, laughing, telling me how I knew I wanted it. But he was wrong. I was devastated. I grabbed my panties, pants and shoes and got dressed.

When I finished dressing, I bolted up the stairs and out the side door. When I got outside, I had another surprise. Big Willie was standing at the side door laughing. He'd heard the whole thing. I was so humiliated. Looking away from him, I ignored him and walked on down the street, my pussy feeling like it had been socked by Mike Tyson. As I walked passed my neighbors, nobody said a word. I wondered silently if they all knew what had just happened.

When I got home, I went straight to the bathroom, ran some bath water and soaked my freshly battered coochie in a tub of nice hot water. As I sat trying to gather my faculties, Victor knocked on the door and I told him to go away. I told him if he had to pee to pee out in the hall. A few minutes after that, a heard another knock and I yelled out the same thing. This time however, it was Nana. Unlike Victor, she demanded that I open the door. Nana always made me feel like I could talk to her and that whatever we talked about was just between me and her, but this time I was not willing to talk. And at least for now, I would not have to. When she looked on the floor and saw my bloody panties, she assumed that I was on my period and immediately understood why I hadn't opened the door. She told me to try and hurry so Victor could use the bathroom then turned and walked out.

Although my coochie would hurt for days to come, I felt so much better after I got out of the tub. After that day, life would never again be the same.

One of the things that me and Di looked forward to during this time in our lives were the monthly hair shows held at the Latin Quarters. Our stylist, Mr. Little, by now was one of the best up and coming hair stylist in the business and we never missed an opportunity to show up and support him. We'd go to the store, 7 Days, get us something fly and we were there. We lived for those shows. The competition was always fierce, but as far as we were concerned, the showdown was always between Mr. Little and Little Willie; both now internationally known hair stylists. Mr. Little was even featured in the 2007 Special Edition of Ripley's Believe it or Not for his one of a kind helicopter hair design.

I remember this one particular day, Me and Di had gone shopping and gotten our outfits for a hair show, when we got back to my house, we were sitting around on the porch kicking it. When I went into the house for something and came back out, this chick was in the street sitting on the back of Booky's Spree. I couldn't believe it. Everybody was out that day. Big Willie, Cedric , the whole crew. Everybody just hanging out in the street. I couldn't believe she was sitting on the back of his Spree like that. Hadn't I given her the heads up on this dude. I'll admit that I hadn't told her about our little romantic interlude but I had told her about the fingering episode. But now there she was, out there skinning and grinning like she'd never heard of Booky. Yes, I'll admit, that he had taken the coochie. But I still had a crush on him and as my best friend, that therefore made him off limits. Nevertheless, he takes off with her on the bike and she comes back twenty minutes later like she's in love. She wasn't gone 20 minutes and you'd thought he'd taken this bitch to Hawaii. So now I had to listen to her talk about this nigga like he the neighborhood prince fucking charming while acting like I didn't give a damn. Ain't that a bitch. And to make things even worse, whenever she wasn't around, the nigga was still tryna get in my panties. A day didn't pass when he wasn't trying. Of course before fucking with Di, I may have let him, but he had blown that. Fuck Booky.

After awhile I even stopped taking Di's calls. I would tell whoever answered the phone to tell her I wasn't home. Before Booky, we use to talk five or six times a day, and if we weren't on the phone we'd be together. But after hooking up with him, I just wasn't in the mood to deal with her. I didn't speak to her for a good two weeks.

When she called, I know she knew I was home, because she knew my schedule so she kept calling. When I finally got tired of not accepting her calls, I answered and the first thing out of her mouth was that she was coming over...but that she would be down the street at Booky's. Come to find out, the whole two weeks I was ignoring her, she was getting in deeper with him. So much so that she was spending the night with him that night.

Chances were she was gone give up the Kitty Cat that night. Maybe I should have told her about him, but my pride wouldn't allow it. I guess she would have to learn the hard way, because with that big dick, and her little ass, she had no idea what she was getting herself into. Booky was a master manipulator who prayed on unsuspecting virgins, and unfortunately, she would just have to learn for herself.

Later on that evening Di stopped by my house so she could change clothes and head down to Booky's. We'd agreed that later that night when she was ready, she could come back down to the house and I would sneak her in and she would stay the rest of the night with me.

Later that night, or early the next morning I should say, I finally heard the tapping of rocks against my window. I jumped up, ran downstairs and as quietly as I could opened the door and snuck back upstairs. Even though I was a little bitter I still wanted to get the dirt. So as soon as we got upstairs I had her tell me everything. After she told me what happened I felt a little guilty because I should have warned her about that Anaconda he had in his pants, but that's what she gets.

A few weeks after Di's first sexual experience, I walked in from hanging out all day and get in the house and no one's home. Of course that was very unusual because there was generally always somebody at our house. So I'm pacing around wondering what's going on and about a half hour later, the phone rings and it's my grandmother telling me that my mother was in the hospital; she was having another baby. Apparently that sickness that Nana had and her sudden weight gain was a pregnancy after all. So I hitched a ride from one of the fiends and headed to the hospital. When I got there, I went straight to labor and delivery. When I walked in, grandma was standing in the room praying. Right then I knew it couldn't be good. Meanwhile, there was my little brother Arcyle, sitting next to her, looking like an old soul who'd been here before.

Just as before, Nana was given an emergency c-section, so again, we had to wait patiently while the doctors completed the operation. After about what seemed like a lifetime the doctor came out to let us know she was ok and the baby was ok. Like Arcyle, he was also premature, barely six pounds, and had to be placed in an incubator to help him maintain his body temperature.

About 20 minutes after the baby was delivereded, they let us see Nana. Again they had numbed her for the procedure so again she lay paralyzed until the medicine wore off. You could tell she'd been crying because her eyes were real puffy and red. I kissed her on the forehead, told her I love her then went and saw the baby. She named him Darshawn. He was a cute little yellow thing with cords and lines running from his little body to a machine to help monitor his progress. Like before my mother had smoked crack, cigarettes and drank night train the whole time she'd been pregnant. So I felt for the baby. I could just imagine what he must have been going through. I wanted to pick him up and hold him close and tell him how much I loved him, but that would have to wait. Meanwhile, I went back to my mother's room and sat with her while she waited for the numbness to wear off.

After three days of being in the hospital, they released Nana, but again the baby had to stay. He was having trouble digesting food so the doctor said that he would have to stay until his body was able to function properly.

Each day Nana would get up and head straight to the hospital to spend the day with the baby. I went a few times. Once the baby even opened his eyes and looked at me like he knew me. Victor went a few times along with grandma but you could tell he was confused about the whole thing because he never knew Nana was pregnant to begin with. None of us did.

When the baby finally came home, I believe he was still addicted because he use to have these tantrums where he would cry for hours. He would start and nothing could stop him. Nana didn't have to take him to a program like she had with Arcyle, probably because somebody had dropped the ball, because she had definitely been just as addicted as she had the first time. Acrcyle was only three when Darshawn was born but he was what I would call a little big man. He was one of those little kids that acted grown, even at a young age. He had seemed to come through his shaky beginnings pretty good. He didn't show any signs of being born to an addicted parent however the jury was still out. He was still very young so I held my breath that he would be o.k.

Well, as if having Booky on the block wasn't enough, a new guy named Deantae had also now moved onto the block. He was also fine as hell with one of those bodies that looked like he'd just spent 10 years in prison. As soon as I saw him I wasted no time introducing myself. Come to find out, not only was he fine like Booky, he had moved in with him. I didn't know why he had moved in or what the relationship was, but I was eager to find out.

Meanwhile, Di and Booky were still hanging strong. By this time, she was in love. You couldn't tell her nothing. Well, I did a little more research on the new boy and come to find out he was Booky's sister's, baby daddy's brother. But I didn't care who he was. My plan was to get his full attention, tie him down, and give him the coochie just to get back at Booky for fucking me and my best friend.

It wouldn't be easy though because Deantae didn't give me the time of day. For a minute I didn't think he even liked girls. I threw the coochie at him for weeks, with no response. Finally, one day, after I had almost given up on him, he decided that he was gone go ahead and tap it. It happened one day clear out of the blue. I was sitting on the porch and he walked up and started talking. One thing led to another and he invited me down to the house. When we got there we first sat on the porch. I guess he wanted to talk. But I didn't. The whole time he was talking I was thinking about fucking. Matter a fact, I was so hot I jumped up and sat on his lap just to let him know how hot I was. That did the trick. It didn't take long for his dick to start to rise and when it did, I knew I had him.

Before I knew it, I was in the basement bucked naked laying spread eagle on the bed. This time the sex didn't hurt, but I also quickly realized that Deantae was no Booky. He wasn't as big nor quite as experienced. But I didn't care. My whole goal was to get back at Booky and as far as I was concerned, that's what I'd done.

Me and Deantae did it a few more times after that, however after seeing that my fucking his boy didn't matter, I got bored and moved on. Hell, matter of fact I felt like I was fucking so much, I was now teasing Di that she had a lot of fucking to do to catch up with me. And believe me, she was willing to try.

Meanwhile, back on the home front, I had convinced my grandmother to let me re-do the basement and move down there. I put a water bed on layaway and with my neighbor Roni's help, proceeded to renovate my brand new apartment.

***June 11, 2008-It's hot as hell out here. I rode my bike to work for the first time. I had to flex on the ones that thought I was lying about riding. My boss is the boss from hell. I asked this woman if she can give us some awards since we have been working short staffed for almost 3 months. I also told her how stressed out we had been because of it. We are so short. I have been encouraging people to not take any days off, which is bold as hell, 'cause everybody got time in they bank and they should be able to use it as they please. One of them has to work six days straight which is crazy. I even showed her the schedule so she can see for herself. This chick says she can't do it and goes to tell me what it says in the policy like I give a fuck about the policy right now. Do it say in the policy to over work your loyal employees and take them for granted because you know they need their jobs. Then she goes to mention how she gave me a spot award a few months a go as I was leaving her office. I turned around so quick to correct her it wasn't funny. I reminded her that she did not give me anything, I earned that spot award because the family I assisted was trying to file a lawsuit against the hospital, and after I spoke with them, they chose not to and on top of that they wrote a letter to corporate office about what I had***

***done. I wanted to snatch her white ass up from behind that desk but I need my job. My goal is to stay at least until I graduate with my bachelor's degree and get a probation job. I don't want to be forced to leave but the way I feel whoever will have me I will go. Then maybe she will realize how much of a valued asset I am, okay***

When Roni finished my room, to say the least, I was a happy teenage. I finally had a door with a lock and to top it off, my water bed was due for delivery the following day. For the bed, I had ordered myself two sets of nice silk sheets. A black set and a red set. They'd already arrived so as soon as the bed arrived I was set to go. I also bought a nice big blanket; red on one side and black on the other. At this point you couldn't tell me nothing.

Chapter 16

## ALL CRACK HEADS WELCOME

Moving downstairs couldn't have come soon enough. My mother was back to her old self and the house was as busy as ever. Every day she was bringing home someone new. At any given time, any and everybody was over our house. She had become the president of the new and improved, east side crack head association. She became known for bringing the curious to the house. People willing to try crack for the first time. People generally already addicted to other things, but now willing to try crack. And she was right there to help them. Usually, after one puff it was over. They were hooked. Crack was that kind of drug. It didn't take a lot to get turned out. After one puff, that cocaine would hit you and that was hit. You were hooked for life.

One night she brought home this white guy driving this raggedy ass orange Chevy. After he had spent all of his money on crack, he and Nana went to my grandmother and asked if she wanted to buy his car for two hundred dollars. So my grandmother goes outside, pops the hood and looks at the engine. I had already given the dude 10 dollars the day before to drive it so I already knew it rode good. So hell I didn't care how raggedy it was. We didn't have a car and I knew if she bought it, I would be able to drive it. So while Nana stood on one side of the car begging, I stood at the other. If she bought it, from that day on, I knew Di and I would be in the streets, and Nana knew that she and her crew would smoke good for a least a few days. So a lot was riding on her decision.

As Nana begged, come to find out, this guy had rich parents, but he done got himself caught up on crack and was now trying to get home. And that's why he needed the money. At least that was the story. So grandma went on ahead and bought the car. I couldn't wait to call Di and let her know I had a grip. It took all of twenty minutes to convince grandma to let me take the car; which by the way had no title, no registration, no insurance and I had no license. But I started driver's training in a few weeks and had learned to drive a stick so she was alright with it. She told me to be back by 8:00 so that gave me three hours to hang.

After I picked up Di we headed straight to Belle Isle. When we got there, we parked, sat out on the hood, and fired up a joint. Mr. Little had done our hair so as we sat out on the hood of the car, nobody could tell us nothing. The more we smoked, the louder we got. Anyway, we had a ball. We flirted with the boys for a couple hours then headed back. When we got to Di's house, there was immediately cause for concern. An E.M.S. truck was parked in front of the house and we didn't know what to think. We didn't know if somebody had gotten shot, her grandmother had had a heart attack. Some crack head had tried to rob the place. We didn't know what to think. Come to find out her crazy ass uncle done got into it with somebody on the block and stabbed him.

After I parked the car, I walked over to the E.M.S and looked in. The man had indeed been stabbed. He looked pretty bad, too. At that point I knew it was over for her uncle. His ass was headed back to Northville. People like him didn't generally get jail because he was on paper as being crazy. But he was definitely going somewhere. The man had probably started teasing him, because her Uncle Feets was slow, but he would tease you back. But once he got mad then he would get violent. The first thing the family did when you came over was warn you that he was crazy because he would immediately start talking shit. He would call you all types of mothafuckas and they would tell you to just ignore him and keep moving. But I guess on this particular day Feets had forgot to take his medication and the end result was somebody almost lost their life.

After dropping her off, I had to hurry. With all the excitement I was now a little behind schedule but I was not yet late. I still had another little stop to make so I hurried so that I could get to Chandler Park, cruise a little and still make it home in time. When I got there, I lit up the lil tail I had left and cruised through the park. It was a nice evening and everybody was out. I didn't have a radio, I guess the fiend had sold it, so I had to make due with the music blasting outside. That was cool though. I was just happy to be out and in the mix.

After driving around a little, I headed home. I had a track meet the next day so I needed to get home and rest. Our team, along with Pershing, King and Cass had made the finals so this was our big chance to prove that we were just as good, if not better than everybody else.

***June 24, 2008- Today my baby starts summer school. He has to take one class. Little bastard... thank God it was only one class because classes are $250.00 which we don't have, but the lord will find a way. He also starts his first day at work today, so he's excited about that. What he doesn't know is I'm more excited than he is. I also had to leave work early because I had a dentist appointment. I have to get a root canal. I never had one and I am so nervous. I am not too fond of the dentist. On a more positive note, I have five more classes till I receive my bachelor's degree. I think that besides the birth of my kids, that will be the most important day of my life. To have a college degree will be quite an accomplishment. There are times I never thought I would see the day.***

***July 4,2008- I'm chilling... debating where I'm gone go and how pretty I want to make myself, but for the life of me I can't get up. I'm in deep thought about my job because the new boss is not working out. This lady came in so nice. I was so impressed with her at first. I was one of those to sit in on her interview and I recall how impressed I was***

*with her resume. I was able to ask her questions and when she finally came I thought she was going to have our back and help us to get what we needed to help run the desk more effectively. We thought she understood our struggles because in the beginning she started off acting like she did. During the first staff meeting she led us to believe that she would help change our titles to receptionist which would improve our pay as well as help make possible the changes that we requested. She also acted like she needed me and respected my input. But that all changed really quick. After the second meeting she proceeds to tell us how she can't make any of our requests happen. So now the morale is down but we're all hoping she can get it done later. They fired one of the patient advocates and I still don't know why. I went from being a major component in our department to an outsider, so even though I felt bad about her being fired that is the next step up for me considering I have been there eight and a half years and I know what the job entails. My former boss was actually grooming me for that position. So I applied but the new boss said that I lack an important piece. A piece in my opinion they could have sent me out to a workshop to get. She didn't even give me an interview. Then she has a meeting and decided that everybody should work weekends including me. Now before the meeting she mentioned it because she said that a few employees were complaining about working weekends so she wanted to make it fair. At the time me and her other two senior people did not work weekends so she said she was not going to put me on weekends. I didn't find out until after another meeting, which I did not attend, because I had to watch the desk, that I had been put back on weekends. And I had to hear that from a co-worker. She didn't even tell me. Two days has gone by and she still hasn't called me into her office to update me about the meeting that I didn't attend. I had to go to her myself to get updated. After that it seemed like everything just started going down hill. Denise was coming to work with me in the morning 'cause her school is located down the street from my job. It made more sense than Edward coming down here to drop her off then going back home then coming back down here. Gas is too high. So she allowed her to come at first, but then one day the surveyors came. Now normally they would come through the front door where I was, however this time someone had them to come through the clinic. So knowing that I had my daughter with me, instead of her sending one of my co-worker's who was just as competent as me, I had to leave my daughter by herself and go greet the surveyors. Well, my daughter cried the entire time I was gone. So after that my boss said that I could no longer bring her to work. Now I have to figure out what we gone do about gas. She still had three more weeks of pre-school before the end of the semester. I did my best to try and explain my situation. I did everything except cry and get on my knees, but she still said no. Now mind you, everybody else bring their kids to the hospital because a lot of the employee's kid's go to the school across the street. So in the morning, the lobby is filled with kids waiting to go to school, but mine can't come. She said it is actually against policy to bring kids however the school is right across the street. Everybody that works here centers their world around this place. It's like one big family. Or at least I thought it was. Well now we have a new rotation. I have to work weekends and on top of that I also have to close. Which I had already worked my way up from not closing but now even though there is another person with less seniority than me who should be closing, I still have to close. I requested that we sit down together and rearrange this change, but before we have a chance, she goes out on medical so I implement the change myself. Everyone is comfortable with the change however when she comes back we have another meeting and again she wants to make changes to our routines. To me, a lot of what she was saying wasn't making sense so I was vocal about it. Other people were too, but I was more vocal than everyone else. So it seemed like every idea she came up with I counteracted it. I didn't mean to, but working the desk for as long as I have, I can just foresee some things and it would have made our job harder. So that pinched a nerve. Everybody at the meeting agreed with what I was saying. So then she goes on to say that she's getting a lot of complaints about us as if we're just sitting at the desk chillin'. But not once has she come out and sat with us to see exactly what we do. I am a firm believer that if it ain't broke don't fix it. Now instead of giving me the promotion, she has hired somebody from the outside to fill the position. I have eight and a half years invested in this department and I should have at least gotten an interview. Now there is no real communication period. If I have to talk to her about something; a clarification, anything, she either sick, in a meeting or her door closed and she won't open it. I remembered her first day and how we had a family in the lobby that had lost a love one. There they were, crying... fallen out. You should have seen her in action. She was on her knees cradling the lady. The lady seemed like she was gonna pass out and she was right there helping. So I complimented her and thought she was gonna do just fine. Same scenario... a few weeks ago someone died, family crying, passing out. I run to get a wheelchair for one of the ladies then look to see If my manger was going to help. Do you know she walked her ass right out the door like nothing was going on. That's when I knew she wasn't all she claimed to be. Since she has been here things have only gotten worse. They have even taken the surgical lounge waiting area away from our department. The reason why we had it was because they weren't doing a good job with it. They have managed to take our rest room and one of our employees so even though we are only really down one employee, it seems like two because whoever was in the lounge was able to cover if we needed. Now they can't. She can't fight for nothing for us and she talks to me like someone has been giving her second hand information about me and it wasn't good nor true. The biggest part of my job is to communicate with her about issues with the department and we can't even talk. When she talks to me its like she looks at me like I'm stupid. I hate that because as it stands, I know more about the department then her. Last but not least, the last meeting we had she said no personal calls and no personal computers at the desk; to use them only on your lunch breaks. So during the meeting when I seen no one was going to correct her about personal calls I chuckled and told her that just because she sees us on the phone does not mean we are on personal calls. Yea, we get them but not as often as she thinks. We're usually way too busy for personal calls. So I goes on to say after a chuckle that I was gone transfer some of the calls so she can see what type of calls we get. Of course that didn't set too well with her.*

*Last week Wednesday I rode my bike to work. I got there at 7a.m. but when I got to the area to park it was a tight fit. Some ass hole parked too close to the wall and I had to cut the bike off and find another way to get in the spot. So when I came up it was eleven minutes after seven. I told the coordinator what happened then I asked if I could put 7:05 because we do get a five-minute grace period. I come in the next day and seven o five was crossed out and 7:11 was put in. I questioned the coordinator about the change and she said she didn't change it my manager did. So when she came in I said good morning can I speak to you about my time. While walking away, not even stopping to hear me out, she throws her hands up in my face and said she had a meeting that she would talk to me later. I thought her walking away like that was so disrespectful. So I did payroll with the tardy and gave it to her. Hours went by and I still have not been called back to talk. Then around 2:00pm she brings the time sheet out and tells me we will talk tomorrow. I look and see the tardy was still there and the slip is signed so what do we have to talk about. You have no intensions on changing my time.*

*Friday it was slow. Nobody in the lobby and we short. I'm still training so lately I haven't been getting a lunch. Today I had my computer out and that created a problem. Yea I know I was wrong to have it out on the desk but it was wrong for me to be working short for the last three and a half months and sometimes not even able to take a lunch for lack of people. So when can I use it. I still got homework. Anyway, she came out looked behind the desk because someone told her I had it out and twenty minutes later she called me into her office and told me how disrespectful I talk to her and how she expected more from me. She said that I had neglected to inform the staff about the new clinic and that I be on personal calls and that she was writing me up for having my personal computer on the desk. Now what type of shit is that. Now because I was written up I can't move out of her department for six months. In eight and a half years I have nothing on my record and you write me up for my computer being out. No verbal, just straight write me up. I had an interview with the security department that Monday so I'm hoping if they do want me the fact that nothing was in my file during the interview that they might be able to work with me. In the meantime, I have been working on a suggestion to submit too corporate to be a voice for the employees that work for the organization. This will be a way for us to vent about our care when we go for our doctor's appointments. A lot of us have the insurance given by he hospital and we use the same doctors from the various hospitals. So hopefully it just don't sit on somebody's desk. Hopefully they will find a need for it. Until then I hope I can hold on until January.*

*July 6, 2008- It's Chavez's birthday. My baby is seventeen. I feel old as hell. Me and my boo been through a lot, thank God I still have him. The way this world is today we losing children in violent ways everyday. A17 year old was brought in yesterday shot in the back. Wrong place at the wrong time. I thank the lord everyday my baby is still here.*

*Well we had a big announcement yesterday. Arcyle came out and told me he was gay but I wasn't shocked. He has no feminine tendencies but I seen other signs over the years. Like the company he keeps. But like I told him, I'm not gone love him no less 'cause he gay, I'm more mad at the other decisions he is making with his life. More than anything his sexual preference is the last thing I'm concerned about. I did tell him though that it is not going to be easy. This is a serious life changing decision he is making and he has to be safe because HIV and Aids is running rapid in the black community with straight and gay people so strap up.*

## *Chapter 17*

## *LIVING THE DREAM*

Having a waterbed was wonderful. Buying it was one of the best decisions of my young life. It even had a knob that allowed me to control the temperature, and in Detroit, that feature came in handy. When I first bought the bed, me and Di chilled down there more than we did in the streets.

Another big thing to happen for me during this time was driver's training. Unlike everybody else who got dropped off by their parents though, grandma let me drive our new clunker to school. Driver's training was exciting. Part of it was set up like a real street, with real stop signs and working lights, while the other side was set up like a classroom.

After a few classes, the instructor kindly let me know that he didn't approve of me driving to drivers training. So I came up with another plan. I started parking down the street and walking the rest of the way to class. I looked forward to completing the class because I knew once I did that I would get my permit, and then I would qualify for my driver's license. After that, I would be able to grip the Chevette.

During this time, me and Di had started partying at this place called the Vice. It was a slight departure from the house parties. The Vice was actually this big hall and every week it would be packed wall to wall with teens humping, grinding, drinking and smoking weed. Di would usually get her mother's car and we along with the rest of the crew would go each Friday. By this time, we had started dressing more like ladies so whereas before, we would be down for anything, we were now limited in our dance choices. As a result, whenever niggas would start jittin' I would have to sit out because I didn't want to look too out of place.

Well, just because we were no longer at the neighborhood house parties, didn't mean that we were any less inclined to get into fights. I remember this one particular night, Di had gotten into a beef with one of her ex's ex and we ran into the girl at the hall. When they saw each other I was thinking that they would maybe just stare each other down. So being that's what I assumed, I went back out on the dance floor and continued doing my thing. Next thing I know I hear a glass break and when I turn around, I see the girl and her crew walking toward Di. The girl with the beef, Dakato, walked over to Di and placed her face right up to Di's. It was obvious that she was ready to do more than stare. However, security was on their job. Before any one could throw a punch, one of the promoters jumped in between them and demanded that they take the fight outside.

Before the promoter could finish his sentence, our crew was already headed out the door. All except Di and Tae. The other crew had not waited until we got outside and had snatched Di and Tae and were tossing them around the hall. Next thing we knew, both of them came flying out the front door. First Di came flying out the door, then Tae. Both of them landed head first on this car parked right outside the hall. After Di and Tae were tossed outside, Dakota's crew didn't waste any time following up. They moved in like a mob on the loose. They went right after Di. But Tae was not about to let them murder her friend. She jumped in front of Di and all I could see after that was Tae's arms blocking blows. She was holding back the entire mob. Me and the other girls were not as brave. We ran to the car and jumped in, leaving the doors open for the other two. After a minute or so, Di and Tae came running to the car, clothes ripped, face bruised, and mad.

After they got in the car, I knew I was gonna hear it. And sure enough, they couldn't wait to get started about how scary I was and blah, blah, blah. It didn't bother me though because the fact is they had gotten snatched back and what did they want me to do. Jump over a whole crowd of people and save them. Had I been a warrior sure, but that just wasn't me. I had to be honest with myself. I didn't have a death wish. I wanted to live. Get married one day...have children...see my grandchildren. But Di and Tae, they could care less. Life or death. They lived for the next fight.

***July 16, 2008 - A friend of mine found Arcyle temporary placement housing. I haven't seen him in a few days and I know he***

*hasn't been taking his medicine so I hope he don't mess this up 'cause he can't stay with me and I'm sticking stern. I have done all I can do for him. Right now he has to do for himself before I can help him any further. I am still waiting on a response from Security and a response on the suggestion that I submitted to administration. Nothing yet though. I did e-mail my supervisor about the concerns we had in our department and I can't wait to see what she has to say about the issues.*

*Me and Edward are wordless and have been for the past few days due to the fact that he got a job offer making three times what he is making now. I was so happy for him. It's out of state but that's o.k. What ticked me off though is I e-mailed him and asked again if he could put his car in my name. His response was "we were not there yet." But I couldn't understand. Were we there yet for me to uproot my kids, move to another state, quit my job, start all over, stop working on my youth program, drop all my connections I have made to get this far. Not to mention give up the janitorial service I am only a few months from starting. We're talking about a car in my name, so that I can get a loan that we would all benefit from and he says we're not there yet. He couldn't make that sacrifice for us but he wanted me to make that ultimate sacrifice for him. It has always been about him. Ever since that dreadful night, I have always made it about him. So now nothing has really been said since I sent the email. He only called*

***yesterday because he needed some gas money but he claimed I was the one acting funny. Other than that, life is good. I'm just being patient. My day will come when everything will fall right in place.***

Growing up brought out all kinds of things in young people from the hood. For some it brought out ambition, for some, lack of ambition, for others a greater need for friends and/or family and for others, it brought out the freak. When I say freak, I mean nasty, fuck anything for money ass freaks. Dusty, dirty and down right disgusting. That's what I call a few of the girls Di sometimes kicked it with. They were flat out hoes, and to make it so bad, they use to try and convince Di to join them in their escapades. They'd be standing around on corners in them skimpy outfits, looking like, I don't know what, and doing everything within their powers to suck her in. Talking about how much money they made, how much they shopped and how many niggas they fucked. To me they didn't look like they could get a dollar from a bum on the street but Di said they were getting paid.

Anyway, whenever we would bump into them and Di would want to stop and talk, I would find something else to do. Go sit down somewhere, because the last thing I needed was a rumor floating around that I was a part of the tittle dancing click. That I did not need.

***July 22, 2008- Edward didn't come home last night. We've been fighting since Sunday. I really feel like he is cheating on me. All the signs point to it. The arguing all the time over nothing, just so he can leave and be gone all day and night. He claims to be at his mother's but when I talk to her she hasn't seen him. Or he claims to be over his friends so I ride by all their houses and don't see his car any where. He is never around on the holidays. When we visit my relatives, he always got something else to do. I'm getting pretty tired of this shit. If he got another woman she needs to get on her job 'cause I'm tired of giving head every morning and giving up all this good pussy every night just for shit still not to be right. We went to the show Friday, then to the golf range Saturday, so I can try out my vintage clubs I got from my boy. We had a good time, too. But, I had to ruin it by bringing up the future. I asked him about the loan again and even though he already said no I thought if I spoke in a soft voice and tried to explain my point of view, and the benefits it would have for us he would change his mind, however he's still under the impression that his only responsibility is just to pay the bills and that he should not be responsible for nothing else, which is absurd. I'm tired of having to use whatever little money I have to fund my dreams and do home repairs. I was hoping for just a little help. My part of the loan would have given me enough to do that. To make his point, he threw up me buying my bike and yea***

*I could have waited a little longer but why should I. I have put everything else before my bike for three years. Plus... I thought he would say yes. I mean with all the shit he has taken me through why wouldn't he. So before we left we both exchanged some unpleasant words. While later riding my bike I felt guilty and pulled over and called him to apologize about some of the things I said just in case something happened to me while I was on the road.*

*July 30, 2008 - I'm a tired ass. We had a power outing at my job and one thing I can say is when we experience a crisis everybody comes together. The elevators were down so me and a few other people actually walked trays to all the floors. I mean even a few managers got in on the act, so for an hour and a half I was walking up and down the damn stairs. At one point I had to stop and freshen up. I ended up taking off my blouse and replacing it with a scrub. The only thing that ticked me off was my supervisor. I have been trying so hard to get along with her and its been cool, I just do my job and go home. Well today she sees what everybody is doing and meanwhile she's on the stairs just looking. It took everything in me not to say bitch, grab a tray. We had a few patients that were in wheelchairs and had to take the stairs, so while I'm was helping them, some ass hole holler from two stories up can we move to one side to let people down. Now my supervisor was standing next to me, so I hollered back up not at this time... it will be a few minutes and before I could finish my sentence she looks at me and says why not, so I said ' cause we have a patient on the stairs and I pointed down thinking why couldn't she see that. So I hollered back up we have a patient on the stairs and they are being assisted on both sides so no one can get through. I wanted to tell her to go back to her office and play in the dark 'cause she wasn't doing shit out here. But before I could build up the nerves, the power started coming back on. Now we have another problem. We have an angry mob of people that want to go up and visit. So security said it would be wise to call up and see how many units were ready for visitors. So me and my staff did just that, just for my supervisor to come out two minutes too late to tell us that command said it was ok to let the visitors up. Mind you most of the units said no, that they still had too little power, so we call the units back to tell them that we are sending visitors up anyway, which sucks. I personally felt it was unsafe. Half the units did not even have their power back. So of course shortly after I start sending people up, I start getting calls from nursing managers and units asking why are we sending up visitors after the nurses have already informed us not to. So I politely gave them my supervisor's name and number and suggested they give her a call. I can't wait until I have my own company and calling the shots. It won't be long*

After awhile, I started getting tired of school. I really couldn't see the point. I wasn't learning shit and the teachers didn't seem like they cared. I was working and making my own money so I really didn't see the point. So right in the middle of the school year, I just stopped going. I concluded that I would take off the rest of the year and then make a decision later as to what to do regarding school. After I quit, I didn't really do nothing, I chilled at home most of the time just sitting around with my mother watching TV. Nana didn't really give me any problems, she said that she loved me but if I wanted to drop out and be a dummy, that was on me. She said she had graduated and was happy she did.

Nevertheless, by the end of the school year, after seeing that I wasn't going to pass, I sort of realized that school was in fact the ticket. However, by then, it was too, late. On top of that, I had made my house the skip house. Every day somebody new came. A lot of the times Di came, but others came too. Anyway, one day I'm chillin' around the house, and I get a call telling me that one of Di's friends is having beef at the school, so to tell Di when she gets to my house that she's needed up to my school. Not Di's school mind you, but mine... and, oh, and my help is needed, too. So Di gets to my house and she's already gotten the news. So I get in the car and they've got hammers, knives and all kinds of fuckin' weapons and there I was right in the car with them headed up to the same school that I'd dropped out of to fight. Now ain't that a bitch. I couldn't get my ass up to go to school to learn but there I was on my way to fuck somebody up. The whole ride there I knew I shouldn't have been in that car but I had no choice. I had to prove to Di and her girls that I was part of the click. I had already let them down at the party so I knew if I didn't fight this time my ass was grass. Fuck... peer pressure was a motha.

So we get to the school, walk in and go over to the Canon side of the school. When we get there I see one of my girls hanging out in the halls so I go over and speak. Meanwhile, people are standing on both sides of the hall like they're waiting on something to go down. I hadn't been to school in months so I'm giving daps... speaking to everybody, so anyway I stop to speak to my girl Tawana. Me and her was cool. She was a bit on the butch side but other than that, she was alright. So I'm kicking it with her and when I finish talking, I give her a little hug then go back over to where Di and Katrina was standing and soon as I get over there they start cussing me out. Come to find out, the girl I was just talking to was the girl whose ass we had come up there to kick. O.k. now I'm fucked. I guess that's why it's important that before you get all pumped up to fight that you know who you're about to battle. So I look over at Tawanna and she does this sign to let me know we're cool. That when the fight goes down, if I don't hit her she won't hit me. At that point I began to feel sick. I couldn't even believe I was in the school about to get involved in a gang fight. Wasn't Little House on the Prairie on. What time was it.

As my mind started drifting into thoughts of going back home, the bell sounded, shaking me back to reality. Within seconds, the hallway was crowded with kids, squeezing in and out, all trying to get to their next class. Meanwhile, Katrina and Tawana were standing in the middle of the hall arguing. They were going at it. They didn't get far though before security saw them and came over and ordered them to class. But it was too, late. By this time Tawana was livid. She was out of her mind with anger. When security told her to move on she refused. When he grabbed her arm to lead her to the office she snatched away and that's when she and the security officer got to fighting. I don't know how he did it, but he somehow managed to wrestle her to the floor, however she was tough. The girl was built like a man. While lying across her back, she grabbed a hold of the post located between the wall and the door and lifted her as well as the security guard up off the floor and to her feet. At that point I looked at Katrina and just shook my head. She was about to get fucked up.

As the security guard escorted Tawana outside, everybody, including the crowd, followed. When we got outside we ended up in the dock receiving area. Tawana and her crew stepped out on the dock first with our crew right behind them. Then the crowd encircled both groups and closed ranks. At that point nobody was going nowhere. Tawana then shouted that the main participants should fight. That meant she and Katrina, and LaKiesha and

Tonya and just like that, the fight was on. Tawana grabbed Katrina and the hammers, fists, and sticks went to flying. I looked around to try and spot Di, and I see this tall pregnant chick, who looks like she's about to deliver, grab Di from behind and swing her to the ground. So at that point I made my way through the crowd. When I reached her, two girls had her on the ground and were wailing away. When I attempt to jump in the pregnant girl shows up again and this time grabs me and hurls me to the ground. Now the dust is flying. Everybody is getting tossed. I'm tossing, the pregnant girl is tossing and in between all of that, somebody manages to get one of our hammers and pops me in the arm with it.

Finally, after what seemed like a life time, security showed back up. They round everybody up and herd us to the office. As we're walking, blood dripping, the only thing I can think is that I'm going to jail. I wasn't even supposed to be at the school and now there I was in the middle of a gang fight. I had to come up with a plan, fast.

When I got to the office, I quickly gave a fake name then complained that I needed to go to the restroom because I was bleeding. Security hesitated for a moment then went on and let me go; unescorted. That was all I needed. I was out.

As I rushed out of the back door, I swore to myself that if I made it home, I would never again put myself in any situation that could cause me to go to jail. I was only 16 years old. What the hell was I thinking?

Later that night I called Di to check on her and see how she was doing. She said she was fine, then said that everybody had told her how I had been the only one out of our crew to help. Of course that was all I needed to hear. I had now proven myself a warrior.

***July 5 2008- I'm taking it easy today. I got in the yard yesterday. The house was starting to look like a flop house so I replanted some flowers and dug a deeper ditch for my little fences. I also bought some lights and put some grass seeds down to cover the few patches. I wanted to do the back but I ran out of energy so I came in the house to take a short nap and ended up sleeping for two hours. After I woke up I got up, jumped on my bike and went to the grocery store. I just needed something light so I bought what I needed for spaghetti, put it in my saddle bags came home and made spaghetti, salad and garlic bread. After that I got on my bike for a few hours and just cruised. Afterwards, since I was on the freeway I went to visit Aunt Mona. The pot holes can drive you crazy. I know it sounds crazy but I prefer to ride on the freeway. I feel safer. On the street cars are switching lanes, people running stop signs, pulling out in front of me, it gets crazy. On the freeway you don't have to worry about all of that. I submitted***

***my part to our team project for school... mission accomplished***

Well, not long after the fight, Booky forced himself into my downstairs apartment and took the coochie again. This time though, while we was doing it, my girl Toyia, who was also cool with Di, knocked on the door and I hollered for her to come back later. Even though I thought we were cool, she some how found out what I was doing and couldn't wait to tell. She immediately called Di, who was now pregnant and within fifteen minutes Di was pulling up in a cab. What made it so bad was that Di wasn't even fucking with Bookie no more. She had been fucking this other dude for the past 6 months. Now on other the other hand, I had been fucking this dude named Stan, who turned out to be the girl down the street baby daddy and the girl was Bookie's baby momma. And to top it off, she was pregnant with Stan's second child, so to make matters worse, Toyia had also made it her business to tell the girl, Roshell, about her man's extra curricular activities with me. So when Bookie left, and I walked outside, both Roshell and Di outside. They both out there crying. And to make this whole thing even crazier, Di was pregnant, so I couldn't figure out what her problem was. It wasn't Bookie's. So I get outside and these hoes standing in front my house. Meanwhile Toyia out there instigating and trying to build the whole thing up. However, with both of them pregnant and in no mood for fighting, a few choice words were exchanged and everybody simply went on back home and I lived to see another day.

Weeks went by before Di spoke to me again. When we did talk, she was so emotional. Like I said she wasn't even with Bookie anymore and like I said she was pregnant by somebody else. Now me and Roshell had gone to Jackson together but she wasn't my friend period, so I could care less about her feelings. She was pretty, hung with the in crowd and was popular. But that was about it. Now because she was pregnant, that even made her more popular because she was carrying Booky's child. I'll never forget the looks of all the girls as she walked through the school big as hell and pregnant by the best looking boy in the school. She was the envy of every teenaged girl with dreams of being pregnant by Booky.

Even thou I didn't know Stan was Rochell's baby daddy, this fool had told me he was her cousin. All this time he was coming to my house and spending time with me; sitting on my porch, hanging out, I had no reason to think that was her man. But that just goes to show you how trifling some niggas can be. Of course I wish he wouldn't have lied because if I would have known he had a baby on the way I would have definitely stayed away.

Well, after a few months passed, Stan finally came down and apologized for lying. He said he just had to have me and that's why he did it. He then started telling me how much he cared about me and, you know, how much he missed me, so you know, I had to go on ahead and give him some more of this coochie because I felt the same way about him as he said he felt about me. Plus, Stan had been the first one to lick my coochie and had done such a good job doing it that how could I kick him to the curb. The first time he licked it I remember going upstairs and cuddling up with my mother like a little baby. That's how good that shit was.

Chapter 18

**LOOK WHO'S DRIVING**

Later on that summer, I finally got the Chevette. Aunt Mona finally got to the point where she felt comfortable with me taking it so I got my license, we got it fixed, and that was the end of me catching the bus.

Getting the car really gave me the opportunity to travel like never before. I went everywhere. East side, west side, of course I mainly just went to Di's house but at least now I had options.

As much as I enjoyed having a car, after several months, I realized that having a car wasn't everything it was cracked up to be. It got to the point where I hated it. Every day, everybody and they momma needed to go someplace. Nana and Auntie Sandra was good for that shit. Sandra and all her kids lived with us as did Uncle Ronald who was back out of jail. I knew it was just a matter of time before they moved back in, but now, having the car made it even worse. Sandra always wanted to go somewhere and it was always far as hell. I hated saying no but she would always promise all this money and when we'd get back home end up giving me half of what we discussed. This last time though was the last straw. She had me take her way on the west side, near six mile and Livernois to some apartment building, then had me sit in the car and wait on her for an hour and a half while she was in there probably getting high. I wanted to leave her ass, but I knew Uncle Ronald would have had a fit had I left his precious Sandra, so I waited. After that day, money or no money, I learned how to say no. Most of the times I would just say that I didn't have any gas, or that I had to pick up somebody, but for the most part, I learned just to say no.

During this time of my life, I began talking on and off to this guy that I went to elementary school with, named Kevin. Nothing serious, he started coming around to get his bike fixed by my brother and after that we just started talking. It wasn't long after that we became close friends. He was nice looking, not really my type, but he was alright. During those first few months together, we never had sex, but in between Bookie, and Stan, and whoever else, we would kiss from time to time.

Well, everything was going good with Kevin, then one day out of the blue, he came over and he started about how much he cared about me and how we never really spent any time together, and blah, blah, blah. I was shocked because that wasn't what our relationship was about. We were supposed to be platonic. But still, I was young, and I have to admit impressed by his behavior, so I went on ahead and gave him some. I figured nothing would shut up a raging teenage boy more than a little piece of pussy. In fact, he ended up shuttin' me up. That shit was good. Kevin had a big black pretty dick and he knew just what to do with it. Before I knew it, Kevin had managed to knock every other boy out the box. After that first time, he was at my house every day. Grandma and Nana loved him and Victor considered him like a big brother.

Everything was going fine with Kevin until one day this nigga up and flipped the script on me. What happened was one day I arrived home from work and my boy Anthony from school pulled up. I hadn't seen him since he'd graduated the year before. So we kicked it for about ten minutes, he gave me a friendly hug and told me that he was headed back down to Georgia where he was stationed in the military. So I wished him luck and he continued his rounds. When I got in the house Kevin ass started tripping. The nigga started talking shit about Anthony coming over, questioning whether I was fucking him, and how dare I disrespect him in his own house. Yea, he had gone crazy. Come to find out Anthony had been over twice when I wasn't home. When we were talking he told me he had come by earlier but I didn't think nothing of it. So when Kevin said it, I knew what he was talking about, but the boy was just a friend. I tried to explain this to Kevin but he wasn't hearing it. Before I knew it, he was huffing and puffing, and grabbing at my clothes trying to snatch me around. Meanwhile, Victor and Travon were on the sidelines instigating because they didn't know no better. They didn't see the danger. They thought the shit was funny. I broke loose and ran into my grandma's room just for her to tell me that Kevin was just playing. So I left out of her room feeling like I was on my own. At that point, I told him to leave, and take his ass home, but this fool gone tell me that he was home. So I go downstairs hoping he'll at least sit his ass down, but after about 10 minutes I hear him coming down the stairs. As I'm sitting on the edge of the bed this fool comes into my room, grabs me by the collar and pulls me down backwards on the bed. That's when we started tussling.

As we wrestled, all I could hear was Victor and Travon near the doorway laughing. But what they didn't know was this fool was down there trying to kill me. This crazy mother fucker pulled my sheets back and tried to smother my face in the waterbed mattress but I twisted around and got up from under him and managed to flip him off of me. I had an advantage in the bed because it was mine and I knew how to maneuver. So I kicked his ass as hard as I could and he fell off the bed and onto the floor. While he was trying to collect himself, I got up, bolted to the door, and ran outside.

When I got outside, I relaxed thinking he'd had enough. But boy was I wrong. When he got outside, he walked up to me and this time slapped the dog shit out of me. He slapped me so hard that my whole left side instantly swelled up and my eye turned black. After that, with him running right behind me, I ran upstairs and back into the house. This time he wasn't trying to hit me, he was trying to apologize for slapping me. But it was too, late. As I stood in the bathroom looking at my face in the mirror, I knew we were over. All while he was talking I was looking in the mirror at how fucked up my face was. I just couldn't believe he had put his hands on me.

After that day, although I didn't want anything else to do with Kevin, he still came over. I was pissed. Grandma and Nana would let him in, but once in, I would do everything in my power to ignore him. To make matters worse, because of my eye, I was stuck in the house. Every day this fool would come over trying to apologize. But I didn't care what he had to say. He had crossed the line when he put his hands on me. My thing was, if a man hit you once he will hit you again and if he loves you, why the fuck would he put his hands on you in the first place.

This fool was crazy though. Even after I told him that we were through, he would try and crawl in the bed with me, and act like we were still together.

I didn't talk to Kevin for months after this. Then one day he pops up and tells me that he caught a case. Turns out he had got caught selling crack and was sentenced to six months in boot camp. So his story was that he was going away at the end of the month, and again that he was sorry and how he didn't mean it and how could I just kick him to the curve when he was on his way to boot camp. So I felt bad...and I gave in. I gave him a little and let him hang around until it was time for him to leave.

Also during this time, I also had sex with this boy named Dee. Dee was one of the most popular boys in school and I loved everything about him. He had hazel eyes, was light skinned and was bowlegged, what happened is one night I was hanging out with my girl Melanie over one of Dee boy's house. Me and Dee ended up going back to my house and having sex. Unlike me and Kevin though, me and Dee used protection.

Anyway, a month after Kevin left, I started feeling sick. I started throwing up and couldn't keep nothing down. I also couldn't seem to crawl out of bed and every smell stank. I had felt this way only once before and that was when I'd gotten pregnant by this boy Deantae, but I had taken care of it.

When I got over Di's house later that day, as soon as she saw me she told me I was pregnant. She told me that my face was fat, my tiddies were bigger, and that all of that sleeping all day wasn't for nothing. But I was not trying to here it. By this time, Di had an eight-month old daughter herself, so I saw how having a baby had sat her down and I was not ready for that.

Nonetheless, on my way home, I bought a pregnancy test and when I got home, I went into the bathroom, peed on the stick and waited.

***August 15, 2008- Chavez went to court today. They gave him 3 months' probation and a hundred dollar fine for just sitting on a porch with his friends. Technically his friends used to live in the house, but they lost it, so it was a vacant dwelling and he got a ticket for it. My baby ain't never been in any trouble so for him to have a fine and probation for a damn loitering ticket I'm pissed. I'm ready to call my congresswoman and complain about the injustice. On the flipside Darshawn got a job. He had an interview yesterday and they told him to pick up his uniform today. It's at taco bell. Way out in bum fuck Egypt but that's ok, I'm so happy. Between Chavez and Darshawn we should be eating good. It was suppose to have been Arcyle getting a job then Darshawn then Chavez but the baby showed them up. He got his job first now hopefully the other two will catch on and follow suit. Me and Edward went to the golf range yesterday. We had a good little day. Also I have four more classes to go. I can't wait. I can almost smell the ink on my degree. I got my ballroom on last night and two of my favorite dancers were there. If I get two good dances from them I'm tight for the night. I got dipped, lifted up in the air and we did double turns. I felt like I was on dancing with the stars. The dream cruise is this***

***weekend so I think I'll ride my bike up Woodward.***

When Di found out I was pregnant, the first thing out of her mouth was that I should have an abortion, but I didn't want to go through that again, thanks to Di showing me how to go about it the first time. To Di, abortion was a method of birth control. To her, why take the pill. If you got knocked up just go and see the good doctor and he would take care of it. But I didn't feel that way. I didn't really want to have another abortion, but at the same time I was not ready to take care of a child. Plus, my father would kill me, not to mention school. How would I finish. I also didn't want to be like my mother and have a baby at 17. So I waited. I couldn't decide what to do. Plus, the new titties were wonderful.

After about a month, I finally decided to tell the family. I told Nana, grandma and Aunt Mona I was pregnant, then in the same breath told them that I wanted an abortion. Aunt Mona wasn't agreeing to that at all. She didn't believe in abortions. Even though I understood, it was me who had to make the decision so in spite of her feelings, I went on ahead and made the appointment.

When it was time for my appointment, my grandmother, Nana, and Aunt Mona rode with me to the clinic. During the entire ride, I had to hear how the baby was already three and a half months, how the legs and arms were already formed, how it had fingers, toes...how it could probably already open its eyes and they went on and on. But my mind was made up. When we got there, in spite of those facts, all I wanted to know was were they gone take the baby right then or did I need to make another appointment and come back.

Well, after the doctor examined me, I had another dilemma. Because the baby was so far along, the price of the abortion would make it impossible for me to afford the procedure. When I looked at my grandmother and saw the way she looked at me, I knew it was over. She had no intentions of paying for an abortion.

I was stuck. I was having a baby. I cried the whole way home. As far as I was concerned, my life as I knew it was over. No high school graduation. No college. No clubbing. Nothing.

When I got home I knew I had to tell Kevin because he was the only person that I'd been with without using a rubber. So I called him and he came right over. When I told him his attitude was the total opposite of mine. He was happy as a lark. He grabbed me and hugged me and kissed my belly. He was so happy. But my feelings were bittersweet. The next day he was leaving to go to boot camp meaning I was going to have to deal with the pregnancy all alone. I was not looking forward to that.

Every week it seemed like something changed on my body. When I went to my first prenatal appointment they did an ultrasound and I could see the baby's body. It looked like a baby doll in my stomach. The Doctor couldn't quite tell what it was but he said he would try again on my next visit. At this point I still hadn't told my father, but I knew that he suspected something, because every time he called Nana would tell him that I wasn't home, nor did I return his calls. In spite of everything I was going through though, I knew I had to tell him because it was only a matter of time before he popped up to see what was going on with his first born.

Once I mustered up the courage to visit my dad, I was so nervous. To make things easier, I put on my orange fitted dress so when I saw him he wouldn't have to ask no questions. As soon as he opened the door he looked me up and down then opened the door wider so my fat ass could come in. He gave me the biggest hug then I went into the den and sat down. He asked me if I was hungry and I said yea. At that point I was always hungry. He brought me a neatly cut bologna and cheese sandwich, some orange slices, and a cup of juice then just sat there on the couch next to me rubbing my stomach.

By the time I reached 5 months, I was tired, fat and all of my normal clothes were too tight. It was also my senior year, which meant while everyone else was saving money for the senior prom, trip, senior dues, etc., I was saving my money for my baby and preparing myself for late night feedings, diaper changes and a whole new life.

***August 21, 2008-God is good. DTE is willing to put me back on the budget plan, which is a relief. They were trying to shut a sister down. I got a shutoff notice last month so I went to social service to try and get some help with the bill. Three weeks done passed and I ain't heard nothing so I thought that they paid it. I opened the bill to see the balance so I could call to make an arraignment and it's a shut off notice for that following week. I have been calling the worker everyday but have gotten no response. I leave messages everyday but still nothing. I called her supervisor only for her to tell me that I was denied because I make a few dollars too much. What is a few dollars too much. Even with Edward being back we still in the hole and falling further in debt. I am living a nightmare, being in a recession with no money saved, behind on every bill, barely paying my truck note, no set plan because every time one is set Edward changes the game in the ninth inning. I hate not being able to do the little things. I literally have to watch every dollar. I'm looking for a 50cent store... can I get a half a loaf of bread. Not being able to cook my family a four course meal with beverages everyday kills me. Not having enough to feed company if we have any... these are things I have grown accustomed to. Now these necessities have***

*turned into luxury's all because I'm trying to be that strong black woman and keep my family together. We eating bullshit pot pies and wing dings almost every night. It's alright every now and then or just because you had a taste for it but try eating it ' cause that is all you got. Everybody in the house is losing weight in addition to the fact that my hair is falling out and I'm getting very little sleep. Meanwhile Edward is picking and choosing what he gone give me every pay while not sticking to the set budget we both agreed to. Then when he spends all his money driving around the city, hanging out and playing golf he comes back and asks me for gas money.*

*August 30, 2008- This is the holiday weekend and I'm trying to decide what to do. A friend gave me some tickets to the Grand prix so I'll probably go tomorrow. I am going to let Chavez drive the truck... he got paid today so he feeling a little bossy. I'm gone cruise behind him on my motorcycle. This was not in my plans but he said the magic word-gas money. There is also a birthday party tonight that I might attend but with money the way it is, I don't know. Lately I have been finding peace through ball rooming. Going back reminded me just how much I loved it before I'd gotten married. Even though things have not been improving with me and Edward's marriage I have still been pushing on with everything else. So the support I need I have to drum up from strangers. So far Edward is the only one besides family that know what I*

***have been working on. Now that I know where me and Edward stand I have to network and share my ideas with niggas and hope that instead of stealing my ideas or trying to fuck and take advantage of me that they will just help me get these ideas off the ground. My goal is to be fully operational before the new year and have my kids in a fully furnished new crib by Christmas, therefore I have to do what I have to do.***

After Kevin went to boot camp, me and my neighbor Cory started spending more time together. Even though I saw him a lot I never really paid much attention to him. But now he was older. He had grown a lot since middle school, and was now quite handsome. So we ended up spending a lot of time together. He started coming around everyday. He even started going to my doctor's appointments and helping me get little things for the baby. After awhile he even started spending the night. We didn't do anything at first, but after awhile it was hard for me to avoid the sexual attraction. So I broke down and went on and gave him some of what he was looking for.

While I was getting older, so was Arcyle and Darshawn. They were now getting big and turning into a handful for grandma and Nana. Victor was now a teenager and was even worse. It was nothing for him to get up in Nana's face and mouth off whenever he felt the urge. I even had to call the police on him once after getting all up in her face and then turning around trying to front on me after I came to her rescue. One thing led to another and before I knew it, he slapped me and if not for Aunt Mona who reminded me I was pregnant, the fight would have been on. So instead I called the police.

Pregnant or not, he may have planted a little fear in everybody else around the house, but I was convinced that I could still lay his ass out if need be. He didn't scare me one bit.

***September 2, 2008- It's Denise's first day of kindergarten. Alexis is going to the fourth grade and the two of them look real cute. Me and Edward are still not speaking but we had our asses up to get the girls ready. I actually almost overslept. This after I had taken off work just to get them settled in on their first day. Edward didn't wake me and when I did wake up, he was in the kitchen doing Denise's hair. Even though I didn't say anything, I was so pissed. I just couldn't understand his rationale for doing things. I had to take back down her hair because the parts were crooked. What the hell was he thinking.***

***After dropping of the girls, I then picked up Chavez and took him to school and got him registered for the 11^th^ grade. He didn't stay but he did get his schedule. I was also happy to find out that they didn't put the little incident he had at the end of the school year on his record. Thank God. Just seeing the way, the counselors and the teachers were talking***

***to him I could see that he had charmed they ass the same way he charms me.***

***After we left the school we went to the Good Will to grab him some pants and a tie. Until I get some more money the second hand store will have to do. After that we hit the dollar store and got him a few notebooks to get him started. Thanks to Edward's sister, the girls had school supplies. That was truly a blessing***

Everybody on both sides of my family has been very supportive of my pregnancy. My aunts encouraged me to keep working, and going to school, and reminded me that it was not the end of the world. Kevin's oldest sister would also stop by to check on me. Meanwhile Cory had a pregnancy to deal with on his own. Before we hooked up he'd gotten his ex girlfriend pregnant and although he spent most of his time with me, he still went with her to her appointments as well. I didn't really have a problem with it, however I have to admit I was a little jealous whenever they were together. It got so bad that one night I snuck down to the house where they hung, which was Cory's aunt's who had rented out Booky's mother's rental property. Yea I know. It's something about that house. Anyway I get down there, creep up the stairs and peek through the window and I see Cory's head. It was either between her legs or lying on her stomach. Either way, I was hurt. My heart just fell to my feet and I broke down crying. I tip toed back down the stairs and headed back down the street heart broken. The further I got from the house the louder I cried. As I walked home I noticed that Cory's little smartass cousin had seen the whole thing. I swear I didn't see his little ass standing out there when I walked up, but at that point I didn't care, I was too hurt to care about anything. Cory was a dog and that's all there was to it.

***September 3, 2008 - I am starting to see that my life will soon revolve around politics. Between school, the news and just everyday life I see if I want to make a change in the world and get my voice heard I will have to run for some sort of office. It's scary though because right now our mayor is catching hell. I know I am currently not politically savvy- as one of my coworkers have told me- but I am learning something new everyday. I firmly believe that as a young black man in power that the Mayor was making moves that a lot of people didn't like. I think for some people he was moving too fast. That scares people, especially the media. If not for the media we would have forgotten all about the little things he was accused of and the whole thing would have been over. We would have forgotten about it in a week. Men cheat every day so I really don't think that issue was worth bringing him down. Name me three men right now who have never cheated. Cheat or not, they still went to work and still functioned normally. Yea he cheated on his wife and I don't condone that but I honestly feel that that***

*was an issue between that man, his wife and his savoir. He was wrong as hell but if his wife is ok with it and she has found it in her heart to forgive him, let it go. I mean he came out on national TV and apologized to her and the city and that took a lot. I mean how humiliating. But no that wasn't enough. You got some people that just want blood and they not gone stop until they get it. Everybody makes mistakes. Its hypocritical to me. I don't think that it affected his ability to still do his job and that is to run the city. Hell he was running it before we knew about the affair... sure they have other issues twisted up in there like the party that supposedly happened at the mansion... that supposedly didn't happen... a stripper that was allegedly at the party and was beaten up by the Mayor's wife and turned around and came up dead... the firing of some officers and a law suit that followed that, then the shoving of a city officer or trooper and the list goes on. But my problem lies with the fact that they have followed the man around every day damn near since he been in office. News reporters following him everywhere he goes... following his kids to school like paparazzi. He ain't no celebrity. They never let him rest and this was before the sex scandal and all the things that followed. You dig too deep into anybody's past you gone find something. I feel he has done a lot for the city. I see a change. I see more paved streets, new houses popping up in what use to be poverty stricken neighborhoods, but nobody gives him credit for*

***that. Every time I bring that up along with the events that we have had since he has been in office and people say that the credit goes to the administrations before him. Whatever the case may be, I am disappointed in the city for not respecting the Mayor's position from the start. Ain't no telling what they gone pull up digging in my past. I just hope that when I get in public office that my accomplishments speak for me. I hope the public sees the person I have become and the lessons I have learned from my mistakes. Mayor... I like the sound of that. It can happen. One word; Obama. I am proud of how far we have come as a people. Back in the sixties being president was just a dream. Hell bathrooms and restaurants were still labeled whites and colored and we were still sitting on the back of the bus and getting rocks thrown at us for trying to go to school. Let's not forget getting attacked by police dogs and sprayed with fire hoses. So I am proud to be an American. Good luck to Obama.***

During the later part of my pregnancy, it started getting really hard to move around. It felt like my coochie was going to fall out. I also started thinking a lot about how the baby would come out. That was a part of the process that not too many people had cared to share, so I went and got one of the little baby dolls sitting around the house and tried to size up the head, but I just couldn't see it. I couldn't imagine anything that big coming out from anywhere between my legs. That's when I started to get scared.

***September 5,2008- The mayor resigned yesterday. I watched his last speech with my Aunt Jackie at her house. She loves the mayor as much as I do. We both appreciated the speech. It was very honorable. He didn't talk too much about the wrong... the only thing he mentioned was if he could turn back the hands of time that he would have made better decisions. But the just of the speech was primarily about all the accomplishments he and his administration have made since he has been in office. I also admired the fact that he was a big enough man to meet with his replacement.***

***I met with my architect today. He will be designing my boot camp. Hopefully this time next year it will be up and operational. He will be working on things like zoning issues, location and what I envision my obstacle course to look like. It's a work in progress, but I'm excited. With the new business ventures and opportunities, I just got to stay prayed up cause the devil never rests.***

During most of my pregnancy, I was able to maintain my job at the nursing home. In the later months though, I asked my boss if she could move me downstairs because it was hard for me to lift patients and she said she had no openings but when one became available she would let me know. Well, when I came to work the following week a new white girl had been hired and was working on the first floor. You talking about somebody pissed. My co-workers

Wendy and Marlo tried to help as much as they could and even the elderly lady, I can't remember her name, she would also help with my load.

I had been to the prom my 9th, 10th, and 11th grade years, but the year of my pregnancy I decided not to go. I had two dates, too. They were just friends but it was too close to my due date to take that chance. Just my luck my water break and I go into labor at the prom. That would have been something to remember, huh. Well, in fact it wasn't long before my water did break. It happened a few weeks later while me and Cory was about to have sex. Yea I know, but we'd made up, and next to Di, he was actually the next closest person to me. So as much as I despised his actions, I really needed him in my life.

Anyway, while he was about to stick it in, warm water starting gushing down my legs, causing him to immediately jump to his feet. He then helped me to my feet, I cleaned myself up, then he ran upstairs to tell my grandmother that I was ready to go to the hospital. I could feel the baby moving around, but at that point I wasn't feeling much pain so I was at least happy about that.

When we got to the hospital they put me in a room with about six other girls. I couldn't see them because the curtains were pulled, but I knew they were there because they were all moaning. It didn't take long before I was moaning, too. The pain felt like hard menstrual cramps, but worse. After a couple hours though, what I considered worse turned into unbearable. At this point the epidural they had given me did nothing to ease the pain. The nurses told me that once the baby got so far down in the canal that the medicine becomes obsolete. Just great.

I had two people in the room with me at all times. They included my grandmother, a friend Cory, a family friend named Constance and my mother. When it was time to deliver, the doctor came in and said that only one person could stay in the room. So Constance, who was trained as a midwife, sort of took charge, thereby sending Nana out in the hall to wait with grandma, Cory and the others.

While I waited to become totally dilated, Constance's coaching helped to ease the pain. I still hurt, but the breathing techniques helped. However, like the medicine, after a certain point, no amount of breathing could help the nagging pain I was feeling. I felt like an alien was stuck in my stomach and was trying to force itself out. Every few minutes it would get tired, then rest then start over again. Just when I didn't think I could take the pain one more second, the doctor rushed in and wheeled me into the operating room. When we got there he placed my feet in stirrups and then placed me in front of this big mirror. With nurses surrounding him, the doctor then told me that my contractions would now come once inside of every minute, and when I felt them, to push. So that's what I did. In spite of the immense pain, I also tried to remain calm, and breath in and out like Constance had shown me. Finally, after about four rounds of contractions, at exactly 3:15 a.m., the doctor made a small cut, I pushed once more and the head popped out.

After the body slid out, a bunch of fluid ran out. After that the nurses began pressing on my stomach in order to push out all the after birth. I was so exhausted I couldn't move. I couldn't even cry. I just laid there until they were done. When they finished pushing out the after birth, they numbed me up, sewed up the cut, then left the room.

After cleaning up the baby, they brought it to me, and announced I'd had a healthy baby boy. He was 7lbs, 3 1/2 ounces, and 21 inches long. The first time I saw my babies face, I fell in love. I counted his fingers and toes then watched as he slowly opened his eyes, which were blue. He was just the cutest thing I had ever seen. Thank God I made it through.

***September 11, 2008- My morning is starting off good. I'm tired as hell because I had class last night then when I got home there was drama with the boys. A gang of boys chased a man through the street, caught him right near our house and began beating him into a pulp. The man somehow broke loose,***

*then ran toward our house at which point the boys ran. After the boys ran away, my next door neighbor had the man to wait on her porch. Thinking I might know who the boys were, I jumped in my truck to see if I knew any of the guys that did it cause somebody said they thought they saw Darshawn in the group. But all I saw when I got to the corner was one of his friend's car pull off with a gang of boys in the car. I didn't see Darshawn; thank God. That was my main concern so I turned around and went back to the house. When I got back, I went and checked on the man they had beaten up. The man's wrist was bleeding really bad so I volunteered to take him to the hospital. Now, even though I didn't see Darshawn in the car, his ass so sneaky he better not have had anything to do with it. He hasn't been giving me any problems lately, but you never know. As we drove to the hospital I asked the man what happened and he said he didn't do nothing, that the boys just started talking shit and ran up on him. He said that he'd defended himself and had stabbed one of them, so when I reached the hospital, I told security what he told me then let them know that I was an innocent bystander, merely helping an assault victim get to the hospital. Meanwhile while they were processing him I walked to the lobby to see if I saw any of the boys and sure enough I saw two of my son's friends, Ricky and Devon. When we made eye contact I looked at them as if to say that they better get the fuck on because the police were waiting on a stab*

***victim to walk through the door. Both of them were good boys with jobs and the last thing they needed was to end up in jail. Hopefully this will be a lesson to them about the company they keep. I could tell they were both shocked to see me, still, when I walked out, they came out after me and walked home. When they got to the hood I chin checked the fuck out of them and they both claimed they didn't have anything to do with it. Every time I turn around its something going on with one of my kids or their friends. It's just too much shit going on in this neighborhood. I am ready to move.***

Since I had a boy, my dream name, Brittany, was no longer viable. I don't know why I hadn't already thought of a name for a boy, I just assumed it was going to be a girl.

After I had the baby, many members of my family came to see me. Cory on the other hand never left. He stayed the entire night. You would have thought it was his baby. When my dad and Pam came, my dad just stood by the window and held the baby looking out the entire time. The thing I couldn't get over was the color of the baby's eyes. I had no idea where they came from. They sure didn't come from me and they sure didn't come from Kevin.

***September 15, 2008- The whole family is up bright and early. We all have dental and vision appointments today. The ladies were nice enough to schedule us all in the same day***

***so once we finish with the dental all we have to do is walk to the other side of the building to vision. Thank God they both in the same office.***

***Edward has started passing me little love notes through Denise. If only he was sincere. I have to catch up on my school work, I am behind. I still have a few papers yet to complete. I had some technical difficulties the first few weeks of class. I needed a cord for my laptop and thanks to Mody Woowoo I got one. Edward claimed he ordered me one but I never got it. He lies for no reason.***

Even though I carried my beautiful baby for nine months and had a safe and speedy delivery I was still not feeling motherly. Don't get me wrong, I cuddled, I goo goo ga gad, I fed him, changed him, bathed him and dressed him; all my favorite part of the day. I kept his little ass fresh with my ADC checks. But I knew that as soon as I healed, I was hitting the streets.

During the past few months leading up to the baby, things had changed somewhat around the house. Nana was now seeing this man named Boo, Victor had practically moved in with his girlfriend and her family, and I was now off work and on ADC. I hated going to the ADC office. It was so depressing sitting there looking at people that looked beyond help. But like Di and Nana said. It was free money so why not.

Boo seemed cool, although they all did at first. He didn't seem to be on any type of drugs, however I couldn't see why he would spend all of his time with somebody who was. He claimed he didn't smoke anything but cigarettes and was going to help get Nana straight. This I had to see!

***October 1, 2008- I am sitting here in class tired as hell. I keep looking at the clock. The only reason I haven't gotten up and left is because I like the teacher. Since Edward has politely let me know that he does not have my back for the upteeth time it is solely up to me to get me and my kids out of this house. They have already started the foreclosure and I don't know how I should feel. Here it is I have been here 14 years taking care of my kids and now after 6 ½ years I am losing my house. I am down to one truck that I am barely holding on to, no money saved… it is like I went completely backwards. This marriage has set me back 14 years. Something is wrong with this picture. I thought that since I have managed to do good by myself all this time that if I took on a life partner I should be a lot further, but instead I am taking steps back.***

***So now I have taken control and I have taken my mind back. I am pushing forward with the notion that I still have to move and get my businesses up and running without him. I have managed to not include him in nothing I am working on right now even though I have been sharing everything with my husband***

*since day one, which don't get me wrong, is not a bad thing, just in my case it was the wrong man. I have cut off communication and although that sounds childish, in this case, he wasn't hearing shit I was saying anyway, so all I did was stop wasting words on dead ears. I have been having meetings every evening with people that are doing what I am trying to do, its just different trying to bring outsiders up to speed on my projects that I have been working on for the last three years instead of just sharing things with my husband. It sounds cruel because I was under the impression that once I got married that my husband was all I needed. But I guess I was wrong.*

## Chapter 19

### Back to normal

It's been a few months since I had the baby and I was now all healed up. I also started taking birth control pills. I should have been taking them since day one.

As soon as I felt ready, I was back in the streets. I stayed home during the day, but as soon as it got dark, I was out. Nana would keep the baby for me. I didn't have any intentions of staying on ADC so I tried to take advantage of my time off. Also, just like I predicted, Nana's new boy friend didn't help her get off crack. As a matter of fact, he started smoking the shit, himself. I actually saw him smoking it. Before I caught him, something told me that he was probably on it because all of a sudden his demeanor changed. He went from this wimpy little shit cooking, cleaning the house, taking care of the boys lil man, to this bossy, argumentative little shit. He would send Nana out with no money to get crack, and when she'd get back he'd want to argue about how she went about getting the money to get it. Of course he wouldn't want to fight until after all the crack was gone. But I didn't give a fuck what he thought, I was just waiting on him to put his hands on her so I could fuck him up.

One day one of my neighbors came running up on the porch to tell me that Boo and my mother was around the corner fighting.

They were up on Warren near the projects. So I jumped in my car and headed to the scene. When I got there I spotted him swinging her around like she was his pet, so I made a quick u-turn jumped out and confronted him. When I jumped in between them, he still had a hold of one arm, so I started pulling at him to let her go. Meanwhile Di who had come with me, started pulling on Nana to get away. Nana then starts yelling at everybody to just calm down. Telling us that he's not hurting her. Meaning that I should just let them do there thing right in the middle of a main street on the east side of Detroit. It was quite obvious to me they were fighting and every thing wasn't alright. Regardless of what my mother was saying, I pulled out my knife and put it to his throat and told him that if he didn't let her go right then and there, that I was gone drop his ass. I pressed the knife so hard against his neck that I broke the skin. He then let her go. After that, we walked her to the car, warned him to stay away from our house, and left him standing against the fence looking like a broke down crack head.

***October 5, 2008- I'm in class and instead of listening to the teacher, I'm sitting there reflecting on my life. Edward been gone since last Tuesday. His clothes still here but I have not seen him or talked to him. The nigga got paid Friday and didn't give me shit, but I'm good. I have been focused on what I have to do for my self and my kids. Last week my family looked out. Aunt Juanita gave us food***

*and gave me some Victoria secret lotion 'cause I have practically no smell good. Aunt Jackie made us a big pan of spaghetti and loaned me a few dollars too. My neighbor also loaned me a few dollars. I swear I am so tired of begging and asking for help because this nigga choose to dip whenever he gets ready. I don't know what he be thinking about half the time. You would think I would have gotten me a boyfriend on the side by now to pick up the slack when Edward do this bullshit, but I can't get around my morals, my values and my vows. This the last time I go through this bullshit though. This time I mean it. This time I am going through with the divorce until it is final. Fuck that nigga.*

*October 9, 2008- I am moving too fast, but not fast enough.*

*October 11, 2008 I picked the baby up from Edward's mama house. As soon as she got in the car she gets to rambling on about her daddy out of town with her tete. I'm thinking hell you can do that when you not taking care of your family, so I'm bitter as hell. We back to eating noodles and hot dogs and this nigga flying from state to state and renting cars and shit. I hope he happy.*

*October 13, 2008- It's the first day of my semi vacation. I took a few days off work to get some things organized and pack up some more things that we're not using right now. I am going to miss this house... I have had so many things happen to me in this house. Some good, some bad. I raised my boys in this house. I have practically fixed everything that ever broke or went wrong in this house. That includes painting, dry wall, plumbing, redecorating and remolding. You name it. I thought I would have the day to myself, however, after getting the girls up and getting ready, the news announced that school was closed due to bad weather. So I was stuck with them. As a result, I had to rearrange some things but that was cool. It was better than being stuck with Chavez. The girls only annoyed me a little. On the other hand, I had to argue with Chavez about simple things. He beefing with this nigga over his ex girlfriend so they're suppose to be fighting so I have to argue with him about the consequences of him fighting and ending up in juvenile. I had Darshawn to drive him to and from school in order to avoid problems but it seemed like he was intent on finding problems. It was bad enough that Darshawn had to use my car to drive him because I hate people driving my car. I can't afford it. If anything happens to the car that's just one more problem and the last thing I need in my life is another major problem. Well before Darshawn could get out the door good, I get a call from Chavez telling me he has just fought. So I call the school to see what happened and now I got to eat humble pie for the next couple of days until the school call me back and let me know what they are going to do. He hates going to this school 'cause*

***everyday it is something with these niggas. Ever since Chavez and that girl broke up its been some shit. I can see they still got feelings for each other and until they get back together the fighting is not gone stop. I can't do nothing but shake my head. I've made sure that he got to school, and got there safely and still I've got to deal with him fighting. It doesn't make sense to transfer him to another school and then get transferred again after a few months when the lord bless us with a new home. Dilemma, dilemma.***

It's been an eventful year, but Chavez is finally turning one. I put up balloons, got a cake and ice cream, put him on some fresh clothes and a touch of cologne and invited the kids from the block to his 1st birthday party. Nobody his age was there, but he had a ball. He was running around the house fresh as hell. Fila hat, Fila shirt, Fila shorts, Fila socks, and last but not least some Fila shoes. Nana calls him Vette because he crawls around the house like one.

A few months after Chavez's birthday, Nana finally got rid of Boo sorry ass. Thank God for that. He had jumped on her several times since that day and each time I'd question her, she always had a story about how it happened. It was always some bullshit and then when I'd approach him she would get in the way crying about how it wasn't worth going to jail.

After Boo she started talking to one of Uncle Ronald's friend's. She met him over the phone. My uncle use to charge people on the inside to set up a phone at our house. It was a separate line from the main phone in the house. The way it went was a person from prison would call, we would accept the call, then call whoever they wanted to talk to on the three way and then sit the phone down. Well this man called Jerome must've had some money because he kept the line on for some months. His people supposedly had money and he supposedly had a lump some of money coming himself through a law suit of some sort. So anyway, he and Nana started talking.

Not long after Nana started talking to Jerome, Ronald came home. So now with he and his woman and the two of her kids that weren't in jail, that made nine people in the house. I could barely breathe. To make the situation even worse, Jerome got out a few months later and he also moved in. I couldn't believe it. Did anybody have a background check? This fool was coming in right out of prison and nobody really even knew his entire background. But like always, our family welcomed him with open arms.

***October 16, 2008-This is the day of my annual doctor's appointment. Every day I dread this day. I'm usually all good but the way this year been going Edward leaving, being separated, coming back leaving again, I just hope my coochie is OK. I have not had any problems but you never know. I'm just gone keep this coochie to myself until Mr. Right***

*comes along. Edward calls himself being concerned this morning as a result of me and Chavez's beef about this school situation. When Edward came to get the girls I don't know what heartbreak story Chavez told him but he asked if he could go to the school. At first I said whatever, I didn't care, then I thought about it. Go up there for what. Now all of a sudden you care. We don't have any food in the fridge thanks to you caring, so I nutted up on Chavez about telling him shit that goes on in this house. This the same nigga flying across state lines and aint gave us shit. I went to the school 'cause I was really thinking about taking him out but it is the middle of the school year and we moving soon. Plus, he still talking that moving to California shit. When I met with the dean he told him the same thing. I was so mad that I was crying. I was also hurt because I don't feel like I should be pleading with no seventeen-year-old about what he want to do with his life. They also had a surveillance tape of the boy who punched Chavez and the tape clearly shows that the boy sucker punched Chavez. That he didn't do anything wrong. Both security and the dean is backing his story but in the back of my mind I still feel like he could have avoided the boy so when I got to the car I gave him an ultimatum. Either go to school tomorrow or find another place to live. I told him when I got off work the following day if he had not gone to school that I was taking him down to juvenile court. The choice was his. I am tired of being the one*

***always compromising. That's why my life is all fucked up as it is. I'm starting to feel like I can't breathe. I'm about to get divorced, I'm on the verge of losing my house, then on top of that...Chavez, I'm at my wits end. All I can do is ask the lord to give me strength because I am almost ready to throw in the towel. All I can think about is what's next.***

Well, as it turned out, Jerome was crazy. He was actually worse than Boo. I walked in the house one day and I see Chavez running from my mother. I couldn't understand why because he was always up under her. But then when I looked at her face I knew why. Thanks to Jerome she had been transformed to the bride of Frankenstein. Jerome had busted up her face and the baby was running to get away. He had started beating her not long after moving in but this last time was enough for me. She refused to let me help, so I had to go. I had to get out of there. I called my dad and asked if I could move in and without hesitation he said yes. So me and Chavez packed our bags and headed west.

As I was walking out the door, I looked at her and shook my head. I wanted to cry I was so hurt. Had I not known she was my mother, I wouldn't have recognized her. Her lip was swollen, eye black, her last boyfriend, Boo had already knocked out her teeth, but this dude had taken her partials, broke them in half and threw one half in the river and put the other one in the mail box with a note telling her what he'd done with the uppers. Now what type of crazy ass mothafucka did dumb shit like that.

## Chapter 20

## HOME SWEET HOME

When I got to my dads, I went into the guest room, made sure Chavez was fine, put away my things, and got comfortable. When I sat down, it hit me. How was I gonna get to work. The Chevette was down. As a matter of fact, it was out for the count. It was dead. I was saving up to get another car but for the time being I was hit. It looked like my only option was the iron pimp-the bus. I hated asking people to do shit for me so that wasn't really an option. They would always expect these huge favors back in return or was always throwing stuff back in my face, so forget begging. I started getting up every day at 4:00 a.m. in order to be out the door by 5:00.

It didn't take long to get burned out from that shit. After a few months I knew I had to make a decision. I just couldn't get to work on time. I knew if I didn't make a change that I was gonna get fired.

Living with my father wasn't bad, but it also wasn't what it was when I would visit during the summers and on weekends. Not to say it was fake, it was just living there allowed me to be a little bit more observant. Maybe stuff was happening all the while and I just didn't pay attention, but living there gave me the opportunity to see that my Dad and Pam did get on each other's nerves. They didn't have too many major arguments, but they did argue.

To make things easier I started staying at my grandma Nanie's a lot. She had a big boarding house not too far from my dad's, so that worked out. She was a nurse and had her business set up pretty good. She had borders living in the house and it appeared that it was going pretty good. So I would go over, help out and spend the night. It took me a minute to get used to the environment, though. There were all kinds of men there. They mostly just walked around all day doing nothing, but then there was a couple of them who scared me.

There was this one guy who walked around and talked to himself all day, and another one who was just the opposite and didn't say nothing to nobody. I was scared of they ass at first but I soon realized that they were harmless.

Another problem that I had with staying with my Dad and Pam was the kids. Those kids were bad as hell. Watching them wasn't the same as dealing with the kids back home. Back home there was some sense of discipline in the home. My brothers and sisters at my dads were bad. Pamela didn't really believe in disciplining them with whippings, she believed in that time out shit. Now that may have been fine for some kids but these kids needed they asses beat. They were hard headed as hell; especially

Matthew. That little boy needed to be on medication.

Whenever I'd watch them, before the day was done my sister would be in the corner and the boys in the closet suffering from fork punctures. I would never draw blood, but I would stick they little asses. It started off just me scaring they ass but they didn't believe I would stick them so they kept trying me, so after awhile I just went ahead and stuck one of 'em just to prove my point. I stuck the first one just to make an example out of 'em. Of course when my Dad got home I got cussed out but I didn't care. I had to do something. After that first time they were like perfect angels.

Because of my attendance at the job, I ended up getting put on midnights. Midnights were even worse. Now I had to wait all times of night downtown for the bus. So after a couple of months of that shit, I ended up getting fired. I was good for awhile, I had saved some money plus I needed a little break anyway, so I created myself a new past time. Male dancing. I don't know how I became so fascinated with it but once I saw them for the first time, I was hooked. There was a club not too far from my dad's and on Wednesday's it would be off the hook. Since I had no real social life I had actually convinced my dad to drop me off and pick me up from the club. Don't ask me how I convinced him, I just did. It was cool seeing them fine ass niggas shaking they ass for a few dollars. I would usually tip a dollar or two. I never went so far as to go home with anybody, but I'll tell you, a few of them could have gotten the coochie had they wanted it.

I couldn't blame some of the girls, they were in love with some of them niggas. Just giving them all they loot. I remember one time they had a birthday party for this dude name Ace and this hoe put a bag of money on the stage. A big ass plastic garbage bag full of money. The size bag that you would pick up leaves in. Then there was this guy named Sexual Healer. Now when his bad ass would dance, you would wanna take off all your clothes, lay butt naked on that stage and let him have all yo pussy. There were a few other cats that would have you wondering what they were like in bed but that Sexual Healer could get it.

***October 23, 2008-It is cold then a motherfucka. I been riding my motorcycle to work because some Jerk hit the side of my truck while Chavez had it at the grocery store. My strut was bent as a result. I'm still grateful because it could have been worse. I won't have any money until tomorrow so for the time being I'm riding my bike. Chavez gets paid Saturday but this happened last Thursday so we had to drive it like that all this week. The tire wabbles and its ruining the tires so we can't drive fast. I've already gone through three tires since Saturday. One I paid for and the other two I have to pay for on Saturday because I got those on credit. So driving it all the way to work was not an option. Plus, lets***

***not forget about my loving son. He has to get dropped off and picked up everyday. I'm numb as hell when I get to work but I have to do what I have to do.***

Everything was going good for me, and then one day I received a call from Aunt Mona crying saying Jerome had jumped on her boyfriend, Mark and had also broken Victor's nose during the fight. So I jumped up in a panic. I called one of my boys to come get me and headed over there. I wanted to call Di but had she come we both would have caught a case. I'd done my best to avoid Jerome. I would stop by my grandmother's but I could never stay long because of him. He was such an asshole. He was always beating on my mother; yelling, and acting like it was his house. Ronald was back in jail so he was not around to defend her so it was basically left up to me.

When I got to the house, I jumped out the car and ran in the house ready to battle. As I walked in Victor was sitting in a chair, nose bleeding, eyes black, with tears running down his face. I asked him what the fuck had happened and before he could explain, Jerome came running out the room like he was the baddest nigga on the east side. At that point I saw red. I flipped out. I ran over to him, shoved him against the wall, put my knife up to his throat and closed my eyes. I was ready to kill that nigga right then and there. Visions of him beating my mother, disrespecting my grandmother and beating Victor was all I could see. Then I envisioned me cutting this nigga throat and dropping his ass and going to jail. But for a split second I didn't care about none of that, the nigga had to die. I pressed the knife harder against his throat breaking the skin. As blood started running down his neck Nana went into her antics. "; Please don't kill him," she shouted. She was now crying and yelling for me to stop but I was intent on killing him. I looked into his eyes and with all the anger I could muster, told him that if I ever had to come back to that house because he had put his hands on anybody, that he was gone die. And I meant every word. Before turning away, I held the knife to his neck for another minute because I wanted him to remember that day. Every time he looked in the mirror I wanted him to see that scar. I then loosened my grip on his shirt, straightened out the wrinkles, then wiped the knife clean with his shirt. The look on his face was priceless. I was surprised he didn't shit on himself. When I stepped back, he took a deep breath, grabbed his neck and then walked backwards into the room and slammed the door. I then turned toward Nana. I told her in no uncertain terms that the nigga had to go. She had a choice. See me go to jail or force that nigga to move out. It was her decision.

***October 29, 2008- God is so good to me and my kids. Yesterday was Alexis's birthday and her father Chauncey came through. She was so happy to see him because since he and his wife had gotten divorced and he had lost one of his closest cousins to a bad car accident,***

***he had somewhat shut everybody out and hadn't been coming around. He brought pizza, cake, ice cream, and candy plus I'd managed to buy her a new pair of boots and some earrings that I'd purchased at my job during one of our clothing and jewelry sales. Him showing up just made every thing right. I told him about me getting a divorce so you know he put his bid in but I was o.k. on that tip. He did help Darshawn get a job at McDonalds though. That was a blessing. It seems like no matter how bad I think things are, something happens to show me how blessed I truly am. I can't wait for all this to be over. I can't think about nothing but getting through this divorce and getting my credit score up. Without that I can't do shit. So I'm taking baby steps. This starting over is no joke. This marriage has put me at ground zero but I am ok.***

After the incident with Jerome, I started going to my grandmother's as much as possible. I was intent on letting him know that I was dead serious about what I said.

When Uncle Ronald finally called, I couldn't wait to tell him about Jerome. Normally when he was locked down, we didn't bother him with things that he couldn't fix, but this time I wanted it to fester. He was getting out in a few weeks so when he got out I wanted him boiling mad and ready to fuck that nigga up.

The day he was due home, Jerome was creeping around the house like a scared rat. He eventually went on and left out however the next thing we know, this dude from around the corner came banging on the door asking if Jerome was home. Come to find out he'd broken into the guy's spot, beat up one of his workers and jumped out the window escaping down the alley. So Ronald was really pissed now. He grabbed his shit and went huffing and puffing out the door. That night, one way or another, Jerome was getting his ass beat.

They looked all over the neighborhood for that niggga. Finally, after a couple of hours, Ronald's boy shouted out from the alley that he found him. As Ronald ran to the alley, he ordered me into the house so I wouldn't see the whipping they was about to put on his ass. But I acted like I didn't hear him. This was one ass whipping that I wasn't about to miss.

When Ronald got to the alley, he commenced to fucking that nigga up. Before I knew what happened he pulled out his pistol and slapped that nigga across the face splitting it to the white meat. As I watched them beat his ass into a messy pulp I couldn't help but feel a sense of satisfaction that he was finally getting what he deserved. A good old fashion east side ass kicking.

After about a week Jerome was back calling Nana. She would let him know when Ronald or I wasn't there and he would then come over. I caught his ass coming out the house once but nothing happened. As he was getting into his car we locked eyes but that was about it. But after that ass whipping, we never had no more problems out of that fool.

Not long after this incident my grandmother had my mother committed to a psychiatric facility. She restricted her visitors to just family thus prohibiting Jerome from seeing her. Whenever he would call the house to see if she was home yet, he would try and disguise his voice, but I knew it was him.

By this time thanks to crack, liquor and Jerome, my mother was now only a mere shell of the beautiful women she once was. During her prime, she was the shit. Men would drive down our street just to get a glimpse at her big pretty legs. Now, those once beautiful legs were nothing more than bony twigs on which she could barely stand. Her face, once compared to some of the most beautiful around, was now merely a bruised and swollen shadow of the past.

I loved visiting my mother at Northville, because she was my mother, and I loved and believed that she would one day wake up. That she would one day come to the realization that she had made a mistake and would turn her life around. On the other hand, Northville was a complete turn off. I hated that place. The patients looked like zombies. Whenever I was there they would always want to walk up and touch me. Like I wasn't real. That always gave me the creeps.

***October 30, 2008 I'm considering running for city counsel. It's a stretch with all this I have on my plate but I still got a little time to get my signatures and get my campaign started. This marriage has been a major set back.***

When Nana got home it didn't take long for her to start back drinking and smoking that shit. I realized then that it didn't matter how much you cared about somebody and tried to help them, if they weren't prepared to help themselves you could forget it.

A few months after her stay in the hospital I came home and before I could walk in the door, Travon was yelling that Victor had just taken Nana to the hospital. So I jumped back in my car and headed to Samaritan. The only information I'd managed to get from Travon was that Victor had found her unconscious on the kitchen floor and had carried her to the car. The closer I got to the hospital, the more afraid I became. If he'd carried her it must have been something serious.

When I got to the hospital, Victor was waiting in the lobby. I asked him what happened and he said he didn't know; that when he walked in the kitchen she was passed out on the kitchen floor with a bottle of beer in her hand. He said that he'd tried to wake her up but she wouldn't respond.

After about forty-five minutes of waiting, a doctor came out asking for family. He said they had revived her three times but she'd gone into a diabetic coma. Me and Victor looked at each other because we didn't even know she was diabetic. He then said that we could go in and see her. I turned to Victor, gave him a hug then went first. As I walked toward the room, I didn't know what to expect. When I walked in she was just lying there motionless, her body connected to a machine, with I.V.'s, tubes, and catheters running to and from. I walked over to the bed, took her by the hand, and whispered her name. I asked if she could hear me but she didn't respond. She just laid there. At that point the tears started flowing. I tried to hold them back because I had always prided myself on being the strong one in the family. I was always the supportive one. But not this time. This time someone was going to have to help lift me up. I stayed a few more minutes, wiped my face and went out so Victor could go in.

After about a half hour, Grandma and Aunt Mona arrived. As others starting coming, the doctor moved her into a private room so as to allow us the opportunity to all see her together. When we got to her room everybody was quiet. Just looking. After a few minutes I couldn't take it so I walked back out in the hall. I was in denial. I couldn't believe she was dead.

After watching her all those years, I still thought that she would live forever. She was only 35. I prayed to the lord for a miracle. She was still hooked up to the machines so I prayed that she would come out of it. But the truth was, that she was dead when Victor brought her in.

She lay in the hospital for another two months before we finally came to the conclusion that she wasn't going to wake up.

I spent a lot of that time apologizing to her for all the things I'd said to her over the years. I knew she could hear me it helped just knowing that I had the opportunity to say them. The bible says to honor thy mother and thy father and I felt that I had fallen short by being over bearing because she was on crack. I used to raise my voice... I used to curse at her, and I'd lose my patience whenever she'd do something I didn't like. I used to put her down and put my father on a pedestal and I shouldn't have done that. She was there for me since day one. Even when he disappointed me she was there to tell me it was gone be okay and that my dad loved me no matter what. I begged the lord to forgive me for treating her like I did and to also forgive her for the things she did that was not pleasing to him.

On May 1st, 1993 my grandmother and Aunt Mona pulled the plug and my mother took her last breath.

www.ingramcontent.com/pod-product-compliance
Lightning Source LLC
Chambersburg PA
CBHW030412100426
42812CB00028B/2932/J

*9780963667816*